Other Books and Series by Jeff Bowen

Applications for Enrollment of Chickasaw Newborn Act of 1905 Volumes I thru VII

Cherokee Intermarried White 1906 Volume I thru X

Applications for Enrollment of Creek Newborn Act of 1905 Volume I

Visit our website at **www.nativestudy.com** to learn more about these and other books and series by Jeff Bowen

APPLICATIONS FOR ENROLLMENT OF CREEK NEWBORN ACT OF 1905

VOLUME II

TRANSCRIBED BY
JEFF BOWEN

NATIVE STUDY
Gallipolis, Ohio
USA

Other Books and Series by Jeff Bowen

1901-1907 Native American Census Seneca, Eastern Shawnee, Miami, Modoc, Ottawa, Peoria, Quapaw, and Wyandotte Indians (Under Seneca School, Indian Territory)

1932 Census of The Standing Rock Sioux Reservation with Births And Deaths 1924-1932

Census of The Blackfeet, Montana, 1897- 1901 Expanded Edition

Eastern Cherokee by Blood, 1906-1910, Volumes I thru XIII

Choctaw of Mississippi Indian Census 1929-1932 with Births and Deaths 1924-1931   Volume I
Choctaw of Mississippi Indian Census 1933, 1934 & 1937, Supplemental Rolls to 1934 & 1935 with Births and Deaths 1932-1938, and Marriages 1936-1938 Volume II

Eastern Cherokee Census Cherokee, North Carolina 1930-1939 Census 1930-1931 with Births And Deaths 1924-1931 Taken By Agent L. W. Page Volume I
Eastern Cherokee Census Cherokee, North Carolina 1930-1939 Census 1932-1933 with Births And Deaths 1930-1932 Taken By Agent R. L. Spalsbury   Volume II
Eastern Cherokee Census Cherokee, North Carolina 1930-1939 Census 1934-1937 with Births and Deaths 1925-1938 and Marriages 1936 & 1938 Taken by Agents R. L. Spalsbury And Harold W. Foght Volume III

Seminole of Florida Indian Census, 1930-1940 with Birth and Death Records, 1930-1938

Texas Cherokees 1820-1839 A Document For Litigation 1921

Choctaw By Blood Enrollment Cards 1898-1914 Volumes I thru XVII

Starr Roll 1894 (Cherokee Payment Rolls) Districts: Canadian, Cooweescoowee, and Delaware Volume One
Starr Roll 1894 (Cherokee Payment Rolls) Districts: Flint, Going Snake, and Illinois   Volume Two
Starr Roll 1894 (Cherokee Payment Rolls) Districts: Saline, Sequoyah, and Tahlequah; Including Orphan Roll   Volume Three

Cherokee Intruder Cases Dockets of Hearings 1901-1909 Volumes I & II

Indian Wills, 1911-1921 Records of the Bureau of Indian Affairs Books One thru Seven;
Native American Wills & Probate Records 1911-1921

Other Books and Series by Jeff Bowen

Turtle Mountain Reservation Chippewa Indians 1932 Census with Births & Deaths, 1924-1932

Chickasaw By Blood Enrollment Cards 1898-1914 Volume I thru V

Cherokee Descendants East An Index to the Guion Miller Applications Volume I
Cherokee Descendants West An Index to the Guion Miller Applications Volume II (A-M)
Cherokee Descendants West An Index to the Guion Miller Applications Volume III (N-Z)

Applications for Enrollment of Seminole Newborn Freedmen, Act of 1905

Eastern Cherokee Census, Cherokee, North Carolina, 1915-1922, Taken by Agent James E. Henderson
   Volume I (1915-1916)
   Volume II (1917-1918)
   Volume III (1919-1920)
   Volume IV (1921-1922)

Complete Delaware Roll of 1898

Eastern Cherokee Census, Cherokee, North Carolina, 1923-1929, Taken by Agent James E. Henderson
   Volume I (1923-1924)
   Volume II (1925-1926)
   Volume III (1927-1929)

Applications for Enrollment of Seminole Newborn Act of 1905 Volumes I & II

North Carolina Eastern Cherokee Indian Census 1898-1899, 1904, 1906, 1909-1912, 1914 Revised and Expanded Edition

1932 Hopi and Navajo Native American Census with Birth & Death Rolls (1925-1931) Volume 1 - Hopi
1932 Hopi and Navajo Native American Census with Birth & Death Rolls (1930-1932) Volume 2 - Navajo

Western Navajo Reservation Navajo, Hopi and Paiute 1933 Census with Birth & Death Rolls 1925-1933

Cherokee Citizenship Commission Dockets 1880-1884 and 1887-1889 Volumes I thru V

Copyright © 2011
by Jeff Bowen

ALL RIGHTS RESERVED
No part of this publication may be reproduced
or used in any form or manner whatsoever
without previous written permission from the
copyright holder or publisher.

Originally published:
Baltimore, Maryland
2011

Reprinted by:

Native Study LLC
Gallipolis, OH
www.nativestudy.com
2020

Library of Congress Control Number: 2020917992

ISBN: 978-1-64968-081-5

Made in the United States of America.

**This series is dedicated to the descendants of the
Creek newborn listed in these applications.**

DEPARTMENT OF THE INTERIOR.

Commissioner to the Five Civilized Tribes.

NOTICE.

Opening of Land Office at Wewoka,
IN THE SEMINOLE NATION, INDIAN TERRITORY.

Notice is hereby given that on Monday, September 4, 1905, the Commissioner to the Five Civilized Tribes will establish a land office at Wewoka, in the Seminole Nation, Indian Territory, for the purpose of allowing citizens and freedmen of the Seminole Nation to select allotments of land for their minor children enrolled under the Act of Congress approved March 3, 1905 (33 Stat. L 1060), and for the further purpose of allowing citizens and freedmen of the Seminole Nation, whose allotments are incomplete, to select additional land in order to bring the value of their allotments up to the standard of $309.09, as nearly as may be practicable.

Each child whose enrollment in accordance with the Act of March 3, 1905, has been duly approved by the Secretary of the Interior, is entitled to receive an alllotment of forty acres without regard to the character or value of the land selected.

Selection of allotments for minor children must be made by their citizen or freedmen parents or by a duly appointed guardian, or curator, or by a duly appointed administrator.

TAMS BIXBY,
Commissioner.

Muskogee, Indian Territory,
July 29, 1905.

This particular notice makes mention of the Act of 1905. The Creek and Seminole were closely related tribes. Both tribes' notices were like similar in nature.

DEPARTMENT OF THE INTERIOR,
Commission to the Five Civilized Tribes.

Closing of Citizenship Rolls
OF THE MUSKOGEE OR CREEK NATION.

WHEREAS, on June 13, 1904, the Secretary of the Interior, under the authority in him vested by the provisions of the act of Congress approved March 3, 1901, (31 Stat., 1058) ordered that September 1, 1904, be and the same is hereby fixed as the time when the rolls of the Muskogee or Creek Nation shall be closed:

Notice is hereby given that the Commission to the Five Civilized Tribes will, at its office in Muskogee, Indian Territory, up to and inclusive of September 1, 1904, receive applications for the enrollment of citizens and freedmen of the Muskogee or Creek Nation, and that after that date the application of no person whomsoever for enrollment as a citizen or freedman of said nation will be received by the Commission.

Commission to the Five Civilized Tribes,
TAMS BIXBY, Chairman,
T. B. NEEDLES,
C. R. BRECKINRIDGE,
Commissioners.

Muskogee, Indian Territory,
June 25, 1904.

A notice like this was printed in newspapers and posted throughout Indian Territory.

INTRODUCTION

This series concerns Applications for Enrollment of Creek Newborn, National Archive film M-1301 (Act of 1905), as described in the National Archives publication *American Indians*. It falls under the heading Applications for Enrollment of the Commission to the Five Civilized Tribes, 1898-1914, M-1301 and is transcribed from microfilm rolls 414-419. This shows the application forms filled out by individuals applying for enrollment in the Five Civilized Tribes under the Dawes Commission. These applications contain additional information that wasn't abstracted to the census cards that you find in series M-1186. This particular roll (Creek by Birth) contains its own series of numbers separate from M-1186. To find each party's roll number you would have to reference M-1186. On July 25, 1898, there was an Indian Territory Division created in the Office of the Department of Interior. This division was created because of the increased work caused by what was called the Curtis Act, named after Senator Charles Curtis. Basically, this law stated that the tribal rolls needed to be descriptive and pointed out that each tribal roll was without description and had to be redone. At this point there was such a struggle among the Creeks to accept that the Government was going to change their way of life, again, that their leaders were refusing to cooperate in handing over their census information. The Commission had found that enrolling the Creeks was a difficult task not only because the Creek feared what was coming but also because their tribal structure was consistent with being a confederacy with forty-four different bands whose tribesmen lived in different towns of which each had a king that was supposed to keep track of their citizenry. The Commission reported that there was very little evidence of any census that existed and what there was had been kept carelessly. There were attempts and tribal conflicts along the way, but the Curtis Act would make it so they had to do it again no matter what effort from the past. In 1899, Agent Wesley Smith educated Washington to the fact that it was difficult to verify Creek eligibility. The acts passed by the Creeks themselves concerning enrollment since 1893 had been strewn amongst the archives of the Creek Council in Muskogee, I.T., and there was no provision ever approved for the printing of the those enrollments. There was confusion and difficulty let alone the fact that surnames were practically unknown among the Creek. But there was no confusion on March 9, 1905, when the Commission stated they would come to seven towns in the Creek Nation and accept applications that had to be made on a standardized blank form and contain a notarized affidavit from the mother and the attending doctor or midwife. A few by mail, but most of them were offered to a field party led by Commissioner Needles. The Commission took in applications for 2,410 children by the deadline of midnight, May 2, 1905.

This series contains applications and correspondence from 1,171 of those claimants. Realizing there were over 2,400 applicants originally, it is understood that not all were accepted. Also included are names of doctors, lawyers, mid-wives, and others who attended to the Creek Nation before and during this time in history.

Jeff Bowen
Gallipolis, Ohio
NativeStudy.com

Applications for Enrollment of Creek Newborn
Act of 1905 Volume II

BIRTH AFFIDAVIT.

DEPARTMENT OF THE INTERIOR.
COMMISSION TO THE FIVE CIVILIZED TRIBES.

IN RE APPLICATION FOR ENROLLMENT, as a citizen of the CREEK Nation, of Millard E. Allen, born on the 7 day of Dec, 1904

Name of Father:	John W. Allen	a citizen of the	Creek	Nation.
Name of Mother:	Cora Lou "	a citizen of the	U.S.	Nation.

Postoffice   Bixby, I.T.

(Child Present)

AFFIDAVIT OF MOTHER.

UNITED STATES OF AMERICA, Indian Territory,
WESTERN   DISTRICT.

I, Cora Lou Allen, on oath state that I am 24 years of age and a citizen by -----, of the U.S. Nation; that I am the lawful wife of John W. Allen, who is a citizen, by blood of the Creek Nation; that a male child was born to me on 7 day of Dec, 1904, that said child has been named Millard E. Allen, and is now living.

Cora Lue[sic] Allen

Witnesses To Mark:
{

Subscribed and sworn to before me this 8" day of March, 1905.

Edw C Griesel
Notary Public.

BIRTH AFFIDAVIT.

DEPARTMENT OF THE INTERIOR.
COMMISSION TO THE FIVE CIVILIZED TRIBES.

IN RE APPLICATION FOR ENROLLMENT, as a citizen of the Creek Nation, of Millard E. Allen, born on the 7th day of Dec, 1904

Name of Father:	John W. Allen	a citizen of the	Creek	Nation.
Name of Mother:	Cora L Allen	~~a citizen of the~~		~~Nation~~.

Postoffice   Bixby, I.T.

1

Applications for Enrollment of Creek Newborn
Act of 1905 Volume II

AFFIDAVIT OF MOTHER.

UNITED STATES OF AMERICA, Indian Territory,
Western DISTRICT.

I, Cora L. Allen, on oath state that I am 24 years of age and ~~a citizen by~~ ——, of the ----- Nation; that I am the lawful wife of John W. Allen, who is a citizen, by blood of the Creek Nation; that a male child was born to me on 7th day of December, 1904, that said child has been named Millard E. Allen, and was living March 4, 1905.

Cora L. Allen

Witnesses To Mark:
{

Subscribed and sworn to before me this 24th day of May, 1905.

Chas. M. Sherrill
Notary Public.

AFFIDAVIT OF ATTENDING PHYSICIAN OR MID-WIFE.

UNITED STATES OF AMERICA, Indian Territory,
Western DISTRICT.

I, Eliza H. Allen, a mid-wife, on oath state that I attended on Mrs. Cora L. Allen, wife of John W. Allen on the 7th day of Dec., 1904; that there was born to her on said date a male child; that said child was living March 4, 1905, and is said to have been named Millard E. Allen.

Eliza H. Allen

Witnesses To Mark:
{

Subscribed and sworn to before me this 24th day of May, 1905.

Chas. M. Sherrill
Notary Public.

BIRTH AFFIDAVIT.

DEPARTMENT OF THE INTERIOR.
COMMISSION TO THE FIVE CIVILIZED TRIBES.

IN RE APPLICATION FOR ENROLLMENT, as a citizen of the CREEK Nation, of Millard E. Allen, born on the 7 day of Dec, 1904

Name of Father:	John W. Allen	a citizen of the	Creek Nation.
Name of Mother:	Cora Lou "	a citizen of the	U.S. Nation.

Applications for Enrollment of Creek Newborn
Act of 1905 Volume II

Postoffice   Bixby, I.T.

(Child present)

AFFIDAVIT OF ~~MOTHER~~. father

UNITED STATES OF AMERICA, Indian Territory, }
WESTERN   DISTRICT.

    I, John W. Allen , on oath state that I am 31 years of age and a citizen by blood, of the Creek Nation; that I am the lawful ~~wife~~ hus of Cora Lou Allen , who is a citizen, by ----- of the U.S. Nation; that a *(blank)* child was born to me on 7 day of Dec. , 1904, that said child has been named Millard E. Allen , and is now living.

                                            John W. Allen

Witnesses To Mark:
{

    Subscribed and sworn to before me this 8 day of March, 1905.

                                             Edw C Griesel
                                                  Notary Public.

BIRTH AFFIDAVIT.
DEPARTMENT OF THE INTERIOR.
COMMISSION TO THE FIVE CIVILIZED TRIBES.

    IN RE APPLICATION FOR ENROLLMENT, as a citizen of the CREEK Nation, of Vetrus Allen , born on the 3 day of June , 1903

Name of Father:	John W. Allen	a citizen of the	Creek	Nation.
Name of Mother:	Cora Lou "	a citizen of the	U.S.	Nation.

                                    Postoffice   Bixby

AFFIDAVIT OF ~~MOTHER~~. father

UNITED STATES OF AMERICA, Indian Territory, }
WESTERN   DISTRICT.

    I, John W. Allen , on oath state that I am 31 years of age and a citizen by blood, of the Creek Nation; that I am the lawful ~~wife~~ hus of Cora Lou Allen , who is a citizen, by ----- of the U.S. Nation; that a *(blank)* child was born to me on 3 day of June , 1903, that said child has been named Vetrus Allen , and ~~is now living~~. died Feb 6, 1904

                                             John W. Allen

Applications for Enrollment of Creek Newborn
Act of 1905   Volume II

Witnesses To Mark:
{

    Subscribed and sworn to before me this 8 day of March, 1905.

                                       Edw C Griesel
                                       Notary Public.

IN RE APPLICATION FOR ENROLLMENT, as a citizen of the CREEK Nation, of Vetrus Allen, born on the 3 day of June, 1903

Name of Father:	John W. Allen	a citizen of the	Creek	Nation.
Name of Mother:	Cora Lou	a citizen of the	U.S.	Nation.

                     Postoffice   Bixby

AFFIDAVIT OF MOTHER.

UNITED STATES OF AMERICA, Indian Territory, }
      WESTERN   DISTRICT.

    I, Cora Lou Allen, on oath state that I am 24 years of age and a citizen by -----, of the U.S. Nation; that I am the lawful wife of John W. Allen, who is a citizen, by blood of the Creek Nation; that a female child was born to me on 3 day of June, 1903, that said child has been named Vetrus Allen, and ~~is now living~~. died Feb 6, 1904

                               Cora Lue[sic] Allen

Witnesses To Mark:
{

    Subscribed and sworn to before me this 8 day of March, 1905.

                                       Edw C Griesel
                                       Notary Public.

    To All whom These Present Come Greeting:
This is to certify that I was in attendance on the little girl, Vetrus Allen, daughter of John W. Allen and Cora L Allen during her sickness and death and she died on the 6th day of February 1904, she was at the time of her death about eight months old

                                      M. D. Taylor, M.D.

Indian Territory Western Judicial District, SS:
    Subscribed and sworn to before me this 25th day of August 1904

Applications for Enrollment of Creek Newborn
Act of 1905   Volume II

My Commission Expires May 4, 1907

Arthur L. *(Illegible)*
Notary Public
Mounds I.T

IN RE APPLICATION FOR ENROLLMENT, as a citizen of the CREEK Nation, of Violet Allen, born on the 21 day of Feb , 1902

Name of Father:	John W. Allen	a citizen of the	Creek	Nation.
Name of Mother:	Cora Lou "	a citizen of the	U.S.	Nation.

Postoffice   Bixby

AFFIDAVIT OF MOTHER.

UNITED STATES OF AMERICA, Indian Territory,
WESTERN   DISTRICT.

I, Cora Lou Allen , on oath state that I am 24 years of age and a citizen by ----- , of the U.S. Nation; that I am the lawful wife of John W. Allen , who is a citizen, by blood of the Creek Nation; that a female   child was born to me on 21 day of Feb , 1902, that said child has been named Violet Allen   , and is now living. died Aug 4, 1902

Cora Lue[sic] Allen

Witnesses To Mark:
{

Subscribed and sworn to before me this 8 day of March , 1905.

Edw C Griesel
Notary Public.

BIRTH AFFIDAVIT.

DEPARTMENT OF THE INTERIOR.
COMMISSION TO THE FIVE CIVILIZED TRIBES.

IN RE APPLICATION FOR ENROLLMENT, as a citizen of the CREEK Nation, of Violet Allen, born on the 21 day of Feb , 1902

Name of Father:	John W. Allen	a citizen of the	Creek	Nation.
Name of Mother:	Cora Lou "	a citizen of the	U.S.	Nation.

Postoffice   Bixby

Applications for Enrollment of Creek Newborn
Act of 1905 Volume II

AFFIDAVIT OF ~~MOTHER~~. father

UNITED STATES OF AMERICA, Indian Territory, ⎫
    WESTERN   DISTRICT. ⎭

    I, John W. Allen , on oath state that I am 31 years of age and a citizen by blood, of the Creek Nation; that I am the lawful ~~wife~~ hus of Cora Lou Allen , who is a citizen, by ----- of the U.S. Nation; that a female child was born to me on 21 day of Feb. , 1902, that said child has been named Violet Allen , and ~~is now living~~. died Aug 4, 1902

                                        John W. Allen

Witnesses To Mark:
⎰
⎱

    Subscribed and sworn to before me this 8 day of March, 1905.

                                        Edw C Griesel
                                            Notary Public.

    To All Whom These Presents Come Greeting:
    This is to certify that I was in attendance on the little girl, Violet Allen, daughter of John W. Allen and Cora L. Allen, during her sickness and death, and that she died on the 4th day of August, 1904[sic], that she was between six months and a year old at time of her death.

                                    W.A. *(Illegible)*   M.D.

    Indian Territory, Western District, SS:
    Subscribed and sworn to before me this 26th day of August, 1904.

                                      Chas. M. Sherrill
                                            Notary Public.
My commission expires Sept. 4, 1904.

N.C. 70.   J.L.De.
                DEPARTMENT OF THE INTERIOR,
      COMMISSIONER TO THE FIVE CIVILIZED TRIBES.

    In the matter of the applications for the enrollment of Violet Allen, deceased, and Vetrus Allen, deceased, as a citizen by blood of the Creek Nation.

                          STATEMENT AND ORDER.

    The record in this case shows that on March 8, 1905, applications were made, in affidavit form, for the enrollment of Violet Allen, deceased, and Vetrus Allen, deceased,

Applications for Enrollment of Creek Newborn
Act of 1905   Volume II

as citizens by blood of the Creek Nation, under the provisions of the act of Congress approved March 3, 1905.

It appears that the affidavits filed in this matter that said Violet Allen and Vetrus Allen were born February 21, 1902, and June 3, 1903, respectively, and died August 4, 1902, and February 6, 1904, respectively.

The Act of Congress approved March 3, 1905, (33 Stats., 1048), in part, provides:

"That the Commission to the Five Civilized Tribes is authorized for sixty days after the date of the approval of this act to receive and consider applications for enrollment, of children, born subsequent to May twenty-fifth, nineteen hundred and one, and prior to March fourth, nineteen hundred and five, and living on said latter date, to citizens of the Creek tribe of Indians whose enrollment has been approved by the Secretary of the Interior prior to the approval of this act; and to enroll and make allotments to such children."

It is, therefore, ordered that the applications for the enrollment of Violet Allen, deceased, and Vetrus Allen, deceased, as citizens by blood of the Creek Nation be, and the same are hereby dismissed.

(Name Illegible) Commissioner.

Muskogee, Indian Territory.
JAN 18 1907

NC 70.

Muskogee, Indian Territory, May 17, 1905.

John W. Allen,
    Bixby, Indian Territory.

Dear Sir:

In the matter of the application for the enrollment of your minor child, Millard E. Allen, as a citizen of the Creek Nation, you are advised that the Commission requires the affidavit of the midwife or physician in attendance at the birth of said child.

There is herewith enclosed a blank form of birth affidavit, and in executing same care should be exercised to see that all blanks are properly filled, all names written in full and in the event that either of the persons signing the affidavit is unable to write, signature by mark must be attested by two witnesses. Each affidavit must be executed before a Notary Public and the notarial seal and signature of the officer must be attached to each separate affidavit.

Respectfully,

BC.   Chairman.

Applications for Enrollment of Creek Newborn
Act of 1905 Volume II

NC 70.

Muskogee, Indian Territory, January 1?, 1907.

John W. Allen,
    Bixby, Indian Territory.

Dear Sir:

    There is herewith enclosed one copy of the Statement and Order of the Commissioner to the Five Civilized Tribes, dated January 18, 1907, dismissing the application made by you for the enrollment of your minor children, Violet and Vetrus Allen, both deceased, as a citizen of the Creek Nation.

        Respectfully,

                Commissioner.

Register.
LM-1113.

NC 71.

Muskogee, Indian Territory, May 17, 1905.

William Sherrill,
    Bixby, Indian Territory.

Dear Sir:

    In the matter of the application for the enrollment of your minor child, Gracie Sherrill, as a citizen of the Creek Nation, you are advised that the Commission requires the affidavit of the midwife or physician in attendance at the birth of said child.

    There is herewith enclosed a blank form of birth affidavit, and in executing same care should be exercised to see that all blanks are properly filled, all names written in full and in the event that either of the persons signing the affidavit is unable to write, signature by mark must be attested by two witnesses. Each affidavit must be executed before a Notary Public and the notarial seal and signature of the officer must be attached to each separate affidavit.

        Respectfully,

BC.   Chairman.

Applications for Enrollment of Creek Newborn
Act of 1905 Volume II

DEPARTMENT OF THE INTERIOR,
COMMISSIONER TO THE FIVE CIVILIZED TRIBES.

REFER IN REPLY TO THE FOLLOWING:

N.C. 71.

Muskogee, Indian Territory, **August 4, 1905.**

Mattie M. Sherrill,
    Care of William Sherrill,
        Bixby, Indian Territory.
Dear Sir:

    You are hereby advised that on **July 28, 1905**, the Secretary of the Interior approved the enrollment of your minor child, **Gracie Sherrill**, as a citizen by blood of the **Creek** Nation, and that the name of said child appears upon the roll of new born citizens of the **Creek** Nation as Number **47**.

    The child is now entitled to an allotment, and application therefor should be made without delay at the Land Office for the Nation in which the prospective allotment is located.

    An entire allotment for said child must be selected at the time of the original application.

                Respectively,

                            Commissioner.

BIRTH AFFIDAVIT.

DEPARTMENT OF THE INTERIOR.
COMMISSION TO THE FIVE CIVILIZED TRIBES.

    IN RE APPLICATION FOR ENROLLMENT, as a citizen of the CREEK Nation, of Gracie Sherrill, born on the 18 day of Oct., 1903

Name of Father:	William Sherrill	a citizen of the U.S.	Nation.
Name of Mother:	Mattie M. "	a citizen of the Creek	Nation.

                Postoffice   Bixby, I.T.

(Child present) HGH

AFFIDAVIT OF MOTHER.

UNITED STATES OF AMERICA, Indian Territory,
    WESTERN   DISTRICT.

    I, Mattie M Sherrill, on oath state that I am 28 years of age and a citizen by blood, of the Creek Nation; that I am the lawful wife of William Sherrill, who is a

Applications for Enrollment of Creek Newborn
Act of 1905   Volume II

citizen, by ----- of the U.S. Nation; that a female child was born to me on 18 day of Oct , 1903 , that said child has been named Gracie Sherrill , and is now living.

                                      Mattie M. Sherrill

Witnesses To Mark:
{

    Subscribed and sworn to before me this 8 day of March , 1905.

                                      Edw C Griesel
                                      Notary Public.

BIRTH AFFIDAVIT.

DEPARTMENT OF THE INTERIOR.
COMMISSION TO THE FIVE CIVILIZED TRIBES.

    IN RE APPLICATION FOR ENROLLMENT, as a citizen of the Creek Nation, of Gracie Sherrill, born on the 18th day of Oct. , 1903

Name of Father: William Sherrill   ~~a citizen of the~~   ~~Nation~~.
Name of Mother: Mattie M. Sherrill   a citizen of the   Creek   Nation.

                            Postoffice   Bixby, I.T.

AFFIDAVIT OF MOTHER.

UNITED STATES OF AMERICA, Indian Territory, }
        Western   DISTRICT.

    I, Mattie M Sherrill , on oath state that I am 28 years of age and a citizen by blood , of the Creek Nation; that I am the lawful wife of William Sherrill , ~~who is a citizen, by~~ ----- of the ----- Nation; that a female child was born to me on 18th day of Oct , 1903 , that said child has been named Gracie Sherrill , and was living March 4, 1905.

                                    Mattie M. Sherrill

Witnesses To Mark:
{
   Subscribed and sworn to before me this 24th day of May , 1905.

          My Commission expires Sept. 4, 1906.   Chas. M. Sherrill
                                            Notary Public.

Applications for Enrollment of Creek Newborn
Act of 1905   Volume II

AFFIDAVIT OF ATTENDING PHYSICIAN OR MID-WIFE.

UNITED STATES OF AMERICA, Indian Territory,
Western   **DISTRICT.**

    I, Eliza H. Allen, a midwife, on oath state that I attended on Mrs. Mattie M Sherrill, wife of William Sherrill on the 18th day of Oct, 1903; that there was born to her on said date a female child; that said child was living March 4, 1905, and is said to have been named Gracie Sherrill.

                                        Eliza H Allen

Witnesses To Mark:
{

    Subscribed and sworn to before me this 24th day of May, 1905.

My Commission expires Sept. 4, 1906.   Chas. M. Sherrill
                                              Notary Public.

                                                          NC 72.

                            Muskogee, Indian Territory, May 17, 1905.

William D. Renfro,
    Wagoner, Indian Territory.

Dear Sir:

    In the matter of the application for the enrollment of your minor child, Alef Adalaid Renfro, as a citizen of the Creek Nation, you are advised that the Commission requires the affidavit of the midwife or physician in attendance at the birth of said child.

    There is herewith enclosed a blank form of birth affidavit, and in executing same care should be exercised to see that all blanks are properly filled, all names written in full and in the event that either of the persons signing the affidavit is unable to write, signature by mark must be attested by two witnesses. Each affidavit must be executed before a Notary Public and the notarial seal and signature of the officer must be attached to each separate affidavit.

                                      Respectfully,

BC.   Chairman.

Applications for Enrollment of Creek Newborn
Act of 1905   Volume II

BIRTH AFFIDAVIT.

DEPARTMENT OF THE INTERIOR.
COMMISSION TO THE FIVE CIVILIZED TRIBES.

IN RE APPLICATION FOR ENROLLMENT, as a citizen of the Creek Nation, of Elza Tillman Renfro, born on the 3 day of April, 1902

Name of Father: William D Renfro   a citizen of the United States Nation.
Name of Mother: Bettie Renfro   a citizen of the   Creek   Nation.

Postoffice   *(blank)*

AFFIDAVIT OF MOTHER.

UNITED STATES OF AMERICA, Indian Territory,
   Western   DISTRICT.

I, Bettie Renfro, on oath state that I am 25 years of age and a citizen by blood, of the Creek Nation; that I am the lawful wife of William D. Renfro, who is a citizen, by blood of the United States ~~Nation~~; that a male child was born to me on Third day of April, 1902, that said child has been named Elza Tillman Renfro, and was living March 4, 1905.

                                      Bettie Renfro
Witnesses To Mark:
{

Subscribed and sworn to before me this First day of May, 1905.

My Commission   Joshua Ross
   expires July 2, 1906.   Notary Public.

AFFIDAVIT OF ATTENDING PHYSICIAN OR MID-WIFE.

UNITED STATES OF AMERICA, Indian Territory,
   Dist 4   DISTRICT.

I, S A Bryan, a Physician, on oath state that I attended on Mrs. Bettie Renfroe[sic], wife of William D Renfroe on the third day of April, 1902; that there was born to her on said date a male child; that said child was living March 4, 1905, and is said to have been named Elza Tilman Renfroe.

                                      S.A. Bryan, M.D.
Witnesses To Mark:
{

Subscribed and sworn to before me this 8 day of May, 1905.

Applications for Enrollment of Creek Newborn
Act of 1905 Volume II

                                 Eli Carr
My Commission expires   Notary Public.
    Feb. 27 – 1906.

BIRTH AFFIDAVIT.

DEPARTMENT OF THE INTERIOR.
COMMISSION TO THE FIVE CIVILIZED TRIBES.

    IN RE APPLICATION FOR ENROLLMENT, as a citizen of the CREEK Nation, of Elza Tillman Renfro , born on the 3 day of Apr , 1902

Name of Father: Will Renfro	a citizen of the	U.S.	Nation.
Name of Mother: Bettie Renfro	a citizen of the	Creek	Nation.

                      Postoffice   Wagoner

AFFIDAVIT OF MOTHER.

UNITED STATES OF AMERICA, Indian Territory,
    WESTERN   DISTRICT.

    I, Bettie Renfro , on oath state that I am 25 years of age and a citizen by blood , of the Creek   Nation; that I am the lawful wife of Will Renfro , who is a citizen, by ----- of the U. S. Nation; that a male child was born to me on 3 day of April , 1902 , that said child has been named Elza Tillman Renfro   , and is now living.

                                Bettie Renfro
Witnesses To Mark:

    Subscribed and sworn to before me this 8 day of March , 1905.

                                Edw C Griesel
                                      Notary Public.

BIRTH AFFIDAVIT.

DEPARTMENT OF THE INTERIOR.
COMMISSION TO THE FIVE CIVILIZED TRIBES.

    IN RE APPLICATION FOR ENROLLMENT, as a citizen of the CREEK Nation, of Alef Adalaid Renfro , born on the 23 day of Feb , 1904

Name of Father: Will Renfro	a citizen of the	U.S.	Nation.
Name of Mother: Bettie "	a citizen of the	Creek	Nation.

Applications for Enrollment of Creek Newborn
Act of 1905 Volume II

Postoffice   Wagoner

AFFIDAVIT OF MOTHER.

UNITED STATES OF AMERICA, Indian Territory, }
WESTERN   DISTRICT.

I, Bettie Renfro , on oath state that I am 25 years of age and a citizen by blood , of the Creek Nation; that I am the lawful wife of Will Renfro , who is a citizen, by ----- of the U. S. Nation; that a female child was born to me on 23 day of Feb , 1904 , that said child has been named Alef Adalaid Renfro , and is now living.

Bettie Renfro

Witnesses To Mark:
{

Subscribed and sworn to before me this 8 day of March , 1905.

Edw C Griesel
Notary Public.

BIRTH AFFIDAVIT.

DEPARTMENT OF THE INTERIOR.
COMMISSION TO THE FIVE CIVILIZED TRIBES.

IN RE APPLICATION FOR ENROLLMENT, as a citizen of the Creek Nation, of Alef Adelaide Renfro , born on the 23d day of February , 1904

Name of Father: William D Renfro   a citizen of the United States Nation.
Name of Mother: Bettie Renfro   a citizen of the   Creek   Nation.

Postoffice   Wagoner, Indian Territory

AFFIDAVIT OF MOTHER.

UNITED STATES OF AMERICA, Indian Territory, }
Western   DISTRICT.

I, Bettie Renfro , on oath state that I am 25 years of age and a citizen by blood , of the Creek Nation; that I am the lawful wife of William D. Renfro , who is a citizen, by *(blank)* of the United States Nation; that a female child was born to me on 23rd day of February , 1904 , that said child has been named Alef Adelaide Renfro , and was living March 4, 1905.

Bettie Renfro

Applications for Enrollment of Creek Newborn
Act of 1905 Volume II

Witnesses To Mark:
{

Subscribed and sworn to before me this First day of May , 1905.

        Eskelle Simpson
        Notary Public.

AFFIDAVIT OF ATTENDING PHYSICIAN OR MID-WIFE.

UNITED STATES OF AMERICA, Indian Territory, }
  Western   DISTRICT.

I, George W. Ruble , a Physician , on oath state that I attended on Mrs. Bettie Renfro , wife of William D Renfro on the 23rd day of February , 1904 ; that there was born to her on said date a female child; that said child was living March 4, 1905, and is said to have been named Alef Adelaide Renfro.

        George W Ruble

Witnesses To Mark:
{

Subscribed and sworn to before me this 8 day of May, 1905.

        Eskelle Simpson
        Notary Public.

NC .73.

DEPARTMENT OF THE INTERIOR,
COMMISSIONER TO THE FIVE CIVILIZED TRIBES.

In the matter of the application for the enrollment of Willie and Johnnie Stephens, as a citizen by blood of the Creek Nation.

MILLIE STEPHENS, being duly sworn, testified as follows:

Examination by the Commissioner:
Q What is your name? A Millie Stephens.
Q What is your age? A 31.
Q What is your post office? A Oktaha.
Q What name were you enrolled under? A Millie Whitfield.

  Witness is identified on Creek Indian Card Field No. 1130, opposite No. 3661, as Millie Whitfield.

Applications for Enrollment of Creek Newborn
Act of 1905   Volume II

Q Have you two children named Willie and Johnnie? A Yes sir, they are here with me. (Children present).
Q What is the name of the father of these children? A Green Stephens.
Q How do you spell your last name? A S-t-e-p-h-e-n-s.
Q Is he a citizen of any Nation in Indian Territory? A No sir.
Q He is living? A Yes sir.
Q Have you a child named Rachel? A Yes sir.
Q Where is she? A She is dead.

    Lona Merrick, being duly sworn, states that the above and foregoing is a true and correct transcript of ~~his~~ her stenographic notes as taken in said case on said date.

Lona Merrick

Subscribed and sworn to before me this 17th day of August, 1905.

Edw C Griesel
Notary Public.

BIRTH AFFIDAVIT.

DEPARTMENT OF THE INTERIOR.
COMMISSION TO THE FIVE CIVILIZED TRIBES.

    IN RE APPLICATION FOR ENROLLMENT, as a citizen of the CREEK Nation, of Johnnie Stevens , born on the 12 day of Dec. , 1904

Name of Father:	Green Stevens	a citizen of the	U S	Nation.
Name of Mother:	Millie "	a citizen of the	Creek	Nation.

Postoffice   Oktaha

Child Present

AFFIDAVIT OF MOTHER.

UNITED STATES OF AMERICA, Indian Territory, ⎫
    WESTERN   DISTRICT. ⎭

    I, Millie Stevens , on oath state that I am 31 years of age and a citizen by blood , of the Creek Nation; that I am the lawful wife of Green Stevens , who is a citizen, by ----- of the U.S. Nation; that a male child was born to me on 12 day of Dec. , 1904, that said child has been named Johnnie Stevens , and was living March 4, 1905.

Millie Stephens

Witnesses To Mark:
{

Applications for Enrollment of Creek Newborn
Act of 1905   Volume II

Subscribed and sworn to before me this 14 day of March , 1905.

Edw C Griesel
Notary Public.

AFFIDAVIT OF ATTENDING PHYSICIAN OR MID-WIFE.

UNITED STATES OF AMERICA, Indian Territory, }
    Western   DISTRICT.

I, Susie Chenubbia , a midwife , on oath state that I attended on Mrs. Millie Stevens , wife of Green Stevens   on the 12 day of Dec. , 1904; that there was born to her on said date a *(blank)* child; that said child was living March 4, 1905, and is said to have been named Johnnie Stevens .

Susie Chenubia[sic]

Witnesses To Mark:
{

Subscribed and sworn to before me this 14 day of March, 1905.

Edw C Griesel
Notary Public.

BIRTH AFFIDAVIT.

DEPARTMENT OF THE INTERIOR.
COMMISSION TO THE FIVE CIVILIZED TRIBES.

IN RE APPLICATION FOR ENROLLMENT, as a citizen of the Creek Nation, of Johnnie Stephens , born on the 12 day of Dec. , 1904

Name of Father:	Green Stephens	a citizen of the	U. S.	Nation.
Name of Mother:	Millie Stephens	a citizen of the	Creek	Nation.

Postoffice   Oktaha, I.T.

AFFIDAVIT OF MOTHER.

UNITED STATES OF AMERICA, Indian Territory, }
    Western   DISTRICT.

I, Millie Stephens , on oath state that I am 31 years of age and a citizen by blood, of the Creek Nation; that I am the lawful wife of Green Stephens , who is a citizen, by ----- of the U.S. Nation; that a male child was born to me on 12 day of December, 1904, that said child has been named Johnnie Stephens , and was living March 4, 1905.

Applications for Enrollment of Creek Newborn
Act of 1905   Volume II

Millie Stephens

Witnesses To Mark:
{

Subscribed and sworn to before me this 17 day of August, 1905.

Henry G. Hains
Notary Public.

BIRTH AFFIDAVIT.

DEPARTMENT OF THE INTERIOR.
COMMISSION TO THE FIVE CIVILIZED TRIBES.

IN RE APPLICATION FOR ENROLLMENT, as a citizen of the Creek Nation, of Willie Stephens, born on the 17 day of April, 1903

Name of Father: Green Stephens   a citizen of the   U. S.   Nation.
Name of Mother: Millie Stephens   a citizen of the   Creek   Nation.

Postoffice   Oktaha, I.T.

AFFIDAVIT OF MOTHER.

UNITED STATES OF AMERICA, Indian Territory, }
    Western   DISTRICT.

I, Millie Stephens, on oath state that I am 31 years of age and a citizen by blood, of the Creek Nation; that I am the lawful wife of Green Stephens, who is a citizen, by ----- of the U.S. Nation; that a male child was born to me on 17 day of April, 1903, that said child has been named Willie Stephens, and was living March 4, 1905.

Millie Stephens

Witnesses To Mark:
{

Subscribed and sworn to before me this 17 day of August, 1905.

Henry G. Hains
Notary Public.

Applications for Enrollment of Creek Newborn
Act of 1905   Volume II

BIRTH AFFIDAVIT.

DEPARTMENT OF THE INTERIOR.
COMMISSION TO THE FIVE CIVILIZED TRIBES.

IN RE APPLICATION FOR ENROLLMENT, as a citizen of the CREEK Nation, of Willie Stevens, born on the 17 day of April, 1903.

Name of Father:	Green Stevens	a citizen of the	U. S.	Nation.
Name of Mother:	Millie "	a citizen of the	Creek	Nation.

Postoffice   Oktaha

Child present

AFFIDAVIT OF MOTHER.

UNITED STATES OF AMERICA, Indian Territory,
    WESTERN   DISTRICT.

I, Millie Stevens, on oath state that I am 31 years of age and a citizen by blood, of the Creek Nation; that I am the lawful wife of Green Stevens, who is a citizen, by ----- of the U.S. Nation; that a male child was born to me on 17 day of April, 1903, that said child has been named Willie Stevens, and was living March 4, 1905.

                          Millie Stevens

Witnesses To Mark:
{

Subscribed and sworn to before me this 14 day of March, 1905.

                          Edw C Griesel
                          Notary Public.

AFFIDAVIT OF ATTENDING PHYSICIAN OR MID-WIFE.

UNITED STATES OF AMERICA, Indian Territory,
    Western   DISTRICT.

I, Sawdubby Chenubbe, a midwife, on oath state that I attended on Mrs. Millie Stevens, wife of Green Stevens on the 17 day of April, 1903; that there was born to her on said date a *(blank)* child; that said child was living March 4, 1905, and is said to have been named Willie Stevens.

                          Her
                  Sawdubby x Chenubbe
Witnesses To Mark: mark
{ J McDermott
  EC Griesel

Applications for Enrollment of Creek Newborn
Act of 1905   Volume II

Subscribed and sworn to before me this 14 day of March, 1905.

                                        Edw C Griesel
                                        Notary Public.

BIRTH AFFIDAVIT.

DEPARTMENT OF THE INTERIOR.
COMMISSION TO THE FIVE CIVILIZED TRIBES.

IN RE APPLICATION FOR ENROLLMENT, as a citizen of the Creek Nation, of Willie Stephens, born on the 17th day of April, 1903

Name of Father:	Green Stephens	a citizen of the United States Nation.
Name of Mother:	Millie Stephens	a citizen of the Creek Nation.

                            Postoffice   Oktaha, Ind. Ter.

AFFIDAVIT OF MOTHER.

UNITED STATES OF AMERICA, Indian Territory, }
      Western   DISTRICT.

I, Millie Stephens, on oath state that I am 31 years of age and a citizen by blood, of the Creek Nation; that I am the lawful wife of Green Stephens, who is a citizen, ~~by~~ *(blank)* of the United States Nation; that a male child was born to me on the 17th day of April, 1903, that said child has been named Willie Stephens, and was living March 4, 1905.

                                      her
                              Millie x Stephens
Witnesses To Mark: mark
  { Charley Evans
    Robt Jetton

Subscribed and sworn to before me this 22nd day of Aug., 1905.

                                        W.A. Cain
                                        Notary Public.

AFFIDAVIT OF ATTENDING PHYSICIAN OR MID-WIFE.

UNITED STATES OF AMERICA, Indian Territory, }
      Western   DISTRICT.

I, Sawdubby Chenubbe, a midwife, on oath state that I attended on Mrs. Millie Stephens, wife of Green Stephens on the 17th day of April, 1903; that there was

Applications for Enrollment of Creek Newborn
Act of 1905 Volume II

born to her on said date a male child; that said child was living March 4, 1905, and is said to have been named Willie Stephens .

Sawdubby x Chenubbe

Witnesses To Mark:
   { Ollie Chunbia[sic]
    Robt Jetton

Subscribed and sworn to before me this 23 day of Aug., 1905.

W.A Cain
Notary Public.

BIRTH AFFIDAVIT.

DEPARTMENT OF THE INTERIOR.
COMMISSION TO THE FIVE CIVILIZED TRIBES.

IN RE APPLICATION FOR ENROLLMENT, as a citizen of the Creek Nation, of Johnnie Stephens , born on the 12th day of December , 1904

Name of Father: Green Stephens   a citizen of the United States Nation.
Name of Mother: Millie Stephens   a citizen of the   Creek Nation.

Postoffice   Oktaha, I.T.

Child Present

AFFIDAVIT OF MOTHER.

UNITED STATES OF AMERICA, Indian Territory, ⎫
    Western   **DISTRICT.** ⎭

I, Millie Stephens , on oath state that I am 31 years of age and a citizen by blood , of the Creek Nation; that I am the lawful wife of Green Stephens , who is a citizen, by *(blank)* of the United States Nation; that a male child was born to me on the 12th day of December , 1904, that said child has been named Johnnie Stephens , and was living March 4, 1905.

her
Millie x Stephens
mark

Witnesses To Mark:
   { Charley Evans
    Robt Jetton

Subscribed and sworn to before me this 22nd day of Aug. , 1905.

W.A. Cain
Notary Public.

Applications for Enrollment of Creek Newborn
Act of 1905   Volume II

AFFIDAVIT OF ATTENDING PHYSICIAN OR MID-WIFE.

UNITED STATES OF AMERICA, Indian Territory, ⎱
     Western   DISTRICT. ⎰

    I, Susie Chenubia , a mid-wife , on oath state that I attended on Mrs. Millie Stephens , wife of Green Stephens on the 12th day of December , 1904; that there was born to her on said date a male child; that said child was living March 4, 1905, and is said to have been named Johnnie Stephens .

                                                Susie Chenubia

Witnesses To Mark:
  ⎰ Robt Jetton
  ⎱

    Subscribed and sworn to before me this 23rd day of Aug., 1905.

                                                W.A. Cain
                                                Notary Public.

                                                                               NC. 73.

                            Muskogee, Indian Territory, July 18, 1905.

Millie Stephens,
    Oktaha, Indian Territory.

Dear Madam:

    In the matter of the application for the enrollment of your minor children, Willie and Johnnie Stephens, as citizens by blood of the Creek Nation, you are advised that you will be allowed ten days from date hereof within which to appear at this office for the purpose of being examined under oath.

                                          Respectfully,

                                                        Commissioner.

NC-73.
                            Muskogee, Indian Territory, July 29, 1905.

Millie Stephens,
    c/o Green Stephens,
        Oktaha, Indian Territory.

Dear Madam:

Applications for Enrollment of Creek Newborn
Act of 1905 Volume II

In the matter of the application for the enrollment of your children Willie Stephens and Johnnie Stephens, as citizens by blood of the Creek Nation, a discrepancy appears in the proof of birth on file with the records of this office as to your surname it appearing in the body of the affidavits as Stevens and your signature being Millie Stephens.

For the purpose of correcting this discrepancy there are inclosed[sic] herewith two blanks properly filled out which you are requested to have executed and return to this office in the inclosed[sic] envelope.

Please give this matter your prompt attention.

                      Respectfully,

                                                Commissioner.

CTD-9
Env.

                                                Cr NC-74.

DEPARTMENT OF THE INTERIOR,
COMMISSION TO THE FIVE CIVILIZED TRIBES.

Muskogee, Indian Territory, May 26, 1905.

In the matter of the application for the enrollment of Martha Chenubbee as a citizen of the Creek Nation.

Susie Chenubbee, being duly sworn, testified as follows (through Jesse McDermott, Official Interpreter):

EXAMINATION BY THE COMMISSION:
Q Give her name, age and postoffice address. A Susie Chenubbee; about 25; Oktaha.
Q Are you a citizen of the Creek Nation? A Yes sir.
Q Is you child, Martha Chenubbee, for whom you have made application, living?
A Yes, there it is.
Q What is the name of the father of this child? A David Hall.
Q You were not married to him, were you? A No, and we are not now married.
Q Are you full-blood? A Yes sir.
Q When was this child born? A Sept 14, 1903.
Q How many years old will it be next September? A Two years old.
Q Then, when you made affidavit here and said it was born September 14, 1904, that was a mistake of one year, was it? A Yes, I said 1903, when I was making the application, but they understood me to say 1904.

Applications for Enrollment of Creek Newborn
Act of 1905 Volume II

Q You now wish to correct the affidavit by this testimony, giving the right year? A Yes sir.

INDIAN TERRITORY, Western District.

I, J. Y. Miller, a stenographer to the Commission to the Five Civilized Tribes, do hereby certify that the above and foregoing is a true and complete translation of my notes as same appear in my stenographic report of this case.

JY Miller

Sworn to and subscribed before me this the 31st day of May, 1905.

Edw C Griesel
Notary Public.

BIRTH AFFIDAVIT.

DEPARTMENT OF THE INTERIOR.
COMMISSION TO THE FIVE CIVILIZED TRIBES.

IN RE APPLICATION FOR ENROLLMENT, as a citizen of the CREEK Nation, of ~~Susie~~ Martha Chenub~~b~~ie, born on the 14 day of Sept, 1904

Name of Father:	(?)	a citizen of the	*(blank)*	Nation.
Name of Mother:	Susie Chenub~~b~~ie	a citizen of the	Creek	Nation.

Postoffice   Oktaha

(child present)

AFFIDAVIT OF MOTHER.

UNITED STATES OF AMERICA, Indian Territory, }
    Western   DISTRICT.

Illigitimate[sic]

I, Susie Chenub~~b~~ie, on oath state that I am 25 years of age and a citizen by blood, of the Creek Nation; that I am the ~~lawful wife of~~ ? —, who is a citizen, by ----- of the ----- Nation; that a female child was born to me on 14 day of Sept, 1904, that said child has been named Martha Chenub~~b~~ie, and was living March 4, 1905.

Susie Chenubie

Witnesses To Mark:
{

Subscribed and sworn to before me this 14 day of March, 1905.

Edw C Griesel
Notary Public.

Applications for Enrollment of Creek Newborn
Act of 1905   Volume II

Illegitimate   Assistant
                                AFFIDAVIT OF ~~ATTENDING PHYSICIAN~~ OR MID-WIFE.

UNITED STATES OF AMERICA, Indian Territory, ⎤
    Western   DISTRICT.   ⎦

    I, Sartarpe Harjo , a assistant midwife , on oath state that I attended on Mrs. Susie Chenubbie , is not wife of David Hall on the 14 day of Sept , 1903 ; that there was born to her on said date a female child; that said child was living March 4, 1905, and is said to have been named Martha Chenubbie.   her

                                          Sartarpe x Harjo
Witnesses To Mark: mark
  { HG Hains
    J McDermott

    Subscribed and sworn to before me this 26 day of May, 1905.

        My Commission   J. McDermott
        Ex. July 25" 1907   Notary Public.

                                         NC 75.

                        Muskogee, Indian Territory, May 17, 1905.

Sandy Hall,
        Oktaha, Indian Territory.

Dear Sir:

    In the matter of the application for the enrollment of your minor child, Marley Hall, as a citizen of the Creek Nation, you are advised that the Commission requires the affidavit of the mother of said child.

    There is herewith enclosed a blank form of birth affidavit, and in executing same care should be exercised to see that all blanks are properly filled, all names written in full and in the event that the person signing the affidavit is unable to write, signature by mark must be attested by two witnesses. Each affidavit must be executed before a Notary Public and the notarial seal and signature of the officer must be attached to each separate affidavit.

                    Respectfully,

BC.   Chairman.

Applications for Enrollment of Creek Newborn
Act of 1905 Volume II

COMMISSIONERS:
TAMS BIXBY,
THOMAS B. NEEDLES,
C.R. BRECKINBRIDGE.

WM. O. BEALL
Secretary

DEPARTMENT OF THE INTERIOR,
COMMISSIONER TO THE FIVE CIVILIZED TRIBES.

REFER IN REPLY TO THE FOLLOWING:

N.C. 75.

ADDRESS ONLY THE
COMMISSION TO THE FIVE CIVILIZED TRIBES.

Muskogee, Indian Territory, June 6, 1905.

Martha Hall,
    Oktaha, Indian Territory.

Dear Madam:

    There are on file with the Commission affidavits executed by yourself and Sandy Hall, relative to the birth of your minor child, in which her name is given as Mollie and Marley Hall.

    You are requested to advise the Commission as to which is the correct name of said child.

                                Respectfully,

                                  (Name Illegible)
                                Commissioner in Charge.

(Copy)

Doctors
SNELSON & SOMERVILLE

                            Oktaha, Ind. Ter. June 21st. 1905.

Mr. Tams Bixby,

    Commissioner to Five Civilized Tribes.

Dear Sir:

    The correct name is Mollie Hall.

                              Yours very truly,

                              (signed) MARTHA HALL
                              (signed) SANDY HALL

Witness:
    O. J. Snelson

Applications for Enrollment of Creek Newborn
Act of 1905 Volume II

BIRTH AFFIDAVIT.

DEPARTMENT OF THE INTERIOR.
COMMISSION TO THE FIVE CIVILIZED TRIBES.

IN RE APPLICATION FOR ENROLLMENT, as a citizen of the CREEK Nation, of Marley Hall, born on the 17 day of Dec , 1904

Name of Father:	Sandy Hall	a citizen of the	Creek	Nation.
Name of Mother:	Martha "	a citizen of the	U.S.	Nation.

Postoffice Oktaha

AFFIDAVIT OF MOTHER.

UNITED STATES OF AMERICA, Indian Territory,
    WESTERN   DISTRICT.

I, Sandy Hall , on oath state that I am 21 years of age and a citizen by blood , of the Creek Nation; that I am the lawful ~~wife~~ hus of Martha Hall , who is a citizen, by ----- of the U.S. Nation; that a female child was born to me on 17 day of Dec , 1904, that said child has been named Marley Hall , and was living March 4, 1905.

                                  Sandy Hall

Witnesses To Mark:
{

Subscribed and sworn to before me this 14 day of March , 1905.

                                  Edw C Griesel
                                  Notary Public.

AFFIDAVIT OF ATTENDING PHYSICIAN OR MID-WIFE.

UNITED STATES OF AMERICA, Indian Territory,
    Western   DISTRICT.

I, Canzada McCaslin , a midwife , on oath state that I attended on Mrs. Martha Hall, wife of Sandy Hall on the 17 day of Dec. , 1904 ; that there was born to her on said date a female child; that said child was living March 4, 1905, and is said to have been named Marley Hall .

                                        her
                            Canzada x McCaslin

Witnesses To Mark: mark
  { H.G. Hains
    EC Griesel

Applications for Enrollment of Creek Newborn
Act of 1905   Volume II

Subscribed and sworn to before me this 14 day of March, 1905.

Edw C Griesel
Notary Public.

BIRTH AFFIDAVIT.

DEPARTMENT OF THE INTERIOR.
COMMISSION TO THE FIVE CIVILIZED TRIBES.

IN RE APPLICATION FOR ENROLLMENT, as a citizen of the Creek Nation, of Mollie Hall, born on the 17 day of Dec. , 1904

Name of Father:	Sandy Hall	a citizen of the Creek Nation.
Name of Mother:	Martha Hall	a citizen of the Creek by marriage.

Postoffice   Oktaha, I.T.

AFFIDAVIT OF MOTHER.

UNITED STATES OF AMERICA, Indian Territory, ⎱
          Western   DISTRICT.   ⎰

I, Martha Hall , on oath state that I am 18 years of age and a citizen by marriage , of the Creek Nation; that I am the lawful wife of Sandy Hall , who is a citizen, by blood of the Creek Nation; that a Female child was born to me on 17 day of December , 1904, that said child has been named Mollie Hall , and was living March 4, 1905.

her
Martha x Hall
mark

Witnesses To Mark:
⎰ Dug *(Illegible)*
⎱ Robt Jetton

Subscribed and sworn to before me this 20 day of May , 1905.

W.A. Cain
Notary Public.

AFFIDAVIT OF ATTENDING PHYSICIAN OR MID-WIFE.

UNITED STATES OF AMERICA, Indian Territory, ⎱
          Western Dist.   DISTRICT.   ⎰

I, Dr. A. J. Snelson , a Physician , on oath state that I attended on Mrs. Martha Hall, wife of Sandy Hall on the 17 day of Dec. , 1904 ; that there was born to her on

Applications for Enrollment of Creek Newborn
Act of 1905   Volume II

said date a Female child; that said child was living March 4, 1905, and is said to have been named Mollie Hall .

Witnesses To Mark:
{

A. J. Snelson
M.D.

Subscribed and sworn to before me this 20 day of May, 1905.

W. A. Cain
Notary Public.

NC 76.

Muskogee, Indian Territory, May 17, 1905.

Henry Carter,
    Oktaha, Indian Territory

Dear Sir:

    In the matter of the application for the enrollment of your minor children, Susie and Jennie Carter, as citizens of the Creek Nation, you are advised that the Commission requires the affidavit of the midwife or physician in attendance at the birth of said child. in attendance at the birth of said children.

    There are herewith enclosed two blank forms of birth affidavits, and in executing same care should be exercised to see that all blanks are properly filled, all names written in full and in the event that the persons signing the affidavits are unable to write, signatures by mark must be attested by two witnesses. Each affidavit must be executed before a Notary Public and the notarial seal and signature of the officer must be attached to each separate affidavit.

Respectfully,

BC.   Chairman.

NC .76

Muskogee, Indian Territory, May 22, 1905.

Henry Carter,
    Oktaha, Indian Territory.

Dear Sir:

Applications for Enrollment of Creek Newborn
Act of 1905 Volume II

The Commission is in receipt of your letter of May 19, in which you ask what was wrong with the affidavits you sent in.

In reply you are advised that the Commission requires the affidavit of the midwife or physician in attendance at the birth of your two children. In the event that no midwife or physician was present at the birth of said children, the affidavits of two disinterested witnesses as to their birth should be supplied.

There are herewith enclosed four blank forms of birth affidavit, and in executing same care should be exercised to see that all blanks are properly filled, all names written in full and in the event that either of the persons signing the affidavits is[sic] unable to write, signature by mark must be attested by two witnesses. Each affidavit must be executed before a Notary Public and the notarial seal and signature of the officer must be attached to each separate affidavit. This matter should receive your prompt attention.

Respectfully,

BC. Chairman.

DEPARTMENT OF THE INTERIOR,
COMMISSIONER TO THE FIVE CIVILIZED TRIBES.

REFER IN REPLY TO THE FOLLOWING:
N.C. 76.

Muskogee, Indian Territory, **August 4, 1905.**

Henry Carter,
Oktaha, Indian Territory.

Dear Sir:

You are hereby advised that on **July 28, 1905**, the Secretary of the Interior approved the enrollment of your minor child, **Susie Carter**, as a citizen by blood of the **Creek** Nation, and that the name of said child appears upon the roll of new born citizens of the **Creek** Nation as Number **48**.

The child is now entitled to an allotment, and application therefor should be made without delay at the Land Office for the Nation in which the prospective allotment is located.

An entire allotment for said child must be selected at the time of the original application.

Respectively,

Commissioner.

Applications for Enrollment of Creek Newborn
Act of 1905   Volume II

DEPARTMENT OF THE INTERIOR,
COMMISSIONER TO THE FIVE CIVILIZED TRIBES.

REFER IN REPLY TO THE FOLLOWING:

N.C. 76.

Muskogee, Indian Territory, **August 4, 1905.**

Henry Carter,
   Oktaha, Indian Territory.

Dear Sir:

You are hereby advised that on **July 28, 1905**, the Secretary of the Interior approved the enrollment of your minor child, **Jennie Carter**, as a citizen by blood of the **Creek** Nation, and that the name of said child appears upon the roll of new born citizens of the **Creek** Nation as Number **49**.

The child is now entitled to an allotment, and application therefor should be made without delay at the Land Office for the Nation in which the prospective allotment is located.

An entire allotment for said child must be selected at the time of the original application.

Respectively,

Commissioner.

BIRTH AFFIDAVIT.

DEPARTMENT OF THE INTERIOR.
COMMISSION TO THE FIVE CIVILIZED TRIBES.

IN RE APPLICATION FOR ENROLLMENT, as a citizen of the CREEK Nation, of Jennie Carter, born on the 14 day of Aug, 1902

Name of Father: Henry Carter   a citizen of the   Creek   Nation.
Name of Mother: Annie   "   a citizen of the   "   Nation.

Postoffice   Oktaha

child present

AFFIDAVIT OF MOTHER.

UNITED STATES OF AMERICA, Indian Territory,
          WESTERN   DISTRICT.

I, Annie Carter, on oath state that I am 27 years of age and a citizen by blood, of the Creek Nation; that I am the lawful wife of Henry Carter, who is a citizen, by blood of the Creek   Nation; that a female child was born to me on 14 day of Aug, 1902, that said child has been named Jennie Carter, and was living March 4, 1905.

Applications for Enrollment of Creek Newborn
Act of 1905   Volume II

                        Annie Carter

Witnesses To Mark:
{

    Subscribed and sworn to before me this 14 day of March , 1905.

                        Edw C Griesel
                        Notary Public.

AFFIDAVIT OF ATTENDING PHYSICIAN OR MID-WIFE.

UNITED STATES OF AMERICA, Indian Territory, }
    Western   DISTRICT.

    I, Henry Carter , am , ~~on oath state that I~~ attended on Mrs. *(blank)* , ~~wife~~ hus of Annie Carter on the 14 day of Aug , 1902 ; that there was born to her on said date a female child; that said child was living March 4, 1905, and is said to have been named Jennie Carter .

                        His
                  Henry x Carter
Witnesses To Mark: mark
{ JY Miller
  EC Griesel

    Subscribed and sworn to before me this 14 day of March, 1905.

                        Edw C Griesel
                        Notary Public.

BIRTH AFFIDAVIT.

DEPARTMENT OF THE INTERIOR.
COMMISSION TO THE FIVE CIVILIZED TRIBES.

    IN RE APPLICATION FOR ENROLLMENT, as a citizen of the Creek Nation, of Jennie Carter, born on the 14th day of August , 1902

Name of Father:	Henry C. Carter	a citizen of the	Creek	Nation.
Name of Mother:	Annie Carter	a citizen of the	Creek	Nation.

                Postoffice   Oktaha Indian Territory

Applications for Enrollment of Creek Newborn
Act of 1905   Volume II

AFFIDAVIT OF MOTHER.

UNITED STATES OF AMERICA, Indian Territory, }
    Western   DISTRICT.

    I, Annie Carter , on oath state that I am 27 years of age and a citizen by blood , of the Creek Nation; that I am the lawful wife of Henry C. Carter , who is a citizen, by blood of the Creek Nation; that a Female child was born to me on the 14th day of August , 1902 , that said child has been named Jennie Carter , and was living March 4, 1905.

                                              Annie Carter

Witnesses To Mark:
{ O. S. *(Illegible)*
  E D Casmean

    Subscribed and sworn to before me this 15th day of April , 1905.

                                              A. M. Darling
                                                  Notary Public.

AFFIDAVIT OF ATTENDING PHYSICIAN OR MID-WIFE.

UNITED STATES OF AMERICA, Indian Territory, }
    Western   DISTRICT.

    I, A. J. Snelson , a physician , on oath state that I attended on Mrs. Annie Carter , wife of Henry C Carter on the 14th day of August , 1902 ; that there was born to her on said date a Female child; that said child was living March 4, 1905, and is said to have been named Jennie Carter .

                                              A. J. Snelson

Witnesses To Mark:
{ E D Casmean

    Subscribed and sworn to before me this 15th day of April, 1905.

                                              A.M. Darling
                                              Notary Public.

Applications for Enrollment of Creek Newborn
Act of 1905 Volume II

BIRTH AFFIDAVIT.

DEPARTMENT OF THE INTERIOR.
COMMISSION TO THE FIVE CIVILIZED TRIBES.

IN RE APPLICATION FOR ENROLLMENT, as a citizen of the CREEK Nation, of Susie Carter, born on the 22 day of Sept., 1904

Name of Father: Henry Carter   a citizen of the   Creek   Nation.
Name of Mother: Annie   "   a citizen of the   "   Nation.

Postoffice   Oktaha

Child Present

AFFIDAVIT OF MOTHER.

UNITED STATES OF AMERICA, Indian Territory, }
    WESTERN   DISTRICT.

    I, Annie Carter, on oath state that I am 27 years of age and a citizen by blood, of the Creek Nation; that I am the lawful wife of Henry Carter, who is a citizen, by blood of the Creek Nation; that a female child was born to me on 22 day of Sept., 1904, that said child has been named Susie Carter, and was living March 4, 1905.

                      Annie Carter

Witnesses To Mark:
{

    Subscribed and sworn to before me this 14 day of March, 1905.

                      Edw C Griesel
                      Notary Public.

AFFIDAVIT OF ATTENDING PHYSICIAN OR MID-WIFE.

UNITED STATES OF AMERICA, Indian Territory, }
    Western   DISTRICT.

    I, Henry Carter, am, ~~on oath state that I~~ attended on Mrs. *(blank)*, ~~wife~~ husband of Annie Carter on the 22 day of Sept., 1904; that there was born to her on said date a female child; that said child was living March 4, 1905, and is said to have been named Susie Carter.

                      His
                      Henry x Carter
Witnesses To Mark: mark
  { JY Miller
    EC Griesel

Applications for Enrollment of Creek Newborn
Act of 1905   Volume II

Subscribed and sworn to before me this 14 day of March, 1905.

(No signature given)
Notary Public.

BIRTH AFFIDAVIT.

DEPARTMENT OF THE INTERIOR.
COMMISSION TO THE FIVE CIVILIZED TRIBES.

IN RE APPLICATION FOR ENROLLMENT, as a citizen of the Creek Nation, of Susie Carter, born on the 22 day of September, 1904

Name of Father: Henry C. Carter   a citizen of the   Creek   Nation.
Name of Mother: Annie Carter   a citizen of the   Creek   Nation.

Postoffice   Oktaha Indian Territory

AFFIDAVIT OF MOTHER.

UNITED STATES OF AMERICA, Indian Territory, ⎫
     Western   DISTRICT.   ⎬

I, Annie Carter, on oath state that I am 27 years of age and a citizen by blood, of the Creek Nation; that I am the lawful wife of Henry C. Carter, who is a citizen, by blood of the Creek Nation; that a female child was born to me on the 22nd day of September, 1904, that said child has been named Susie Carter, and was living March 4, 1905.

Annie Carter

Witnesses To Mark:
 { O. S. *(Illegible)*
 { E D Casmean

Subscribed and sworn to before me this 15 day of April, 1905.

A. M. Darling
Notary Public.

AFFIDAVIT OF ATTENDING PHYSICIAN OR MID-WIFE.

UNITED STATES OF AMERICA, Indian Territory, ⎫
     Western   DISTRICT.   ⎬

I, A. J. Snelson, a physician, on oath state that I attended on Mrs. Annie Carter, wife of Henry C Carter on the 22nd day of September, 1904; that there was born to

Applications for Enrollment of Creek Newborn
Act of 1905   Volume II

her on said date a female child; that said child was living March 4, 1905, and is said to have been named Susie Carter.

A. J. Snelson

Witnesses To Mark:
{ E D Casmean

Subscribed and sworn to before me this 15th day of April, 1905.

A.M. Darling
Notary Public.

NC 77.

Muskogee, Indian Territory, May 17, 1905.

William S. Murphy,
    Muskogee, Indian Territory.

Dear Sir:

    In the matter of the application for the enrollment of your minor child, Eva Doris Murphy, as a citizen of the Creek Nation, you are advised that the Commission requires the affidavit of the mother of said child.

    There is herewith enclosed a blank form of birth affidavit, and in executing same care should be exercised to see that all blanks are properly filled, all names written in full and in the event that the person signing the affidavit is unable to write, signature by mark must be attested by two witnesses. Each affidavit must be executed before a Notary Public and the notarial seal and signature of the officer must be attached to each separate affidavit.

Respectfully,

BC.   Chairman.

Cr NC-77

Muskogee, Indian Territory, May 27, 1905.

William S. Murphy,
    Muskogee, Indian Territory.

Dear Sir:

Applications for Enrollment of Creek Newborn
Act of 1905 Volume II

In the matter of the application for the enrollment of your minor child, Eva Doris Murphy, as a citizen of the Creek Nation, you are advised that the Commission required the affidavits of two disinterested parties as to the death of Nettie Murphy, and to the fact that she was the mother of said Eva Doris Murphy.

This matter should be attended to at your earliest convenience.

Respectfully,

Chairman.

DEPARTMENT OF THE INTERIOR,
COMMISSIONER TO THE FIVE CIVILIZED TRIBES.

REFER IN REPLY TO THE FOLLOWING:
N.C. 77.

Muskogee, Indian Territory, **August 4, 1905.**

William S. Murphy,
    Muskogee, Indian Territory.

Dear Sir:

You are hereby advised that on **July 28, 1905**, the Secretary of the Interior approved the enrollment of your minor child, **Eva Dorcas**[sic] **Murphy**, as a citizen by blood of the **Creek** Nation, and that the name of said child appears upon the roll of new born citizens of the **Creek** Nation as Number **50**.

The child is now entitled to an allotment, and application therefor should be made without delay at the Land Office for the Nation in which the prospective allotment is located.

An entire allotment for said child must be selected at the time of the original application.

Respectively,

Commissioner.

DEPARTMENT OF THE INTERIOR.
COMMISSION TO THE FIVE CIVILIZED TRIBES.

In the matter of the death of ~~Eva~~ Nettie Murphy a citizen of the U.S. Nation, who formerly resided at or near Muskogee, Ind. Ter., and died on the 2 day of March, 1905.

Applications for Enrollment of Creek Newborn
Act of 1905 Volume II

AFFIDAVIT OF RELATIVE.

UNITED STATES OF AMERICA, Indian Territory, }
Western DISTRICT.

    I, Wm S. Murphy, on oath state that I am 23 years of age and a citizen by blood, of the Creek Nation; that my postoffice address is Muskogee, Ind. Ter.; that I am husband of Nettie Murphy who was a citizen, by -----, of the U.S. Nation and that said Nettie Murphy died on the 2 day of March, 1905.

                                Wm S. Murphy

Witnesses To Mark:
{

    Subscribed and sworn to before me this 1 day of June, 1905.

                                Henry G. Hains
                                Notary Public.

BIRTH AFFIDAVIT.

DEPARTMENT OF THE INTERIOR.
COMMISSION TO THE FIVE CIVILIZED TRIBES.

    IN RE APPLICATION FOR ENROLLMENT, as a citizen of the Creek Nation, of Eva Dorris Murphy, born on the 3rd day of October, 1904

Name of Father: William S. Murphy   a citizen of the   Creek   Nation.
Name of Mother: Nettie Murphy   a citizen of the   U.S.   Nation.

                    Postoffice   Muskogee, IT.

AFFIDAVIT OF ATTENDING PHYSICIAN OR MID-WIFE.

UNITED STATES OF AMERICA, Indian Territory, }
Western DISTRICT.

    I, J. O. Callahan, a Physician, on oath state that I attended on Mrs. Nettie Murphy, wife of William S. Murphy on the 3rd day of Oct, 1904; that there was born to her on said date a Female child; that said child was living March 4, 1905, and is said to have been named Eva Dorris Murphy.

                                J.O. Callahan M.D.

Witnesses To Mark:
{

Applications for Enrollment of Creek Newborn
Act of 1905 Volume II

Subscribed and sworn to before me this 22" day of April, 1905.

                     Edward Merrick
                     Notary Public.

BIRTH AFFIDAVIT.

DEPARTMENT OF THE INTERIOR.
COMMISSION TO THE FIVE CIVILIZED TRIBES.

IN RE APPLICATION FOR ENROLLMENT, as a citizen of the Creek Nation, of Eva Doris Murphy, born on the about 3" day of October, 1904

Name of Father:	Wm S. Murphy	a citizen of the	Creek	Nation.
Name of Mother:	Nettie Murphy	a citizen of the	U.S.	Nation.

               Postoffice   Muskogee

                     disinterested witness

AFFIDAVIT OF MOTHER.

UNITED STATES OF AMERICA, Indian Territory, ⎫
       Western   DISTRICT. ⎭

     I, W. F. Blakemore, on oath state that I am 30 years of age and a citizen by -----, of the U.S. Nation; that I am the lawful wife of was acquainted with Nettie Murphy, who is was a citizen, by ----- of the U.S. Nation; that a female child was born to me her on about 3" day of October, 1904, that said child has been named Eva Doris Murphy, and was living March 4, 1905.

                     W. F. Blakemore

Witnesses To Mark:
{

Subscribed and sworn to before me this 1st day of June, 1905.

                     Henry G. Hains
                     Notary Public.

BIRTH AFFIDAVIT.

DEPARTMENT OF THE INTERIOR.
COMMISSION TO THE FIVE CIVILIZED TRIBES.

IN RE APPLICATION FOR ENROLLMENT, as a citizen of the Creek Nation, of Eva Doris Murphy, born on the about 3 day of October, 1904

Applications for Enrollment of Creek Newborn
Act of 1905 Volume II

Name of Father: Wm S. Murphy   a citizen of the   Creek   Nation.
Name of Mother: Nettie " (dec'd)   a citizen of the   U.S.   Nation.

Postoffice   Muskogee

disinterested witness

AFFIDAVIT OF ~~MOTHER.~~

UNITED STATES OF AMERICA, Indian Territory, ⎱
     Western   DISTRICT. ⎰

     I, Joseph M. Lightle , on oath state that I am 46 years of age and a citizen by ----- , of the U.S. Nation; that I ~~am the lawful wife of~~ was acquainted with Nettie Murphy , who ~~is~~ was a citizen, by ----- of the U.S. Nation; that a female child was born to ~~me~~ her on about 3" day of October , 1904, that said child has been named Eva Doris Murphy, and was living March 4, 1905.

Joseph M. Lightle

Witnesses To Mark:
     ⎰
     ⎱

     Subscribed and sworn to before me this 1st day of June , 1905.

Henry G. Hains
Notary Public.

BIRTH AFFIDAVIT.

DEPARTMENT OF THE INTERIOR.
COMMISSION TO THE FIVE CIVILIZED TRIBES.

Doris

     IN RE APPLICATION FOR ENROLLMENT, as a citizen of the CREEK Nation, of Eva ~~Doreas~~ Murphy , born on the 3 day of Oct , 1904

Name of Father: William S. Murphy   a citizen of the   Creek   Nation.
Name of Mother: Nettie Murphy   a citizen of the   U.S.   Nation.

Postoffice   Muskogee

AFFIDAVIT OF ~~MOTHER.~~ father

UNITED STATES OF AMERICA, Indian Territory, ⎱
     WESTERN   DISTRICT. ⎰

     I, William S. Murphy , on oath state that I am 23 years of age and a citizen by blood , of the Creek Nation; that I am the lawful ~~wife~~ husb of Nettie Murphy (dec'd) , who is a citizen, by ----- of the U.S. Nation; that a female child was born to me on 3

Applications for Enrollment of Creek Newborn
Act of 1905 Volume II

day of Oct , 1904 , that said child has been named Eva Dorcas Murphy , and is now living.

Wm S. Murphy

Witnesses To Mark:
{

Subscribed and sworn to before me this 8 day of March, 1905.

Edw C Griesel
Notary Public.

NC 78.

Muskogee, Indian Territory, May 17, 1905.

John Palmer,
    Sharper, Indian Territory.

Dear Sir:

    In the matter of the application for the enrollment of your minor children, Jim and Daniel Palmer, as a citizen of the Creek Nation, you are advised that the Commission requires the affidavit of the midwife or physician in attendance at the birth of said children.

    There are herewith enclosed two blank forms of birth affidavits, and in executing same care should be exercised to see that all blanks are properly filled, all names written in full and in the event that the person signing the affidavits is unable to write, signature by mark must be attested by two witnesses. Each affidavit must be executed before a Notary Public and the notarial seal and signature of the officer must be attached to each separate affidavit.

Respectfully,

BC.   Chairman.

COPY   N.C.78.

Muskogee, Indian Territory, May 31, 1905.

Liza Palmer,
    Sharpe, Indian Territory.

Dear Madam:

Applications for Enrollment of Creek Newborn
Act of 1905   Volume II

      There are on file with the Commission affidavits relative to your new born children, in which your name is given as Liza and Eliza Palmer, and the children's names variously as Jim and James W., Daniel and Daniel B. Palmer.

      You are requested to advise the Commission as to the correct names of said children. You have been identified on the Creek rolls as Eliza Ryan.

Respectfully,

Tams Bixby, Chairman.

B.

Dear Sir:-Refering to the above would say My name is Eliza Palmer, nee Ryan, andnot[sic] 'Liza' Palmer, and that the correct names of my children are James W. Palmer and Daniel B. Palmer as stated in my affidavits of May 26th/05. You will also observe that my name appears on the Creek rolls as Eliza Ryan and not ' 'Liza' ', I presume the name ' 'Liza' ' was given you by some one. The record of my marriage to John W. Palmer you can find in the U. S. Clerk's office at Muskogee, I.T. This 3rd day of June 1905.
                              (Signed) Eliza Palmer
Seal
Sworn and subscribed to before me this 3rd day of June 1905.
  My commission expires July 8/05.
                        B. Nicholas
                        NOTARY PUBLIC.

BIRTH AFFIDAVIT.

DEPARTMENT OF THE INTERIOR.

COMMISSION TO THE FIVE CIVILIZED TRIBES.

      IN RE APPLICATION FOR ENROLLMENT, as a citizen of the Creek Nation, of Jim Palmer, born on the 17 day of Oct , 1901

Name of Father: John Palmer	a citizen of the	*(blank)*	Nation.
Name of Mother: Liza "	a citizen of the	Creek	Nation.

Postoffice   Sharpe

Applications for Enrollment of Creek Newborn
Act of 1905 Volume II

AFFIDAVIT OF MOTHER.

UNITED STATES OF AMERICA, Indian Territory, }
    Western   DISTRICT.

    I, Liza Palmer , on oath state that I am 25 years of age and a citizen by blood, of the Creek Nation; that I am the lawful wife of John Palmer , who is a citizen, by blood of the Creek Nation; that a male child was born to me on 17 day of Oct , 1901 , that said child has been named Jim Palmer , and is now living.

                                      Mrs Eliza Palmer

Witnesses To Mark:
{

    Subscribed and sworn to before me this 13 day of March , 1905.

                                      Edw C Griesel
                                        Notary Public.

BIRTH AFFIDAVIT.

DEPARTMENT OF THE INTERIOR.
COMMISSION TO THE FIVE CIVILIZED TRIBES.

    IN RE APPLICATION FOR ENROLLMENT, as a citizen of the CREEK Nation, of Jim Palmer, born on the ----- day of Oct , 1901

Name of Father: John Palmer   a citizen of the   U. S.   Nation.
Name of Mother: Liza   "   a citizen of the   Creek   Nation.

                            Postoffice   Sharpe, I.T.

---

                                    acquaintance
AFFIDAVIT OF ~~MOTHER~~.

UNITED STATES OF AMERICA, Indian Territory, }
    WESTERN   DISTRICT.

    I, Mary L Harred[sic] , on oath state that I am 72 years of age and a citizen by blood, of the Creek Nation; that I am the ~~lawful wife~~ great grand-aunt of Jim Palmer , ~~who is a citizen, by~~ *(blank)* ~~of the~~ *(blank)* ~~Nation; that a~~ *(blank)* ~~child~~ who was born ~~to me~~ on ----- day of Oct , 1901 , that said child has been named *(blank)* , and ~~is now living~~. I saw said Jim alive in December 1904.

                                      Mary L Herrod

Witnesses To Mark:
{

Applications for Enrollment of Creek Newborn
Act of 1905   Volume II

Subscribed and sworn to before me this 8 day of March, 1905.

           Edw C Griesel
            Notary Public.

BIRTH AFFIDAVIT.

DEPARTMENT OF THE INTERIOR.
COMMISSION TO THE FIVE CIVILIZED TRIBES.

IN RE APPLICATION FOR ENROLLMENT, as a citizen of the Creek Nation, of James W. Palmer, born on the 17th day of October, 1901

Name of Father: John W. Palmer by marriage	a citizen of the Creek	Nation.
Name of Mother: Eliza Palmer	a citizen of the Creek	Nation.

        Postoffice Sharp, Ind. Ter.

AFFIDAVIT OF MOTHER.

UNITED STATES OF AMERICA, Indian Territory, ⎱
  Western Judicial DISTRICT. ⎰

  I, Eliza Palmer, on oath state that I am 25 years of age and a citizen by birth, of the Creek Nation; that I am the lawful wife of John W. Palmer, who is a citizen, by marriage of the Creek Nation; that a male child was born to me on 17th day of October, 1901 ; that said child has been named James W. Palmer, and was living March 4, 1905.

           Eliza Palmer

Witnesses To Mark:
 {

Subscribed and sworn to before me this 26th day of May, 1905.
My commission expires July 8/06.

           Bhirholas
            Notary Public.

AFFIDAVIT OF ATTENDING PHYSICIAN OR MID-WIFE.

UNITED STATES OF AMERICA, Indian Territory, ⎱
  Western Judicial DISTRICT. ⎰

  I, Mary McCormick, a midwife, on oath state that I attended on Mrs. Eliza Palmer, wife of John W. Palmer on the 17th day of October, 1901; that there was

Applications for Enrollment of Creek Newborn
Act of 1905 Volume II

born to her on said date a male child; that said child was living March 4, 1905, and is said to have been named James W. Palmer .

Mary McCormick

Witnesses To Mark:
{

Subscribed and sworn to before me this 26th day of May , 1905. My commission expires July 8/06.

Bhirholas
Notary Public.

BIRTH AFFIDAVIT.

DEPARTMENT OF THE INTERIOR.
COMMISSION TO THE FIVE CIVILIZED TRIBES.

IN RE APPLICATION FOR ENROLLMENT, as a citizen of the CREEK Nation, of Daniel Palmer, born on the ----- day of Sept , 1904

Name of Father: John Palmer	a citizen of the U. S. Nation.
Name of Mother: Liza "	a citizen of the Creek Nation.

Postoffice Sharpe, I.T.

Great Grand Aunt

AFFIDAVIT OF ~~MOTHER~~.

UNITED STATES OF AMERICA, Indian Territory, ⎫
    WESTERN   DISTRICT. ⎭

I, Mary L Harred[sic] , on oath state that I am 72 years of age and a citizen by blood, of the Creek Nation; that I am the ~~lawful wife~~ great grand-aunt of Daniel Palmer , who ~~is a citizen, by~~ *(blank)* ~~of the~~ *(blank)* ~~Nation; that a~~ *(blank)* ~~child who~~ was born ~~to me~~ on ----- day of Sept , 1904 , that said child has been named *(blank)* , and is now living.

Mary L Herrod

Witnesses To Mark:
{

Subscribed and sworn to before me this 8 day of March , 1905.

Edw C Griesel
Notary Public.

Applications for Enrollment of Creek Newborn
Act of 1905 Volume II

BIRTH AFFIDAVIT.

DEPARTMENT OF THE INTERIOR.
COMMISSION TO THE FIVE CIVILIZED TRIBES.

IN RE APPLICATION FOR ENROLLMENT, as a citizen of the Creek Nation, of Daniel Palmer, born on the 8 day of Sept, 1904

| Name of Father: | John Palmer | a citizen of the | U. S. | Nation. |
| Name of Mother: | Liza " | a citizen of the | Creek | Nation. |

Postoffice Sharpe

Child Present

AFFIDAVIT OF MOTHER.

UNITED STATES OF AMERICA, Indian Territory,
Western Judicial DISTRICT.

I, Liza Palmer, on oath state that I am 25 years of age and a citizen by blood, of the Creek Nation; that I am the lawful wife of John Palmer, who is a citizen, by blood of the ~~Sept.~~ Creek Nation; that a male child was born to me on 8 day of Sept, 1904; that said child has been named Daniel Palmer, and is now living.

Mrs Eliza Palmer

Witnesses To Mark:
{

Subscribed and sworn to before me this 13 day of March, 1905.

Edw C Griesel
Notary Public.

BIRTH AFFIDAVIT.

DEPARTMENT OF THE INTERIOR.
COMMISSION TO THE FIVE CIVILIZED TRIBES.

IN RE APPLICATION FOR ENROLLMENT, as a citizen of the Creek Nation, of Daniel B. Palmer, born on the 8th day of September, 1904

| Name of Father: | John W. Palmer by marriage | a citizen of the | Creek | Nation. |
| Name of Mother: | Eliza Palmer | a citizen of the | Creek | Nation. |

Postoffice Sharp, Ind. Ter.

Applications for Enrollment of Creek Newborn
Act of 1905   Volume II

AFFIDAVIT OF MOTHER.

UNITED STATES OF AMERICA, Indian Territory, }
    Wester[sic] Judicial   DISTRICT.

    I, Eliza Palmer, on oath state that I am 25 years of age and a citizen by birth, of the Creek Nation; that I am the lawful wife of John W. Palmer, who is a citizen, by marriage of the Creek Nation; that a male child was born to me on 8th day of September, 1904; that said child has been named Daniel B. Palmer, and is now living.

                                     Eliza Palmer

Witnesses To Mark:
{

    Subscribed and sworn to before me this 26th day of May, 1905.
My commission expires July 8/06.

                                     Bhirholas
                                            Notary Public.

AFFIDAVIT OF ATTENDING PHYSICIAN OR MID-WIFE.

UNITED STATES OF AMERICA, Indian Territory, }
    Western Judicial   DISTRICT.

    I, Sarah Palmer, a midwife, on oath state that I attended on Mrs. Eliza Palmer, wife of John W. Palmer on the 8th day of September, 1904; that there was born to her on said date a male child; that said child is now living and is said to have been named Daniel B. Palmer.

                                       her
                                 Sarah X Palmer

Witnesses To Mark: mark
{ Mollie Farr
  Carrel Farr

Subscribed and sworn to before me this 26th day of May, 1905.
My commission expires July 8/06.

                                   Bhirholas
                                   Notary Public.

(Note: Original application form badly damaged.)

NC 79.

Muskogee, Indian Territory, May 17, 1905.

Joseph H. Land,
    Sapulpa, Indian Territory.

Applications for Enrollment of Creek Newborn
Act of 1905   Volume II

Dear Sir:

In the matter of the application for the enrollment of your minor child, Helen Land, as a citizen of the Creek Nation, you are advised that the Commission requires the affidavit of the midwife or physician in attendance at the birth of said child.

There is herewith enclosed a blank form of birth affidavit, and in executing same care should be exercised to see that all blanks are properly filled, all names written in full and in the event that the person signing the affidavit is unable to write, signature by mark must be attested by two witnesses. Each affidavit must be executed before a Notary Public and the notarial seal and signature of the officer must be attached to each separate affidavit.

Respectfully,

BC.   Chairman.

DEPARTMENT OF THE INTERIOR.
COMMISSION TO THE FIVE CIVILIZED TRIBES.

NC. 79.

Muskogee, Indian Territory, July 18, 1905.

Salina Land,
    Sapulpa, Indian Territory.

Dear Madam:

There are on file at this office affidavits executed by you and your husband, Joseph H. Land, in which the date of the birth of your minor child Helen Land is given as November 3, 1902.

You are requested to sign and execute the enclosed affidavit before an officer authorized to administer oaths, taking care to insert the correct date of birth of said child, and return same to this office in the enclosed envelope.

Respectfully,

Tams Bixby

LM-7-18-79.   Commissioner.

(The above was copied again.)

Applications for Enrollment of Creek Newborn
Act of 1905   Volume II

BIRTH AFFIDAVIT.

DEPARTMENT OF THE INTERIOR.
COMMISSION TO THE FIVE CIVILIZED TRIBES.

IN RE APPLICATION FOR ENROLLMENT, as a citizen of the Creek Nation, of Helen Land, born on the 3rd day of November, 1902

Name of Father: Joseph H. Land   a citizen of the   Creek   Nation.
Name of Mother: Salina Land   a citizen of the   Creek   Nation.
                        Postoffice   Sapulpa, I.T.

AFFIDAVIT OF MOTHER.

UNITED STATES OF AMERICA, Indian Territory,
   Western   DISTRICT.

I, Joseph H. Land, on oath state that I am 47 years of age and a citizen by blood, of the Creek Nation; that I am the lawful ~~wife~~ husband of Salina Land, who is a citizen, by blood of the Creek Nation; that a female child was born to me on 3rd day of November, 1902, that said child has been named Helen Land, and is now living.

                                Joseph Henry Land
Witnesses To Mark:
   {

   Subscribed and sworn to before me this 26th day of July, 1905.

My Commission expires 10/20-1906   Joseph Bruner
                                          Notary Public.

AFFIDAVIT OF ATTENDING PHYSICIAN OR MID-WIFE.

UNITED STATES OF AMERICA, Indian Territory,
   Western   DISTRICT.

I, H. O. Lyford, a Physician, on oath state that I attended on Mrs. Salina Land, wife of Joseph H. Land on the 3rd day of November, 1902; that there was born to her on said date a female child; that said child is now living and is said to have been named Helen Land.

                                H. O. Lyford M.D.
Witnesses To Mark:
   {

   Subscribed and sworn to before me this ~~25~~ 26th day of July, 1905.

49

Applications for Enrollment of Creek Newborn
Act of 1905   Volume II

My Commission expires 10/20-1906   Joseph Bruner
                                     Notary Public.

BIRTH AFFIDAVIT.

DEPARTMENT OF THE INTERIOR.
COMMISSION TO THE FIVE CIVILIZED TRIBES.

IN RE APPLICATION FOR ENROLLMENT, as a citizen of the Creek Nation, of Helen Land, born on the 3rd day of November, 1902

Name of Father: Joseph H. Land   a citizen of the   Creek   Nation.
Name of Mother: Salina Land   a citizen of the   Creek   Nation.

Postoffice   Sapulpa, I.T.

AFFIDAVIT OF MOTHER.

UNITED STATES OF AMERICA, Indian Territory,
     Western   DISTRICT.

I, Salina Land, on oath state that I am 33 years of age and a citizen by blood, of the Creek Nation; that I am the lawful wife of Joseph H. Land, who is a citizen, by blood of the Creek Nation; that a female child was born to me on 3rd day of November, 1902, that said child has been named Helen Land, and is now living.

                                     her
                              Salina x Land
Witnesses To Mark: mark
 { J.R. Langley
 { W Y Mason

Subscribed and sworn to before me this 26th day of November, 1905.

My Commission expires 10/20-1906   Joseph Bruner
                                     Notary Public.

BIRTH AFFIDAVIT.

DEPARTMENT OF THE INTERIOR.
COMMISSION TO THE FIVE CIVILIZED TRIBES.

IN RE APPLICATION FOR ENROLLMENT, as a citizen of the CREEK Nation, of Helen Land, born on the 4 day of November, 1902

Name of Father: Joseph H. Land   a citizen of the   Creek   Nation.
Name of Mother: Salina   "   a citizen of the   "   Nation.

Applications for Enrollment of Creek Newborn
Act of 1905 Volume II

Postoffice   Sapulpa, I.T.

(Child Present)

AFFIDAVIT OF ~~MOTHER~~. father

UNITED STATES OF AMERICA, Indian Territory,
    WESTERN   DISTRICT.

I, Joseph H. Land , on oath state that I am 47 years of age and a citizen by blood, of the Creek   Nation; that I am the lawful ~~wife~~ hus of Salina Land , who is a citizen, by blood of the Creek   Nation; that a female   child was born to me on 4 day of Nov. , 1902 , that said child has been named Helen Land   , and is now living.

Joseph H. Land

Witnesses To Mark:
{

Subscribed and sworn to before me this 9 day of March, 1905.

Edw C Griesel
Notary Public.

BIRTH AFFIDAVIT.

DEPARTMENT OF THE INTERIOR.
COMMISSION TO THE FIVE CIVILIZED TRIBES.

IN RE APPLICATION FOR ENROLLMENT, as a citizen of the Creek Nation, of Helen Land , born on the 3' day of November , 1902

Name of Father: Joseph H. Land   a citizen of the   Creek   Nation.
Name of Mother: Salina G Land   a citizen of the   Creek   Nation.

Postoffice   Sapulpa, I.T.

AFFIDAVIT OF ATTENDING PHYSICIAN OR MID-WIFE.

UNITED STATES OF AMERICA, Indian Territory,
        Western   DISTRICT.

I, H. O. Lyford , a Physician   , on oath state that I attended on Mrs. Silina[sic] Land, wife of Joseph H. Land on the 3" day of November , 1902 ; that there was born to her on said date a Female child; that said child was living March 4, 1905, and is said to have been named Helen .

H. O. Lyford

Witnesses To Mark:
{

Applications for Enrollment of Creek Newborn
Act of 1905 Volume II

Subscribed and sworn to before me this 22 day of May , 1905.
My Commission expires 10/20-1906   Joseph Bruner
                                                    Notary Public.

BIRTH AFFIDAVIT.

DEPARTMENT OF THE INTERIOR.
COMMISSION TO THE FIVE CIVILIZED TRIBES.

IN RE APPLICATION FOR ENROLLMENT, as a citizen of the CREEK Nation, of Helen Land , born on the 4 day of Nov. , 1902

Name of Father: Joseph H. Land   a citizen of the   Creek   Nation.
Name of Mother: Salina   "   a citizen of the   "   Nation.

                            Postoffice   Sapulpa, I.T.

(Child Present)
AFFIDAVIT OF MOTHER.

UNITED STATES OF AMERICA, Indian Territory, ⎫
      WESTERN   DISTRICT. ⎭

I, Salina Land , on oath state that I am 33 years of age and a citizen by blood, of the Creek Nation; that I am the lawful wife of Joseph H. Land , who is a citizen, by blood of the Creek Nation; that a female child was born to me on 4 day of Nov. , 1902 , that said child has been named Helen Land , and is now living.

                                              her
                                      Salina x Land
Witnesses To Mark: mark
  { Irwin Donovan
  { Edw C Griesel

Subscribed and sworn to before me this 9 day of March, 1905.

                                      Edw C Griesel
                                        Notary Public.

NC 80.

Muskogee, Indian Territory, May 17, 1905.

Earnest Drew,
    Tulsa, Indian Territory.

Applications for Enrollment of Creek Newborn
Act of 1905   Volume II

Dear Sir:

In the matter of the application for the enrollment of your minor children, Earl B. and Ray W. Drew, as citizens of the Creek Nation, you are advised that the Commission requires the affidavit of the midwife or physician in attendance at the birth of said children.

There are herewith enclosed two blank forms of birth affidavits, and in executing same care should be exercised to see that all blanks are properly filled, all names written in full and in the event that the person signing the is unable to write, signature by mark must be attested by two witnesses. Each affidavit must be executed before a Notary Public and the notarial seal and signature of the officer must be attached to each separate affidavit.

Respectfully,

BC.   Chairman.

BIRTH AFFIDAVIT.

DEPARTMENT OF THE INTERIOR.
COMMISSION TO THE FIVE CIVILIZED TRIBES.

IN RE APPLICATION FOR ENROLLMENT, as a citizen of the Creek Nation, of Roy W Drew, born on the 23 day of Augst., 1904

Name of Father:	Ernest Drew	a citizen of the	Creek	Nation.
Name of Mother:	Alice Drew	a citizen of the	Creek	Nation.

Postoffice   Tulsa, I.T.

AFFIDAVIT OF MOTHER.

UNITED STATES OF AMERICA, Indian Territory,
       Western   DISTRICT.

I, Alice Drew, on oath state that I am 24 years of age and a citizen by blood, of the Creek Nation; that I am the lawful wife of Ernest Drew, who is a citizen, by marriage of the Creek Nation; that a male child was born to me on 23rd day of August, 1904, that said child has been named Roy W Drew, and is now living.

Alice Drew

Witnesses To Mark:
   Jessie Clark
   John W. Terryman

Subscribed and sworn to before me this 15 day of March, 1905.

Applications for Enrollment of Creek Newborn
Act of 1905   Volume II

My Commission Expires Dec. 15, 1907.   Wm *(Illegible)*
                                                                            Notary Public.

AFFIDAVIT OF ATTENDING PHYSICIAN OR MID-WIFE.

UNITED STATES OF AMERICA, Indian Territory, ⎫
    Western   DISTRICT. ⎬

I, Sallie Drew , a midwife , on oath state that I attended on Mrs. Alice Drew , wife of Ernest Drew on the 23^d day of August , 1904 ; that there was born to her on said date a male child; that said child is now living and is said to have been named Roy W. Drew.

                                      Sallie Drew

Witnesses To Mark:
  { Jessie Clark
    John W Terryman

Subscribed and sworn to before me this 15 day of March, 1905.

My Commission Expires Dec. 15, 1907.   Wm *(Illegible)*
                                                                            Notary Public.

BIRTH AFFIDAVIT.

DEPARTMENT OF THE INTERIOR.
COMMISSION TO THE FIVE CIVILIZED TRIBES.

IN RE APPLICATION FOR ENROLLMENT, as a citizen of the CREEK Nation, of Roy W Drew , born on the 23 day of Aug. , 1904

| Name of Father: | Ernest Drew | a citizen of the | U. S. | Nation. |
| Name of Mother: | Alice Drew | a citizen of the | Creek | Nation. |

                            Postoffice   Tulsa

Child present
                       AFFIDAVIT OF MOTHER.

UNITED STATES OF AMERICA, Indian Territory, ⎫
    WESTERN   DISTRICT.⎬

I, Alice Drew , on oath state that I am 24 years of age and a citizen by blood , of the Creek Nation; that I am the lawful wife of Ernest Drew , who is a citizen, by ----- of the U. S. Nation; that a male child was born to me on 23 day of Aug , 1904 , that said child has been named Roy W Drew , and is now living.

Applications for Enrollment of Creek Newborn
Act of 1905   Volume II

Alice Drew

Witnesses To Mark:
{

Subscribed and sworn to before me this 14 day of March , 1905.

Edw C Griesel
Notary Public.

BIRTH AFFIDAVIT.

DEPARTMENT OF THE INTERIOR.
COMMISSION TO THE FIVE CIVILIZED TRIBES.

IN RE APPLICATION FOR ENROLLMENT, as a citizen of the Creek Nation, of Roy W. Drew, born on the 23 day of Aug. , 1904

Name of Father:	Ernest Drew	a citizen of the	U S.	Nation.
Name of Mother:	Alice T. Drew	a citizen of the	Creek	Nation.

Postoffice   Tulsa, I.T.

AFFIDAVIT OF MOTHER.

UNITED STATES OF AMERICA, Indian Territory, ⎱
   Western   DISTRICT. ⎰

I, Alice T. Drew , on oath state that I am 24 years of age and a citizen by Blood , of the Creek Nation; that I am the lawful wife of Ernest Drew , who is a citizen, by marriage of the Creek Nation; that a male child was born to me on 23 day of August , 1904 , that said child has been named Roy W Drew , and was living March 4, 1905.

Alice T. Drew

Witnesses To Mark:
{

Subscribed and sworn to before me this 20 day of May , 1905.

My Commission Expires Dec. 15, 1907.   Wm *(Illegible)*
Notary Public.

Applications for Enrollment of Creek Newborn
Act of 1905   Volume II

AFFIDAVIT OF ATTENDING PHYSICIAN OR MID-WIFE.

UNITED STATES OF AMERICA, Indian Territory, }
Western   DISTRICT.

I, Sallie Drew , a mid-wife , on oath state that I attended on Mrs. Alice T. Drew, wife of Ernest Drew on the 23^d day of August , 1904 ; that there was born to her on said date a *(blank)* child; that said child was living March 4, 1905, and is said to have been named Roy W. Drew.

Sallie Drew

Witnesses To Mark:
{

Subscribed and sworn to before me this 20 day of May, 1905.

My Commission Expires Dec. 15, 1907.   Wm *(Illegible)*
Notary Public.

BIRTH AFFIDAVIT.

DEPARTMENT OF THE INTERIOR.
COMMISSION TO THE FIVE CIVILIZED TRIBES.

IN RE APPLICATION FOR ENROLLMENT, as a citizen of the CREEK Nation, of Roy W. Drew, born on the 23 day of Aug. , 1904

Name of Father:	Ernest Drew	a citizen of the	U. S.	Nation.
Name of Mother:	Alice Drew	a citizen of the	Creek	Nation.

Postoffice   Tulsa

Child present

AFFIDAVIT OF MOTHER.

UNITED STATES OF AMERICA, Indian Territory, }
   WESTERN   DISTRICT.

I, Alice Drew , on oath state that I am 24 years of age and a citizen by blood , of the Creek Nation; that I am the lawful wife of Earnest[sic] Drew , who is a citizen, by ----- of the U. S. Nation; that a male   child was born to me on 23 day of Aug , 1904; that said child has been named Roy W. Drew   , and is now living.

Alice Drew

Witnesses To Mark:
{

Applications for Enrollment of Creek Newborn
Act of 1905   Volume II

Subscribed and sworn to before me this 14 day of March , 1905.
Edw C Griesel
Notary Public.

BIRTH AFFIDAVIT.

DEPARTMENT OF THE INTERIOR.
COMMISSION TO THE FIVE CIVILIZED TRIBES.

IN RE APPLICATION FOR ENROLLMENT, as a citizen of the Creek Nation, of Roy W. Drew, born on the 23 day of Aug. , 1904

Name of Father:	Ernest Drew	a citizen of the	U S.	Nation.
Name of Mother:	Alice T. Drew	a citizen of the	Creek	Nation.

Postoffice   Tulsa, I.T.

AFFIDAVIT OF MOTHER.

UNITED STATES OF AMERICA, Indian Territory,
Western   DISTRICT.

I, Alice T. Drew , on oath state that I am 24 years of age and a citizen by Blood , of the Creek Nation; that I am the lawful wife of Ernest Drew , who is a citizen, by marriage of the Creek Nation; that a male child was born to me on 23 day of August , 1904 , that said child has been named Roy W Drew , and was living March 4, 1905.

Alice T. Drew

Witnesses To Mark:
{

Subscribed and sworn to before me this 20 day of May , 1905.

My Commission Expires Dec. 15, 1907.   Wm *(Illegible)*
Notary Public.

AFFIDAVIT OF ATTENDING PHYSICIAN OR MID-WIFE.

UNITED STATES OF AMERICA, Indian Territory,
Western   DISTRICT.

I, Sallie Drew , a mid-wife , on oath state that I attended on Mrs. Alice T. Drew, wife of Ernest Drew on the 23^d day of August , 1904 ; that there was born to her on said date a *(blank)* child; that said child was living March 4, 1905, and is said to have been named Roy W. Drew.

Sallie Drew

Applications for Enrollment of Creek Newborn
Act of 1905   Volume II

Witnesses To Mark:
{

    Subscribed and sworn to before me this 20 day of May, 1905.

        My Commission Expires Dec. 15, 1907.   Wm *(Illegible)*
                                                            Notary Public.

BIRTH AFFIDAVIT.

DEPARTMENT OF THE INTERIOR.
COMMISSION TO THE FIVE CIVILIZED TRIBES.

      IN RE APPLICATION FOR ENROLLMENT, as a citizen of the Creek Nation, of Earl E Drew, born on 11 day of Sept, 1902

Name of Father: Ernest Drew   a citizen of the U. S.   Nation.
Name of Mother: Alice T. Drew   a citizen of the Creek   Nation.

                          Postoffice   Tulsa I.T.

AFFIDAVIT OF MOTHER.

UNITED STATES OF AMERICA, Indian Territory, }
      Western   DISTRICT. }

      I, Alice T. Drew, on oath state that I am *(blank)* years of age and a citizen by Blood, of the Creek Nation; that I am the lawful wife of Ernest Drew, who is a citizen, by marrage[sic] of the Creek Nation; that a male child was born to me on 11 day of September, 1902, that said child has been named Earl E. Drew, and was living March 4, 1905.

                                                  Alice T. Drew
Witnesses To Mark:
{

    Subscribed and sworn to before me this 20 day of May, 1905.

        My Commission Expires Dec. 15, 1907.   Wm *(Illegible)*
                                                            Notary Public.

Applications for Enrollment of Creek Newborn
Act of 1905 Volume II

AFFIDAVIT OF ATTENDING PHYSICIAN OR MID-WIFE.

UNITED STATES OF AMERICA, Indian Territory, ⎱
    Western   DISTRICT. ⎰

    I, Sarah E. Pearce, a mid-wife , on oath state that I attended on Mrs. Alice T. Drew , wife of Ernest Drew on the 11 day of September , 1902 ; that there was born to her on said date a *(blank)* child; that said child was living March 4, 1905, and is said to have been named Earl E. Drew .

                                          her
                                 Sarah E. x Pierce

Witnesses To Mark: mark
   A.R. *(Illegible)*
   Anna Van Pelt

    Subscribed and sworn to before me this 20 day of May, 1905.

    My Commission Expires Dec. 15, 1907.   Wm *(Illegible)*
                                                    Notary Public.

BIRTH AFFIDAVIT.

DEPARTMENT OF THE INTERIOR.
COMMISSION TO THE FIVE CIVILIZED TRIBES.

    IN RE APPLICATION FOR ENROLLMENT, as a citizen of the CREEK Nation, of Earl E Drew, born on 11 day of Sept , 1902

| Name of Father: | Ernest Drew | a citizen of the | U. S. | Nation. |
| Name of Mother: | Alice Drew | a citizen of the | Creek | Nation. |

                        Postoffice   Tulsa

child present

AFFIDAVIT OF MOTHER.

UNITED STATES OF AMERICA, Indian Territory, ⎱
    WESTERN   DISTRICT. ⎰

    I, Alice Drew, on oath state that I am 24 years of age and a citizen by blood , of the Creek Nation; that I am the lawful wife of Ernest Drew , who is a citizen, by ----- of the U. S. Nation; that a male child was born to me on 11 day of Sept , 1902, that said child has been named Earl E. Drew , and was living March 4, 1905.

                                     Alice Drew

Witnesses To Mark:

Applications for Enrollment of Creek Newborn
Act of 1905   Volume II

Subscribed and sworn to before me this 14 day of March , 1905.

                                  Edw C Griesel
                                  Notary Public.

BIRTH AFFIDAVIT.

DEPARTMENT OF THE INTERIOR.
COMMISSION TO THE FIVE CIVILIZED TRIBES.

IN RE APPLICATION FOR ENROLLMENT, as a citizen of the Creek Nation, of Earl E Drew, born on 11 day of September , 1902

Name of Father: Ernest Drew	a citizen of the Creek Nation.
Name of Mother: Alice Drew	a citizen of the Creek Nation.

                      Postoffice   Tulsa Ind. Ter.

AFFIDAVIT OF MOTHER.

UNITED STATES OF AMERICA, Indian Territory,
     Western   **DISTRICT.**

    I, Alice Drew, on oath state that I am 24 years of age and a citizen by blood , of the Creek Nation; that I am the lawful wife of Ernest Drew , who is a citizen, by marrage[sic] of the Creek Nation; that a male child was born to me on 11th day of September , 1902, that said child has been named Earl E. Drew , and was living March 4, 1905.

                                  Alice Drew

Witnesses To Mark:
  { Jessie Clark
    Carl C. Magee

Subscribed and sworn to before me this 16 day of March , 1905.

      My Commission Expires Dec. 15, 1907.   Wm *(Illegible)*
                                                Notary Public.

AFFIDAVIT OF ATTENDING PHYSICIAN OR MID-WIFE.

UNITED STATES OF AMERICA, Indian Territory,
     Western   **DISTRICT.**

    I, Sarah E. Pearce, a mid wife , on oath state that I attended on Mrs. Alice Drew , wife of Ernest Drew   on the 11th day of September , 1902 ; that there was born to her

Applications for Enrollment of Creek Newborn
Act of 1905 Volume II

on said date a male child; that said child was living March 4, 1905, and is said to have been named Earl E. Drew.

                                                  her
                                Sarah E. x Pearce

Witnesses To Mark: mark
  { Jessie Clark
  { Carl C. Magee

Subscribed and sworn to before me this 16 day of March, 1905.

My Commission Expires Dec. 15, 1907.   Wm *(Illegible)*
                                                  Notary Public.

DEPARTMENT OF THE INTERIOR,
COMMISSIONER TO THE FIVE CIVILIZED TRIBES.

REFER IN REPLY TO THE FOLLOWING:
N.C. 81.

Muskogee, Indian Territory, **August 4, 1905.**

Pefeny Fixico,
    Okemah, Indian Territory.

Dear Sir:

    You are hereby advised that on **July 28, 1905**, the Secretary of the Interior approved the enrollment of your minor child, **Icey Fixico**, as a citizen by blood of the **Creek** Nation, and that the name of said child appears upon the roll of new born citizens of the **Creek** Nation as Number **51**.

    The child is now entitled to an allotment, and application therefor should be made without delay at the Land Office for the Nation in which the prospective allotment is located.

    An entire allotment for said child must be selected at the time of the original application.

                        Respectively,

                                          Commissioner.

Applications for Enrollment of Creek Newborn
Act of 1905 Volume II

BIRTH AFFIDAVIT.

DEPARTMENT OF THE INTERIOR.
COMMISSION TO THE FIVE CIVILIZED TRIBES.

IN RE APPLICATION FOR ENROLLMENT, as a citizen of the Creek Nation, of Icey Fixico, born on the 23rd day of November, 1902

Name of Father: Unknown   ~~a citizen of the~~   ~~Nation~~.
Name of Mother: Pefeny Fixico   a citizen of the   Creek   Nation.

           Postoffice   Okemah, Indian Territory

AFFIDAVIT OF MOTHER.

UNITED STATES OF AMERICA, Indian Territory, ⎫
     Western   DISTRICT. ⎭

     I, Pefeny Fixico, on oath state that I am Twenty-eight years of age and a citizen by birth, of the Creek Nation; that I am the lawful wife of unmarried, ~~who is a citizen, by~~ ~~of the~~ ~~Nation~~; that a Female child was born to me on 23rd day of November, 1902, that said child has been named Icey Fixico, and was living March 4, 1905.

                                        Pefeney[sic] Fixico
Witnesses To Mark:
{

     Subscribed and sworn to before me this 14th day of March, 1905.

                               A. Z. Martin
                                    Notary Public.
     My commission expires Sept 19, 1907.

AFFIDAVIT OF ATTENDING PHYSICIAN OR MID-WIFE.

UNITED STATES OF AMERICA, Indian Territory, ⎫
     Western   DISTRICT. ⎭

     I, Peggy Simmons, a mid-wife, on oath state that I attended on Mrs. Pefeny Fixico, ~~wife of~~ *(blank)* on the 23rd day of November, 1902; that there was born to her on said date a Female child; that said child was living March 4, 1905, and is said to have been named Icey Fixico.   Her
                               Peggie x Simmons
Witnesses To Mark: mark
    { J. W. Moore
      John *(Illegible)*

Applications for Enrollment of Creek Newborn
Act of 1905 Volume II

Subscribed and sworn to before me this 14th day of March, 1905.

A. Z. Martin
Notary Public.

My commission expires Sept 19, 1907.

DEPARTMENT OF THE INTERIOR,
COMMISSIONER TO THE FIVE CIVILIZED TRIBES.

REFER IN REPLY TO THE FOLLOWING:

N.C. 82.

Muskogee, Indian Territory, **August 4, 1905.**

Mary M. Williams,
    Care of Nat Williams,
        Weer, Indian Territory.

Dear Madam:

You are hereby advised that on **July 28, 1905** , the Secretary of the Interior approved the enrollment of your minor child, **Charley Williams** , as a citizen by blood of the **Creek** Nation, and that the name of said child appears upon the roll of new born citizens of the **Creek** Nation as Number **52** .

The child is now entitled to an allotment, and application therefor should be made without delay at the Land Office for the Nation in which the prospective allotment is located.

An entire allotment for said child must be selected at the time of the original application.

Respectively,

Commissioner.

BIRTH AFFIDAVIT.

DEPARTMENT OF THE INTERIOR.
COMMISSION TO THE FIVE CIVILIZED TRIBES.

IN RE APPLICATION FOR ENROLLMENT, as a citizen of the CREEK Nation, of Charley Williams , born on the 15 day of Aug , 1902

Name of Father: Matt[sic] Williams   a citizen of the   U. S.   Nation.
Name of Mother: Mary ~~Ann~~ M.   a citizen of the   Creek   Nation.

Postoffice   Weer

Applications for Enrollment of Creek Newborn
Act of 1905   Volume II

Child Present – **MAR 24 1905**

AFFIDAVIT OF MOTHER.

UNITED STATES OF AMERICA, Indian Territory, ⎱
      Western   DISTRICT.   ⎰
                    M.

I, Mary ~~Ann~~ Williams, on oath state that I am 34 years of age and a citizen by blood, of the Creek Nation; that I am the lawful wife of Nat[sic] Williams, who is a citizen, by ----- of the U. S. Nation; that a male child was born to me on 15 day of Aug, 1902, that said child has been named Charley Williams, and is now living.

                                        Mary M. Williams

Witnesses To Mark:
{

Subscribed and sworn to before me this 16 day of March, 1905.

                                        Edw C Griesel
                                            Notary Public.

BIRTH AFFIDAVIT.

DEPARTMENT OF THE INTERIOR.
COMMISSION TO THE FIVE CIVILIZED TRIBES.

IN RE APPLICATION FOR ENROLLMENT, as a citizen of the Creek Nation, of Charley Williams, born on the 14 day of Aug, 1902

                              non
Name of Father: Matt Williams   a ^ citizen of the   Creek   Nation.
Name of Mother: Mary Williams formerly *(Illegible)* a citizen of the   Creek   Nation.

                    Postoffice   Catoosa I.T.

Child Present – **MAR 24 1905**

AFFIDAVIT OF MOTHER.

UNITED STATES OF AMERICA, Indian Territory, ⎱
      Western   DISTRICT.   ⎰
               formerly *(Illegible)*

I, Mary Williams, on oath state that I am 32 years of age and a citizen by blood, of the Creek Nation; that I am the lawful wife of Matt Williams, who is a non citizen, ~~by~~ *(blank)* of the Creek Nation; that a male child was born to me on 14th day of Aug, 1902, that said child has been named Charley Williams, and is now living.

                                        Mary Williams

Witnesses To Mark:
{

Applications for Enrollment of Creek Newborn
Act of 1905 Volume II

Subscribed and sworn to before me this 7th day of January , 1903.

L.E. Nero
Notary Public.

AFFIDAVIT OF ATTENDING PHYSICIAN OR MID-WIFE.

UNITED STATES OF AMERICA, Indian Territory,
Western   DISTRICT.

I, Caroline Fletcher , a midwife , on oath state that I attended on Mrs. Mary Williams , wife of Matt Williams on the 14th day of August , 1902 ; that there was born to her on said date a male child; that said child is now living and is said to have been named Charley Williams .

Caroline Fletcher

Witnesses To Mark:

Subscribed and sworn to before me this 7th day of Jan., 1903.

L.E. Nero
Notary Public.

(Note: the following print very difficult to read, extremely light)

In Re Application For Enrollment as a citizen of the Creek Nation, of Charley Williams, born on the 14" day of August, 1902.

Name of Father Mat Williams, a non citizen of the Creek Nation.
Name of Mother Mary M. Williams, a citizen of the Creek Nation.

Postoffice, Weer, I.T.

Affidavit of Attending Mid-Wife.

United States of America,
Indian Territory,
Western District.

I, Caroline Fletcher, a mid-wife on oath state that I attended on Mrs. Mary M. Williams, wife of Mat Williams on the 14" day of August, 1902; that there was born to her on said date a male child; that said child is now living and is said to have been named Charley Williams.

Caroline Fletcher

Applications for Enrollment of Creek Newborn
Act of 1905   Volume II

Witness to mark.

_____

_____

Subscribed and sworn to before me this 23" day of March A.D. 1905.

Z I J Holt
Notary Public.
My commission expires May 9", 1907

Cr NC-83

DEPARTMENT OF THE INTERIOR,
COMMISSION TO THE FIVE CIVILIZED TRIBES.

Muskogee, Indian Territory, June 8, 1905

In the matter of the application for the enrollment of George Simon as a citizen of the Creek Nation.

Mary Byrd, being duly sworn, testified as follows (through Jesse McDermott, Official Interpreter).

EXAMINATION BY THE COMMISSION:
Q What is your name? A Mary Byrd.
Q Tell her that we have here affidavits that have been signed by her as Mary Byrt[sic], Mary Byrt Simon, and that her name in the body in the affidavit is given as Mary Simon; another place, it is Mary Bird; the correct name is now Mary Simon, is it? A No.
Q You signed one affidavit as Mary Byrt Simon? A That was not correct, but the lawyer took hold of my hand and had me to write that way.
Q Then, your correct name is as it appears on deeds and the Commission's rolls—Mary Byrd? A Yes sir.
Q What is the name of your father? A Chissoe.
Q What is the name of your mother? A Mahaley.
Q Were you ever married to Caesar Simon, the father of this child that you have in your arms, George Simon? A We intended to get married but his parents would not consent and sent him away to school.
Q Who was present when that child, George Simon was born? A Minnie Noble, my sister.
Q When was this child George Simon Born, about? I see she signed affidavits that it was born about September 25, 1904, also that it was born 30th of September, 1904, and another one that is was born 3rd of September, 1904. A The notary made a guess when they put down the date of the child's birth.
Q You think it was born now in the month of September, 1904. –
A It will be one year old this coming September? A Yes sir.

Applications for Enrollment of Creek Newborn
Act of 1905   Volume II

INDIAN TERRITORY, Western District.

I, J. Y. Miller, a stenographer to the Commission to the Five Civilized Tribes, do hereby certify that the above and foregoing is a true and complete translation of my notes as same appear in my stenographic report of this case.

JY Miller

Sworn to and subscribed before me
this the 17 day of June, 1905

Edw C Griesel
Notary Public.

BIRTH AFFIDAVIT.

DEPARTMENT OF THE INTERIOR.
COMMISSION TO THE FIVE CIVILIZED TRIBES.

IN RE APPLICATION FOR ENROLLMENT, as a citizen of the CREEK Nation, of George Simon, born on the 3 day of Sept. , 1904

Name of Father: Caesar Simon	a citizen of the Creek Nation.
Name of Mother: Mary "	a citizen of the " Nation.

Postoffice   Coweta

child present

AFFIDAVIT OF MOTHER.

UNITED STATES OF AMERICA, Indian Territory,
WESTERN DISTRICT.

I, Mary Simon , on oath state that I am 23 years of age and a citizen by blood , of the Creek Nation; that I am the lawful wife of Caesar Simon , who is a citizen, by blood of the Creek Nation; that a male child was born to me on 3 day of Sept. , 1904, that said child has been named George Simon , and is now living.

Mary Byrt

Witnesses To Mark:

Subscribed and sworn to before me this 16 day of March , 1905.

J. McDermott
Notary Public.

Applications for Enrollment of Creek Newborn
Act of 1905   Volume II

DEPARTMENT OF THE INTERIOR.
COMMISSION TO THE FIVE CIVILIZED TRIBES.

In the matter of the **enrollment of George Simon, a minor**   a citizen of the Creek Nation ~~Nation~~, who ~~formerly~~ resides at or near   **Coweta** , Ind. Ter., and ~~died~~ **born** on ~~the~~ **or about 30th** day of **September** , **1904** .

AFFIDAVIT OF RELATIVE.

UNITED STATES OF AMERICA, Indian Territory, }
   Western   DISTRICT.

I, **Mary Bird** , on oath state that I am **over 21** years of age and a citizen by **birth & blood** , of the **Creek**   Nation; that my postoffice address is **Coweta** , Ind. Ter.; that I am **the mother** of **George Simon, a minor**   who ~~was~~ **is** a citizen, by **blood**, of the **Creek**   Nation and that said **George Simon was born about the** ~~died on the~~ **30th**   day of **September**   , **1904**.

                                    Mary Byrd

Witnesses To Mark:
{ Joe Fennell
{ William Sudduth

   Subscribed and sworn to before me this **20th** day of **March**, 1905.

                            R. Callen
                                    Notary Public.
My commission expires March 15, 1908.

AFFIDAVIT OF ACQUAINTANCE.

UNITED STATES OF AMERICA, Indian Territory, }
   Western   DISTRICT.

I, **Ben Noble** , on oath state that I am   **30**   years of age, and a citizen by **blood** of the **Creek**   Nation; that my postoffice address is **Coweta,**   , Ind. Ter.; that I ~~was~~ **am** personally acquainted with   **George Simon, a minor,**   who ~~was~~ **is** a citizen, by **blood** , of the **Creek**   Nation; and that said   **George Simon was born about the** ~~died on the~~   **30th** day of **September**   , **1904**.

                                    Ben Noble

Witnesses To Mark:
{ Joe Fennell
{ William Sudduth

Applications for Enrollment of Creek Newborn
Act of 1905 Volume II

Subscribed and sworn to before me this **30th** day of **March**, 1905.

        R. Callen
         Notary Public.

BIRTH AFFIDAVIT.

DEPARTMENT OF THE INTERIOR.
COMMISSION TO THE FIVE CIVILIZED TRIBES.

  IN RE APPLICATION FOR ENROLLMENT, as a citizen of the Creek Nation, of George Simon, born on the 25th day of Sept., 1904

Name of Father: Caesar Simon	a citizen of the Creek	Nation.
Name of Mother: Mary Simon	a citizen of the Creek	Nation.

      Postoffice Coweta IT

AFFIDAVIT OF MOTHER.

UNITED STATES OF AMERICA, Indian Territory, }
  WESTERN   DISTRICT.}

  I, Mary Simon, on oath state that I am about 34 years of age and a citizen by blood, of the Creek Nation; that 4-23-05 am was the lawful wife of Caesar Simon, who is a citizen, by blood of the Creek Nation; that a male child was born to me on or 5-23-05 about the 25th day of September, 1904, that said child has been named George Simon, and is was living March 4, 1905.

        Mary Byrd Simon

Witnesses To Mark:
{ Ned Sarty
{ James Perryman

  Subscribed and sworn to before me this 23rd day of May, 1905.

        B.J. Beavers
         Notary Public.
My commission expires Dec 19-1908.

AFFIDAVIT OF ATTENDING PHYSICIAN OR MID-WIFE.

UNITED STATES OF AMERICA, Indian Territory, }
  Western   DISTRICT. }

  I, Minnie Noble, a midwife, on oath state that I attended on Mrs. Mary Simon, wife of Caesar Simon on or about the 25th day of Sept., 1904; that there was born

Applications for Enrollment of Creek Newborn
Act of 1905 Volume II

to her on said date a male child; that said child was living March 4, 1905, and is said to have been named George Simon .

Minnie Noble

Witnesses To Mark:
{ Ned Sarty
{ James Perryman

Subscribed and sworn to before me this 23rd day of May, 1905.

B.J. Beavers
Notary Public.

My commission expires Dec 19-1908.

NC 83.

Muskogee, Indian Territory, May 17, 1905.

Caesar Simon,
    Coweta, Indian Territory.

Dear Sir:

In the matter of the application for the enrollment of your minor child, George Simon, as a citizen of the Creek Nation, you are advised that the Commission requires the affidavit of the midwife or physician in attendance at the birth of said child.

There is herewith enclosed a blank form of birth affidavit, and in executing same care should be exercised to see that all blanks are properly filled, all names written in full and in the event that the person signing the affidavit is unable to write, signature by mark must be attested by two witnesses. Each affidavit must be executed before a Notary Public and the notarial seal and signature of the officer must be attached to each separate affidavit.

Respectfully,

BC.   Chairman.

NC-83

Muskogee, Indian Territory, May 29, 1905.

Mary Simon,
    Coweta, Indian Territory.

Dear Madam:

Applications for Enrollment of Creek Newborn
Act of 1905 Volume II

In the matter of the application for the enrollment of your minor child, George Simon, as a citizen of the Creek Nation, there are on file with the Commission affidavits in which your name is variously given as Mary Byrd, Mary Bird, Mary Simon and Mary Byrd Simon. You have been identified on the Commission's rolls as Mary Byrd.

For the purpose of correcting the discrepancy in your name, you are requested to appear before the Commission, at its office in Muskogee, Indian Territory, at an early date, to be examined under oath.

Respectfully,

Chairman.

NC 84.

Muskogee, Indian Territory, May 17, 1905.

John Baugh,
    Broken Arrow, Indian Territory.

Dear Sir:

In the matter of the application for the enrollment of your minor child, Willie E. Baugh, as a citizen of the Creek Nation, you are advised that the Commission requires the affidavit of the midwife or physician in attendance at the birth of said child.

There is herewith enclosed a blank form of birth affidavit, and in executing same care should be exercised to see that all blanks are properly filled, all names written in full and in the event that the person signing the affidavit is unable to write, signature by mark must be attested by two witnesses. Each affidavit must be executed before a Notary Public and the notarial seal and signature of the officer must be attached to each separate affidavit.

Respectfully,

BC.   Chairman.

BIRTH AFFIDAVIT.

DEPARTMENT OF THE INTERIOR.
COMMISSION TO THE FIVE CIVILIZED TRIBES.

IN RE APPLICATION FOR ENROLLMENT, as a citizen of the Creek Nation, of Willie Edward Bough , born on the 9" day of October , 1903

Name of Father: John Bough   a non   a citizen of the   Creek   Nation.
Name of Mother: Rachel Childers Bough a   a citizen of the   Creek   Nation.

Applications for Enrollment of Creek Newborn
Act of 1905   Volume II

Postoffice   Broken Arrow, I.T.

AFFIDAVIT OF ATTENDING PHYSICIAN OR MID-WIFE.

UNITED STATES OF AMERICA, Indian Territory, ⎫
    Western   DISTRICT. ⎭

    I, A.J. Pollard , a Physician , on oath state that I attended on Mrs. Rachel Childers Bough , wife of John Bough on the 9" day of October , 1903 ; that there was born to her on said date a male child; that said child is now living and is said to have been named Willie Edward Bough .

                                  AJ Pollard, M.D.

Witnesses To Mark:
{

    Subscribed and sworn to before me this 24" day of May A.D., 1905.

                              Z.I.J. Holt
                                  Notary Public.
My commission expires May 9" 1907.

BIRTH AFFIDAVIT.

DEPARTMENT OF THE INTERIOR.
COMMISSION TO THE FIVE CIVILIZED TRIBES.

    IN RE APPLICATION FOR ENROLLMENT, as a citizen of the CREEK Nation, of Willie E. Bough , born on the 9 day of Oct , 1903

Name of Father: John Bough	a citizen of the U. S.	Nation.
Name of Mother: Rachel "	a citizen of the Creek	Nation.

                          Postoffice   Broken Arrow

(Child present)

AFFIDAVIT OF MOTHER.

UNITED STATES OF AMERICA, Indian Territory, ⎫
    WESTERN   DISTRICT. ⎭

    I, Rachel Bough , on oath state that I am 20 years of age and a citizen by blood , of the Creek   Nation; that I am the lawful wife of John Bough , who is a citizen, by ----- of the U. S. Nation; that a male child was born to me on 9 day of Oct , 1903, that said child has been named Willie E. Bough , and is now living.

Applications for Enrollment of Creek Newborn
Act of 1905 Volume II

                                                    Her
                                        Rachel x Baugh[sic]
Witnesses To Mark: mark
  { John Bough
    EC Griesel

Subscribed and sworn to before me this 17" day of March , 1905.

                                          Edw C Griesel
                                              Notary Public.

                        Department of the Interior.
                Commission to the Five Civilized Tribes.

In re Application for Enrollment as a citizen of the Creek Nation, of Willie Edward Bough, born on the 9" day of October 1903.

Name of Father: John Bough a non-citizen of the Creek Nation.
Name of Mother: Rachel Bough a citizen of the Creek Nation.

                          Postoffice, Broken Arrow, I. T.

                    Affidavit of Attending Physician.

United States of America,
Indian Territory
Western District.

    I, A. J. Pollard a Physician on oath states[sic] that I attended on Mrs. Rachel Bough, wife of John Bough, on the 9" day of October 1903; that there was born to her on said date a male child; that said child is now living and is said to have been named Willie Edward Bough.

      (SEAL)   A. J. Pollard, M. D.

Subscribed and sworn to before me this 25" day of March 1905.

                                          Z. I. J. Holt
                                          Notary Public
My Commission expires May 9", 1907.

Applications for Enrollment of Creek Newborn
Act of 1905 Volume II

DEPARTMENT OF THE INTERIOR,
COMMISSIONER TO THE FIVE CIVILIZED TRIBES.

REFER IN REPLY TO THE FOLLOWING:

N.C. 85.

Muskogee, Indian Territory, **August 4, 1905.**

Amos Drew,
Broken Arrow, Indian Territory.

Dear Sir:

You are hereby advised that on **July 28, 1905**, the Secretary of the Interior approved the enrollment of your minor child, **Clarence Drew**, as a citizen by blood of the **Creek** Nation, and that the name of said child appears upon the roll of new born citizens of the **Creek** Nation as Number **53**.

The child is now entitled to an allotment, and application therefor should be made without delay at the Land Office for the Nation in which the prospective allotment is located.

An entire allotment for said child must be selected at the time of the original application.

Respectively,

Commissioner.

BIRTH AFFIDAVIT.

DEPARTMENT OF THE INTERIOR.
COMMISSION TO THE FIVE CIVILIZED TRIBES.

IN RE APPLICATION FOR ENROLLMENT, as a citizen of the CREEK Nation, of Clarence Drew, born on the 1 day of Nov., 1903

Name of Father: Amos Drew   a citizen of the   Creek   Nation.
Name of Mother: Nettie "   a citizen of the   "   Nation.

Postoffice   Broken Arrown

Child present

AFFIDAVIT OF MOTHER.

UNITED STATES OF AMERICA, Indian Territory, ⎱
      WESTERN   DISTRICT.⎰

I, Nettie Drew, on oath state that I am 23 years of age and a citizen by blood, of the Creek Nation; that I am the lawful wife of Amos Drew, who is a citizen, by blood of the Creek Nation; that a male child was born to me on 1 day of Nov., 1903, that said child has been named Clarence Drew, and is now living.

Applications for Enrollment of Creek Newborn
Act of 1905 Volume II

                                    Nettie x Drew

Witnesses To Mark:
{ Irwin Donovan
{ J. McDermott

    Subscribed and sworn to before me this 17 day of March, 1905.

                                    J. McDermott
                                    Notary Public.

AFFIDAVIT OF ATTENDING PHYSICIAN OR MID-WIFE.

UNITED STATES OF AMERICA, Indian Territory, }
      Western   DISTRICT.

    I, Sukey Haynes, a midwife, on oath state that I attended on Mrs. Nettie Drew, wife of Amos Drew on the 1 day of Nov, 1903; that there was born to her on said date a male child; that said child is now living and is said to have been named Clarence.

                                          her
                                Sukey x Haynes
Witnesses To Mark: mark
{ Irwin Donovan
{ J. McDermott

    Subscribed and sworn to before me this 17 day of March, 1905.

                                    J. McDermott
                                    Notary Public.

BIRTH AFFIDAVIT.
DEPARTMENT OF THE INTERIOR.
COMMISSION TO THE FIVE CIVILIZED TRIBES.

    IN RE APPLICATION FOR ENROLLMENT, as a citizen of the CREEK Nation, of Jessie Haikey, born on the 9 day of March, 1904

Name of Father: John Haikey   a citizen of the   Creek   Nation.
Name of Mother: Sussannah Haikey   a citizen of the   Creek   Nation.

                          Postoffice   Helum

Applications for Enrollment of Creek Newborn
Act of 1905   Volume II

AFFIDAVIT OF MOTHER.

UNITED STATES OF AMERICA, Indian Territory, }
WESTERN   DISTRICT.

    I, Susannah[sic] Haikey, on oath state that I am 20 years of age and a citizen by blood , of the Creek   Nation; that I am the lawful wife of John Haikey , who is a citizen, by blood of the Creek   Nation; that a male   child was born to me on 9 day of March , 1904 , that said child has been named Jessie Haikey , and is now living.

                                              her
                                   Sussannah x Haikey

Witnesses To Mark: mark
  { Irwin Donovan
     EC Griesel

    Subscribed and sworn to before me this 17" day of March , 1905.

                                   J. McDermott
                                   Notary Public.

AFFIDAVIT OF ATTENDING PHYSICIAN OR MID-WIFE.

UNITED STATES OF AMERICA, Indian Territory, }
WESTERN   DISTRICT.

    I, Sukey Haynes , a midwife , on oath state that I attended on Mrs. Susannah Haikey , wife of John Haikey   on the 9 day of March , 1904 ; that there was born to her on said date a *(blank)* child; that said child is now living and is said to have been named Jessie Haikey .

                                   her
                             Sukey x Haynes

Witnesses To Mark: mark
  { Irwin Donovan
      EC Griesel

    Subscribed and sworn to before me this 17 day of March, 1905.

                               J. McDermott
                               Notary Public.

Applications for Enrollment of Creek Newborn
Act of 1905   Volume II

DEPARTMENT OF THE INTERIOR,
COMMISSIONER TO THE FIVE CIVILIZED TRIBES.

REFER IN REPLY TO THE FOLLOWING:

N.C. 1.

Muskogee, Indian Territory, **August 4, 1905.**

Eliza Cooper,
    Care of Grant Cooper,
        Broken Arrow, Indian Territory.

Dear Madam:

You are hereby advised that on **July 28, 1905**, the Secretary of the Interior approved the enrollment of your minor child, **Effie Cooper**, as a citizen by blood of the **Creek** Nation, and that the name of said child appears upon the roll of new born citizens of the **Creek** Nation as Number **56**.

The child is now entitled to an allotment, and application therefor should be made without delay at the Land Office for the Nation in which the prospective allotment is located.

An entire allotment for said child must be selected at the time of the original application.

        Respectively,

               Commissioner.

DEPARTMENT OF THE INTERIOR,
COMMISSIONER TO THE FIVE CIVILIZED TRIBES.

REFER IN REPLY TO THE FOLLOWING:

N.C. 87.

Muskogee, Indian Territory, **August 4, 1905.**

Eliza Cooper,
    Care of Grant Cooper,
        Broken Arrow, Indian Territory.

Dear Madam:

You are hereby advised that on **July 28, 1905**, the Secretary of the Interior approved the enrollment of your minor child, **Wheeler Cooper**, as a citizen by blood of the **Creek** Nation, and that the name of said child appears upon the roll of new born citizens of the **Creek** Nation as Number **55**.

The child is now entitled to an allotment, and application therefor should be made without delay at the Land Office for the Nation in which the prospective allotment is located.

Applications for Enrollment of Creek Newborn
Act of 1905   Volume II

An entire allotment for said child must be selected at the time of the original application.

Respectively,

Commissioner.

BIRTH AFFIDAVIT.

DEPARTMENT OF THE INTERIOR.
COMMISSION TO THE FIVE CIVILIZED TRIBES.

IN RE APPLICATION FOR ENROLLMENT, as a citizen of the CREEK Nation, of Effie Cooper, born on the 2 day of February, 1905

Name of Father:	Grant Cooper	a citizen of the U. S.	Nation.
Name of Mother:	Liza Cooper	a citizen of the Creek	Nation.

Postoffice   Broken Arrow

Child present

AFFIDAVIT OF MOTHER.

UNITED STATES OF AMERICA, Indian Territory, }
  WESTERN   DISTRICT.

I, Liza Cooper, on oath state that I am 21 years of age and a citizen by blood, of the Creek Nation; that I am the lawful wife of Grant Cooper, who is a citizen, by ----- of the U. S. Nation; that a female child was born to me on 2 day of February, 1905, that said child has been named Effie Cooper, and is now living.

Eliza Cooper

Witnesses To Mark:
{

Subscribed and sworn to before me this 17 day of March, 1905.

J. McDermott
Notary Public.

Applications for Enrollment of Creek Newborn
Act of 1905 Volume II

AFFIDAVIT OF ATTENDING PHYSICIAN OR MID-WIFE.

UNITED STATES OF AMERICA, Indian Territory, }
   WESTERN   DISTRICT.

    I, Suke[sic] Haynes , a midwife , on oath state that I attended on Mrs. Liza Cooper , wife of Grant Cooper on the 2 day of February , 1905 ; that there was born to her on said date a female child; that said child is now living and is said to have been named Effie Cooper .

                                her
                        Sukey x Haynes

Witnesses To Mark: mark
   { Irwin Donovan
     J. McDermott

    Subscribed and sworn to before me this 17" day of March, 1905.

                              J. McDermott
                              Notary Public.

BIRTH AFFIDAVIT.

DEPARTMENT OF THE INTERIOR.
COMMISSION TO THE FIVE CIVILIZED TRIBES.

    IN RE APPLICATION FOR ENROLLMENT, as a citizen of the CREEK Nation, of Wheeler Cooper , born on the 6 day of October , 1903

Name of Father: Grant Cooper   a citizen of the U. S.   Nation.
Name of Mother: Liza Cooper   a citizen of the   Creek   Nation.

                    Postoffice   Broken Arrow

Child present

AFFIDAVIT OF MOTHER.

UNITED STATES OF AMERICA, Indian Territory, }
   WESTERN   DISTRICT.

    I, Liza Cooper , on oath state that I am 21 years of age and a citizen by blood , of the Creek Nation; that I am the lawful wife of Grant Cooper , who is a citizen, by ----- of the U. S. Nation; that a male child was born to me on 6 day of October , 1903, that said child has been named Wheeler Cooper , and is now living.

                              Eliza Cooper

Witnesses To Mark:
   {

Applications for Enrollment of Creek Newborn
Act of 1905   Volume II

Subscribed and sworn to before me this 17 day of Mar , 1905.

                               J. McDermott
                               Notary Public.

AFFIDAVIT OF ATTENDING PHYSICIAN OR MID-WIFE.

UNITED STATES OF AMERICA, Indian Territory, ⎫
   WESTERN   DISTRICT. ⎬

I, Sukey Haynes , a midwife , on oath state that I attended on Mrs. Liza Cooper , wife of Grant Cooper on the 6 day of October , 1903 ; that there was born to her on said date a male child; that said child is now living and is said to have been named Wheeler Cooper .

                                          her
Witnesses To Mark: Sukey x Haynes
   { Irwin Donovan   mark

Subscribed and sworn to before me this 17 day of March, 1905.

                               J. McDermott
                               Notary Public.

                               NC 88.

                Muskogee, Indian Territory, May 18, 1905.

Josiah Looney,
      Weeletka[sic], Indian Territory.

Dear Sir:

      In the matter of the application for the enrollment of your minor child, Sullivan Looney, as a citizen of the Creek Nation, you are advised that the Commission requires the affidavit of the midwife or physician in attendance at the birth of said child.

      There is herewith enclosed a blank form of birth affidavit, and in executing same care should be exercised to see that all blanks are properly filled, all names written in full and in the event that the person signing the affidavit is unable to write, signature by mark must be attested by two witnesses. Each affidavit must be executed before a Notary Public and the notarial seal and signature of the officer must be attached to each separate affidavit.

Applications for Enrollment of Creek Newborn
Act of 1905 Volume II

Respectfully,

BC.   Chairman.

Cr NC-88.

Muskogee, Indian Territory, June 9, 1905.

Fannie Looney,
    Weleetka, Indian Territory.

Dear Madam:

    In the matter of the application for the enrollment of your minor child, Sullivan Looney, as a citizen of the Creek Nation, you are advised that there are on file with the Commission affidavits executed by you in which the date of the child's birth is given as September 8 and September 16, 1902.

    You are requested to advise the Commission as to the correct date of the birth of said child.

Respectfully,

Chairman.

Weleetka, Indian Territory, June 26, 1905.

to the commission to the five civilized tribes.

    Your letter of J 9 is to hand and in reply I will enform your Great commission that the said Sullivan looney my son was born September 8, 1902.

Yours
(Signed) fannie looney

(Letter typed as given on microfilm)

Applications for Enrollment of Creek Newborn
Act of 1905   Volume II

BIRTH AFFIDAVIT.

DEPARTMENT OF THE INTERIOR.
COMMISSION TO THE FIVE CIVILIZED TRIBES.

IN RE APPLICATION FOR ENROLLMENT, as a citizen of the Muskogee (Creek) Nation, of Sullivan Looney , born on the 16 day of Sept. , 1902

Name of Father: Josiah Looney　　　　a citizen of the　　Creek　　Nation.
Name of Mother: Fannie Looney　　　　a citizen of the　　Creek　　Nation.

　　　　　　　　　　Postoffice　　Weleetka, Ind. Ter.

AFFIDAVIT OF MOTHER.

UNITED STATES OF AMERICA, Indian Territory,
　　　Western　　　　DISTRICT.

　　I, Fannie Looney , on oath state that I am 28 years of age and a citizen by Birth , of the Muskogee (Creek)   Nation; that I am the lawful wife of Josiah Looney , who is a citizen, by Birth of the Muskogee (Creek) Nation; that a male   child was born to me on 16 day of September , 1902, that said child has been named Sullivan Looney , and was living March 4, 1905.
　　　　　　　　　　　　　　　　　her
　　　　　　　　　　　　　Fannie x Looney
Witnesses To Mark:　　　　　　mark
　{ S. F. Jones
　{ *(Illegible)* Pemberton

　　Subscribed and sworn to before me this 20 day of March , 1905.

　　　　　MY COMMISSION EXPIRES FEBY. 29, 1908　　John B. Patterson
　　　　　　　　　　　　　　　　　　Notary Public.

AFFIDAVIT OF ATTENDING PHYSICIAN OR MID-WIFE.

UNITED STATES OF AMERICA, Indian Territory,
　　　Western　　　　DISTRICT.

　　I, Malinda Jones , a midwife , on oath state that I attended on Mrs. Fannie Looney , wife of Josiah Looney   on the 16 day of September , 1902 ; that there was born to her on said date a male child; that said child was living March 4, 1905, and is said to have been named Sullivan Looney.
　　　　　　　　　　　　　　　　her
　　　　　　　　　　　　Malinda x Jones
Witnesses To Mark:　　　　　　mark
　{ S. F. Jones
　{ *(Illegible)* Pemberton

Applications for Enrollment of Creek Newborn
Act of 1905 Volume II

Subscribed and sworn to before me this 20 day of September, 1905.

MY COMMISSION EXPIRES FEBY. 29, 1908

John B. Patterson
Notary Public.

Father
AFFIDAVIT OF ~~ATTENDING PHYSICIAN OR MID-WIFE~~.

UNITED STATES OF AMERICA, Indian Territory,
　　Western　　DISTRICT.

I, Josiah Looney , ~~a~~ *(blank)* , on oath state that I attended on ~~Mrs~~. my wife ~~of~~ *(blank)* on the 8 day of Sept , 1902 ; that there was born to her on said date a male child; that said child is now living and is said to have been named Sullivan Looney .

Witnesses To Mark:
{

Josiah Looney
Weleetka, I.T.

Subscribed and sworn to before me this 17" day of March, 1905.

J. McDermott
Notary Public.

BIRTH AFFIDAVIT.

DEPARTMENT OF THE INTERIOR.
COMMISSION TO THE FIVE CIVILIZED TRIBES.

IN RE APPLICATION FOR ENROLLMENT, as a citizen of the Creek Nation, of Sullivan Looney , born on the 8 day of Sept. , 1902

Name of Father:　Josiah Looney　　　　a citizen of the　Creek　Nation.
Name of Mother:　Fannie Looney　　　　a citizen of the　Creek　Nation.

Postoffice　Weleetka

AFFIDAVIT OF MOTHER.

UNITED STATES OF AMERICA, Indian Territory,
　　Western　　DISTRICT.

I, Fannie Looney , on oath state that I am 28 years of age and a citizen by blood, of the Creek Nation; that I am the lawful wife of Josiah Looney , who is a citizen, by blood of the Creek Nation; that a male child was born to me on 8 day of Sept , 1902, that said child has been named Sullivan Looney , and is now living.

Applications for Enrollment of Creek Newborn
Act of 1905 Volume II

                                                    her
                                       Fannie x Looney
Witnesses To Mark: mark
  { W M Beer
    Fanny Lawley

Subscribed and sworn to before me this 18 day of Mar , 1905.

                                       Amos R. Robison
                                       Notary Public.

BIRTH AFFIDAVIT.

DEPARTMENT OF THE INTERIOR.
COMMISSION TO THE FIVE CIVILIZED TRIBES.

     IN RE APPLICATION FOR ENROLLMENT, as a citizen of the Creek Nation, of James Henry Leath , born on the 12th day of September , 1904

Name of Father: Thomas Jefferson Leath   a citizen of the   Creek   Nation.
Name of Mother: Ida Jane Leath   a citizen of the   Creek   Nation.

                          Postoffice   Quitman, Texas

AFFIDAVIT OF MOTHER.

UNITED STATES OF AMERICA, Indian Territory,
                   DISTRICT.

     I, Ida Jane Leath , on oath state that I am twenty two years of age and a citizen by enrollment and by marriage with Thomas Jefferson Leath , of the Creek Nation; that I am the lawful wife of Thomas Jefferson Leath , who is a citizen, by enrollment and birth of the Creek Nation; that a male child was born to me on twelfth day of September , 1904, that said child has been named James Henry Leath , and is now living.

                                       Ida Jane Leath
Witnesses To Mark:
  { L F Lloyd
    Walter Smart

     Subscribed and sworn to before me this 15th day of March , 1905.

                                     V.B. Harris
                                     Notary Public.
                                     Wood Co, Texas

Applications for Enrollment of Creek Newborn
Act of 1905 Volume II

AFFIDAVIT OF ATTENDING PHYSICIAN OR MID-WIFE.

UNITED STATES OF AMERICA, Indian Territory,
DISTRICT.

I, J. A. Fowler , a physician , on oath state that I attended on Mrs. Ida Jane Leath , wife of Thomas Jefferson Leath on the 12th day of September , 1904; that there was born to her on said date a male child; that said child is now living and is said to have been named James Henry Leath.

J. A. Fowler M.D.

Witnesses To Mark:
  Robt L Buttes
  J. D. Conger

Subscribed and sworn to before me this 15th day of March, 1905.

V.B. Harris
Notary Public.
Wood Co, Texas

BIRTH AFFIDAVIT.

DEPARTMENT OF THE INTERIOR.
COMMISSION TO THE FIVE CIVILIZED TRIBES.

IN RE APPLICATION FOR ENROLLMENT, as a citizen of the Creek Nation, of Jessie May Leath , born on the 1st day of July , 1902

Name of Father: Thomas Jefferson Leath   a citizen of the   Creek   Nation.
Name of Mother: Ida Jane Leath   a citizen of the   Creek   Nation.

Postoffice   Quitman, Texas

AFFIDAVIT OF MOTHER.

UNITED STATES OF AMERICA, Indian Territory,
DISTRICT.

I, Ida Jane Leath , on oath state that I am twenty two years of age and a citizen by enrollment and by marriage with Thomas Jefferson Leath , of the Creek Nation; that I am the lawful wife of Thomas Jefferson Leath , who is a citizen, by birth & enrollment of the Creek Nation; that a female child was born to me on first day of July , 1902, that said child has been named Jessie May Leath , and is now living.

Applications for Enrollment of Creek Newborn
Act of 1905 Volume II

Ida Jane Leath

Witnesses To Mark:
- L F Lloyd
- Walter Smart

Subscribed and sworn to before me this 15th day of March , 1905.

V.B. Harris
Notary Public.
Wood Co, Texas

AFFIDAVIT OF ATTENDING PHYSICIAN OR MID-WIFE.

UNITED STATES OF AMERICA, Indian Territory,
DISTRICT.

I, J. A. Fowler , a physician , on oath state that I attended on Mrs. Ida Jane Leath , wife of Thomas Jefferson Leath on the 1st day of July , 1902; that there was born to her on said date a female child; that said child is now living and is said to have been named Jessie May Leath.

J. A. Fowler M.D.

Witnesses To Mark:
- Robt L Buttes
- J. D. Conger

Subscribed and sworn to before me this 15th day of March, 1905.

V.B. Harris
Notary Public.
Wood Co, Texas

DEPARTMENT OF THE INTERIOR,
COMMISSIONER TO THE FIVE CIVILIZED TRIBES.

REFER IN REPLY TO THE FOLLOWING:

N.C. 90.

Muskogee, Indian Territory, **August 4, 1905.**

Winey Yahola,
    Care of Haffy Yahola,
        Braggs Station, Indian Territory.

Dear Sir:

You are hereby advised that on **July 28, 1905** , the Secretary of the Interior approved the enrollment of your minor child, **Jennetta Yahola** , as a citizen by blood of

Applications for Enrollment of Creek Newborn
Act of 1905   Volume II

the **Creek** Nation, and that the name of said child appears upon the roll of new born citizens of the **Creek** Nation as Number **57**.

The child is now entitled to an allotment, and application therefor should be made without delay at the Land Office for the Nation in which the prospective allotment is located.

An entire allotment for said child must be selected at the time of the original application.

Respectively,

Commissioner.

BIRTH AFFIDAVIT.

DEPARTMENT OF THE INTERIOR.
COMMISSION TO THE FIVE CIVILIZED TRIBES.

IN RE APPLICATION FOR ENROLLMENT, as a citizen of the Creek Nation, of Jennetta Yahola, born on the 10 day of Sept, 1904

Name of Father: Haffy Yahola   a citizen of the   Cherokee   Nation.
Name of Mother: Winey   "   (nee Washington) a citizen of the   Creek   Nation.

Postoffice   Braggs Sta. I.T.

(Child Present)

AFFIDAVIT OF MOTHER.

UNITED STATES OF AMERICA, Indian Territory, ⎫
      Western   DISTRICT.   ⎬

I, Winey Yahola, on oath state that I am 28 years of age and a citizen by blood, of the Creek Nation; that I am the lawful wife of Haffy Yahola, who is a citizen, by blood of the Cherokee Nation; that a female child was born to me on 10 day of Sept, 1904, that said child has been named Jennetta Yahola, and is now living.

        her
Winey x Yahola
       mark

Witnesses To Mark:
{ J. McDermott
{ EC Griesel

Subscribed and sworn to before me this 17" day of March, 1905.

J. McDermott
Notary Public.

Applications for Enrollment of Creek Newborn
Act of 1905 Volume II

AFFIDAVIT OF ATTENDING PHYSICIAN OR MID-WIFE.

UNITED STATES OF AMERICA, Indian Territory, }
         DISTRICT. }

  I, Taylor Parnaskey , a ------- , on oath state that I attended on Mrs. Winey Yahola , wife of Haffy Yahola on the 10 day of Sept , 1904 ; that there was born to her on said date a female child; that said child is now living and is said to have been named Jennetta Yahola.

             his
         Taylor x Parnaskey
Witnesses To Mark: mark
 { J. McDermott
  EC Griesel

  Subscribed and sworn to before me this 17 day of March, 1905.

         J McDermott
         Notary Public.

          NC 91.

     Muskogee, Indian Territory, May 17, 1905.

Jacob Gooden,
  Beggs, Indian Territory.

Dear Sir:

  In the matter of the application for the enrollment of your minor child, Charlie Gooden, as a citizen of the Creek Nation, you are advised that the Commission requires the affidavit of the midwife or physician in attendance at the birth of said child.

  There is herewith enclosed a blank form of birth affidavit, and in executing same care should be exercised to see that all blanks are properly filled, all names written in full and in the event that the person signing the affidavit is unable to write, signature by mark must be attested by two witnesses. Each affidavit must be executed before a Notary Public and the notarial seal and signature of the officer must be attached to each separate affidavit.

      Respectfully,

BC.   Chairman.

Applications for Enrollment of Creek Newborn
Act of 1905 Volume II

NC. 91.

Muskogee, Indian Territory, July 18, 1905.

Louisa Gooden,
    Beggs, Indian Territory.

Dear Madam:

    In the matter of the application for the enrollment of your minor child, Charley Gooden, as a citizen of the Creek Nation, you are advised that this office requires the affidavit of the midwife or physician in attendance at the birth of said child.

    There is herewith enclosed a blank form of birth affidavit, and in executing same care should be exercised to see that all blanks are properly filled, all names written in full and in the event that the person signing the affidavit is unable to write, signature by mark must be attested by two witnesses. Each affidavit must be executed before a Notary Public and the notarial seal and signature of the officer must be attached to each separate affidavit.

                    Respectfully,

1 BC   Commissioner.

BIRTH AFFIDAVIT.
DEPARTMENT OF THE INTERIOR.
COMMISSION TO THE FIVE CIVILIZED TRIBES.

    IN RE APPLICATION FOR ENROLLMENT, as a citizen of the Creek Nation, of Charley Gooden, born on the 7th day of Aug, 1904

Name of Father: Jacob Gooden   a citizen of the Creek   Nation.
Name of Mother: Louisa Gooden   a citizen of the Creek   Nation.

                      Postoffice   Beggs, I.T.

AFFIDAVIT OF MOTHER.

UNITED STATES OF AMERICA, Indian Territory,
    Western   DISTRICT.

    I, Louisa Gooden, on oath state that I am 26 years of age and a citizen by blood, of the Creek Nation; that I am the lawful wife of Jacob Gooden, who is a citizen, by Blood of the Creek Nation; that a male child was born to me on 7th day of Aug, 1904, that said child has been named Charley Gooden, and was living March 4, 1905.

Applications for Enrollment of Creek Newborn
Act of 1905   Volume II

Witnesses To Mark:
{

Louisa Gooden

Subscribed and sworn to before me this 4 day of Oct , 1905.

(Name Illegible)
Notary Public.

AFFIDAVIT OF ATTENDING PHYSICIAN OR MID-WIFE.

UNITED STATES OF AMERICA, Indian Territory,
    Western   **DISTRICT.**
}

    I, Rosana Cooper   , a midwife   , on oath state that I attended on Mrs. Louisa Gooden , wife of Jacob Gooden on the 7th day of Aug , 1904 ; that there was born to her on said date a male child; that said child was living March 4, 1905, and is said to have been named Charley Gooden .

                                her
                             Rosana x Cooper

Witnesses To Mark: mark
{ *(Illegible)* Clark
  (Name Illegible)

Subscribed and sworn to before me this 4 day of Oct. , 1905.

(Name Illegible)
Notary Public.

BIRTH AFFIDAVIT.

DEPARTMENT OF THE INTERIOR.
COMMISSION TO THE FIVE CIVILIZED TRIBES.

    IN RE APPLICATION FOR ENROLLMENT, as a citizen of the CREEK Nation, of Charley Gooden , born on the 7 day of Aug , 1904

Name of Father:	Jacob Gooden	a citizen of the	Creek	Nation.
Name of Mother:	Louisa Gooden	a citizen of the	"	Nation.

Postoffice   Beggs

Applications for Enrollment of Creek Newborn
Act of 1905 Volume II

Child Present

AFFIDAVIT OF ~~MOTHER~~. father

UNITED STATES OF AMERICA, Indian Territory, }
WESTERN DISTRICT.

    I, Jacob Gooden , on oath state that I am 26 years of age and a citizen by blood, of the Creek Nation; that I am the lawful ~~wife~~ hus of Louisa Gooden , who is a citizen, by blood of the Creek Nation; that a male child was born to me on 7 day of Aug , 1904 , that said child has been named Charley Gooden , and is now living.

                                       Jacob Gooden

Witnesses To Mark:
{

Subscribed and sworn to before me this 15 day of March, 1905.

                                       Edw C Griesel
                                            Notary Public.

BIRTH AFFIDAVIT.

DEPARTMENT OF THE INTERIOR.
COMMISSION TO THE FIVE CIVILIZED TRIBES.

IN RE APPLICATION FOR ENROLLMENT, as a citizen of the CREEK Nation, of Charley Gooden ~~Jr~~ , born on the 7 day of Aug , 1904

Name of Father: ~~Charles~~ Jacob Gooden   a citizen of the Creek   Nation.
Name of Mother: Louisa   "   a citizen of the   "   Nation.

                         Postoffice   Beggs

Child Present

AFFIDAVIT OF MOTHER.

UNITED STATES OF AMERICA, Indian Territory, }
WESTERN DISTRICT.

    I, Louisa Gooden , on oath state that I am 24 years of age and a citizen by blood, of the Creek Nation; that I am the lawful wife of ~~Charley~~ Jacob Gooden , who is a citizen, by blood of the Creek Nation; that a male child was born to me on 7 day of Aug , 1904, that said child has been named Charley Gooden ~~Jr~~ , and is now living.

                                     Louisa Gooden

Witnesses To Mark:
{

Applications for Enrollment of Creek Newborn
Act of 1905   Volume II

Subscribed and sworn to before me this 10 day of March , 1905.

>Edw C Griesel
>Notary Public.

DEPARTMENT OF THE INTERIOR,
COMMISSIONER TO THE FIVE CIVILIZED TRIBES.

REFER IN REPLY TO THE FOLLOWING:

N.C. 92.

Muskogee, Indian Territory, **August 4, 1905.**

Susanne Barnett Strouvelle,
   Care of C. E. Strouvelle,
      Tulsa, Indian Territory.

Dear Madam:

    You are hereby advised that on **July 28, 1905** , the Secretary of the Interior approved the enrollment of your minor child, **Charles Edward Strouvelle, Jr.** , as a citizen by blood of the **Creek** Nation, and that the name of said child appears upon the roll of new born citizens of the **Creek** Nation as Number **58** .

    The child is now entitled to an allotment, and application therefor should be made without delay at the Land Office for the Nation in which the prospective allotment is located.

    An entire allotment for said child must be selected at the time of the original application.

>Respectively,

>Commissioner.

DEPARTMENT OF THE INTERIOR,
COMMISSIONER TO THE FIVE CIVILIZED TRIBES.

REFER IN REPLY TO THE FOLLOWING:

N.C. 92.

Muskogee, Indian Territory, **August 4, 1905.**

Susanne Barnett Strouvelle,
   Care of C. E. Strouvelle,
      Tulsa, Indian Territory.

Dear Madam:

    You are hereby advised that on **July 28, 1905** , the Secretary of the Interior approved the enrollment of your minor child, **Alice Kendall Strouvelle** , as a citizen by

Applications for Enrollment of Creek Newborn
Act of 1905   Volume II

blood of the **Creek** Nation, and that the name of said child appears upon the roll of new born citizens of the **Creek** Nation as Number **59**.

    The child is now entitled to an allotment, and application therefor should be made without delay at the Land Office for the Nation in which the prospective allotment is located.

    An entire allotment for said child must be selected at the time of the original application.

                                 Respectively,

                                              Commissioner.

BIRTH AFFIDAVIT.

DEPARTMENT OF THE INTERIOR.
COMMISSION TO THE FIVE CIVILIZED TRIBES.

    IN RE APPLICATION FOR ENROLLMENT, as a citizen of the Creek Nation, of Alice Kendall Strouvelle, born on the 8 day of August, 1904

Name of Father: C E Strouvelle   a citizen of the   U S   Nation.
Name of Mother: Susanne Barnett Strouvelle a citizen of the   Creek   Nation.

                             Postoffice   Tulsa Ind Ter

AFFIDAVIT OF MOTHER.

UNITED STATES OF AMERICA, Indian Territory, ⎫
    Western   DISTRICT. ⎭

    I, Susanne Barnett Strouvelle, on oath state that I am 25 years of age and a citizen by birth, of the Creek Nation; that I am the lawful wife of CE Strouvelle, who is a citizen, by birth of the U. S. Nation; that a female child was born to me on Eighth day of August, 1904, that said child has been named Alice Kendall Strouvelle, and was living March 4, 1905.

                                        Susanne Barnett Strouvelle

Witnesses To Mark:
    {

    Subscribed and sworn to before me this 14" day of March, 1905.

                                    Robert E Lynch
    Com Ex 7/3/1906   Notary Public.

Applications for Enrollment of Creek Newborn
Act of 1905 Volume II

AFFIDAVIT OF ATTENDING PHYSICIAN OR MID-WIFE.

UNITED STATES OF AMERICA, Indian Territory, }
Western DISTRICT.

I, Fred S. Clinton , a physician , on oath state that I attended on Mrs. C.E. Strouvelle nee Barnett , wife of C.E. Strouvelle on the 8 day of August , 1904; that there was born to her on said date a female child; that said child was living March 4, 1905, and is said to have been named Alice Kendall Strouvelle .

Fred S Clinton M.D.

Witnesses To Mark:
{

Subscribed and sworn to before me this 14" day of March , 1905.

Com Ex 7/3/1906

Robert E Lynch
Notary Public.

BIRTH AFFIDAVIT.

DEPARTMENT OF THE INTERIOR.
COMMISSION TO THE FIVE CIVILIZED TRIBES.

IN RE APPLICATION FOR ENROLLMENT, as a citizen of the Creek Nation, of Charles Edward Strouvelle , born on the 12 day of November , 1902

Name of Father: C E Strouvelle   a citizen of the   U. S.   Nation.
Name of Mother: Susanne Barnett Strouvelle   a citizen of the   Creek   Nation.

Postoffice   Tulsa Ind Ter

AFFIDAVIT OF MOTHER.

UNITED STATES OF AMERICA, Indian Territory, }
Western DISTRICT.

I, Susanne Barnett Strouvelle , on oath state that I am 25 years of age and a citizen by birth , of the Creek Nation; that I am the lawful wife of CE Strouvelle , who is a citizen, by birth of the U. S. Nation; that a male child was born to me on twelfth day of November , 1902, that said child has been named Charles Edward Strouvelle , and is now living.

Susanne Barnett Strouvelle

Witnesses To Mark:
{

Applications for Enrollment of Creek Newborn
Act of 1905   Volume II

Subscribed and sworn to before me this 14 day of March , 1905.

                                    Robert E Lynch
Com Ex 7/3/1906   Notary Public.

AFFIDAVIT OF ATTENDING PHYSICIAN OR MID-WIFE.

UNITED STATES OF AMERICA, Indian Territory,
     Western   **DISTRICT.**

    I, Fred S. Clinton , a physician , on oath state that I attended on Mrs. Susanne Barnette Strouvelle , wife of C.E. Strouvelle on the 12 day of November , 1902; that there was born to her on said date a male child; that said child is now living and is said to have been named Charles Edward Strouvelle .

                                  Fred S Clinton M.D.
Witnesses To Mark:

Subscribed and sworn to before me this 14" day of March , 1905.

                                  Robert E. Lynch
Com Ex 7/3/1906   Notary Public.

BIRTH AFFIDAVIT.
                          DEPARTMENT OF THE INTERIOR.
                    COMMISSION TO THE FIVE CIVILIZED TRIBES.

    IN RE APPLICATION FOR ENROLLMENT, as a citizen of the Creek Nation, of Clarence Fryday , born on the 29th day of April , 1904

Name of Father: Berry Fryday	a citizen of the Creek	Nation.
Name of Mother: Susan Fryday (nee Gooden)	a citizen of the Creek	Nation.

                          Postoffice   Beggs, I.T.

AFFIDAVIT OF MOTHER.

UNITED STATES OF AMERICA, Indian Territory,
     Western   **DISTRICT.**

    I, Susan Fryday, nee Gooden , on oath state that I am 27 years of age and a citizen by blood, of the Creek Nation; that I am the lawful wife of Berry Fryday , who is a

Applications for Enrollment of Creek Newborn
Act of 1905   Volume II

citizen, by adoption of the Creek Nation; that a male child was born to me on the 29th day of April, 1904, that said child has been named Clarence Fryday, and was living March 4, 1905.

Susan Gooden

Witnesses To Mark:
{

Subscribed and sworn to before me this 22nd day of July, 1905.

Richard d[sic] Hill
Notary Public.

My Commission expires Mar. 25th, 1909

AFFIDAVIT OF ATTENDING PHYSICIAN OR MID-WIFE.

UNITED STATES OF AMERICA, Indian Territory,}
Western DISTRICT.

I, Amie Isac, a mid wife, on oath state that I attended on Mrs. Susan Fryday nee Gooden, wife of Berry Fryday on the 29th day of April, 1904; that there was born to her on said date a male child; that said child was living March 4, 1905, and is said to have been named Clarence Fryday.

her
Annie x Isac
mark

Witnesses To Mark:
{ Richard d Hill
{ George Miller

Subscribed and sworn to before me this 22nd day of July, 1905.

Richard d[sic] Hill
Notary Public.

My Commission expires Mar. 25th, 1909

BIRTH AFFIDAVIT.

DEPARTMENT OF THE INTERIOR.
COMMISSION TO THE FIVE CIVILIZED TRIBES.

IN RE APPLICATION FOR ENROLLMENT, as a citizen of the Creek Nation, of Clarence Friday, born on the 29 day of April, 1904

Name of Father: Berry Friday   a citizen of the   Creek   Nation.
Name of Mother: Susan Gooden   a citizen of the   Creek   Nation.

Postoffice   Beggs, I.T.

Applications for Enrollment of Creek Newborn
Act of 1905   Volume II

AFFIDAVIT OF MOTHER.

UNITED STATES OF AMERICA, Indian Territory,
   Western   DISTRICT.

I, Susan Gooden , on oath state that I am 27 years of age and a citizen by blood, of the Creek   Nation; that I am the lawful wife of Berry Friday , who is a citizen, by Freedman of the Creek   Nation; that a male   child was born to me on the 29" day of Apr , 1904 , that said child has been named Clarence Friday , and was living March 4, 1905.

Susan Gooden

Witnesses To Mark:

Subscribed and sworn to before me this 10" day of Mar , 1905.

Edw C Griesel
Notary Public.

N.C. 93.   F.H.W.

DEPARTMENT OF THE INTERIOR,
COMMISSIONER TO THE FIVE CIVILIZED TRIBES.

In the matter of the application for the enrollment of Clarence Friday as a citizen by blood of the Creek Nation.

DECISION.

The record in this case shows that on March 10, 1905, application was filed, in affidavit form, for the enrollment of Clarence Friday as a citizen by blood of the Creek Nation. A supplemental affidavit filed on July 25, 1905, is attached to and made part of the record herein.

The evidence shows that the said Clarence Friday is the child of Berry Friday and Susan Gooden. The said Berry Friday is identified on a partial schedule of Creek freedmen approved by the Secretary of the Interior March 13, 1902, opposite roll No. 1189. The said Susan Gooden is identified on a partial schedule of citizens by blood of the Creek Nation approved by the Secretary of the Interior March 13, 1902, opposite roll No. 3854.

It further appears that the name Friday is spelled Fryday in the supplemental affidavit but inasmuch as the father is identified as Berry Friday the said discrepancy is hereby corrected and in the future consideration of this case the applicant will be known as Clarence Friday.

The evidence also shows that the said Clarence Friday was born on April 29, 1904, and was still living March 10, 1905.

Applications for Enrollment of Creek Newborn
Act of 1905   Volume II

      The act of Congress approved March 3, 1905, (33 Stats., 1048), provides in part as follows:

> "That the Commission to the Five Civilized Tribes is authorized for sixty days after the date of the approval of this Act to receive and consider applications for enrollments of children born subsequent to May twenty five, nineteen hundred and one, and prior to March fourth, nineteen hundred and five, and living on said latter date, to citizens of the Creek tribe of Indians whose enrollment has been approved by the Secretary of the Interior prior to the date of approval of this Act; and to enroll and make allotments to such children."

      It is therefore, ordered and adjudged that the said Clarence Friday is entitled to be enrolled as a citizen by blood of the Creek Nation, in accordance with the provisions of law above quoted, and the application for his enrollment as such is accordingly granted.

Muskogee, Indian Territory,   *(Name Illegible)*   Commissioner.

NC. 93.

Muskogee, Indian Territory, July 18, 1905.

Susan Gooden,
    Beggs, Indian Territory.

Dear Madam:

      In the matter of the application for the enrollment of your minor child, Clarence Friday, as a citizen by blood of the Creek Nation, you are advised that the affidavit of the midwife or physician in attendance at the birth of said child is required.

      There is herewith enclosed a blank form of birth affidavit, and in executing same care should be exercised to see that all blanks are properly filled, all names written in full and in the event that the person signing the affidavit is unable to write, signature by mark must be attested by two witnesses. The affidavit must be executed before a Notary Public and the notarial seal and signature of the officer must be attached to each separate affidavit.

                                           Respectfully,

1 BC   Commissioner.

Applications for Enrollment of Creek Newborn
Act of 1905   Volume II

N.C.93

Muskogee, Indian Territory, July 25, 1905.

Susan Friday,
    Muskogee, Indian Territory.

Dear Madam:

    In the matter of the application for the enrollment of your minor child, Clarence Friday, there are on file at this office, affidavits in which it appears that your name is Susan Friday and you have signed said affidavits under your maiden name, Susan Gooden.

    For the purpose of correcting this discrepancy, you are requested to sign the enclosed affidavit correctly and after having same properly executed before an officer authorized to administer oaths, return it to this office in the inclosed[sic] envelope.

    Respectfully,

    Commissioner.

REFER IN REPLY TO THE FOLLOWING:
N.C.93

DEPARTMENT OF THE INTERIOR,
COMMISSIONER TO THE FIVE CIVILIZED TRIBES.

Muskogee, Indian Territory, July 7, 1905.

Susan Friday (or Gooden),
    Care Berry Friday,
        Muskogee, Indian Territory.

Dear Madam:

    In the matter of the application for the enrollment of your minor child, Clarence Friday, as a citizen of the Creek Nation, you are advised that you will be allowed fifteen days from date hereof within which to appear at this office and be examined under oath.

    Respectfully,

    (Name Illegible) Commissioner.

Applications for Enrollment of Creek Newborn
Act of 1905   Volume II

NBC 93.

Muskogee, Indian Territory, March 7, 1907.

Susan Gooden,
    Care of Berry Friday,
        Beggs, Indian Territory.

Dear Madam:

    You are hereby advised that on March 2, 1907, the Secretary of the Interior approved the enrollment of your minor child, Clarence Friday, as a citizen by blood of the Creek Nation, and that the name of said child appears upon the roll of new born citizens by blood of the Creek Nation, enrolled under the Act of Congress approved March 3, 1905 as number 1226.

    This child is now entitled to an allotment and application therefor should be made without delay at the Creek Land Office, Muskogee, Indian Territory.

                Respectfully,

                      Commissioner.

DEPARTMENT OF THE INTERIOR,
COMMISSIONER TO THE FIVE CIVILIZED TRIBES.

REFER IN REPLY TO THE FOLLOWING:
N.C. 94.

Muskogee, Indian Territory, **August 4, 1905.**

Stanwaitte Bighead,
    Mounds, Indian Territory.

Dear Sir:

    You are hereby advised that on **July 28, 1905**, the Secretary of the Interior approved the enrollment of your minor child, **Lizzie Bighead**, as a citizen by blood of the **Creek** Nation, and that the name of said child appears upon the roll of new born citizens of the **Creek** Nation as Number **60**.

    The child is now entitled to an allotment, and application therefor should be made without delay at the Land Office for the Nation in which the prospective allotment is located.

    An entire allotment for said child must be selected at the time of the original application.

Applications for Enrollment of Creek Newborn
Act of 1905   Volume II

Respectively,

Commissioner.

BIRTH AFFIDAVIT.

DEPARTMENT OF THE INTERIOR.
COMMISSION TO THE FIVE CIVILIZED TRIBES.

IN RE APPLICATION FOR ENROLLMENT, as a citizen of the CREEK Nation, of Lizzie Bighead, - - - - - - - -, born on the 8th, day of February, 1904

Name of Father: Standwaitie Bighead - - - -   a citizen of the Creek, - - - Nation.
Name of Mother: Millie Bighead, - - - - - -   a citizen of the Creek , - - - Nation.

Postoffice   Mounds, I.T.

AFFIDAVIT OF MOTHER.

UNITED STATES OF AMERICA, Indian Territory, ⎫
    WESTERN   DISTRICT.⎭

I, Millie Bighead, - - - - - - - - - -, on oath state that I am thirty five years of age and a citizen by Blood - - - - -, of the Creek - - - - - - - - - - - Nation; that I am the lawful wife of Standwaitie Bighead, - - - - - - - - - - - - who is a citizen, by Blood, - - - - of the Creek, - - --- - - - -   Nation; that a female child was born to me on the eighth day of February, - - - - - -1904, that said child has been named Lizzie Bighead, - - - - - - - -, and is now living.

                                    her
                          Millie x Bighead
                            mark

Witnesses To Mark:
  { W.R. Castell
    Daniel Bigpond

Subscribed and sworn to before me this 15th, day of March, - - - - - - , 1905.

(No signature given)
My Commission expires Feb. 21, 1907.   Notary Public.

Applications for Enrollment of Creek Newborn
Act of 1905 Volume II

AFFIDAVIT OF ATTENDING PHYSICIAN OR MID-WIFE.

UNITED STATES OF AMERICA, Indian Territory, }
    WESTERN   DISTRICT.

    I, Nancy Bigpond, - -- - - -, a Mid wife, - -, on oath state that I attended on Mrs. Lizzie[sic] Bighead, - - - - - -, wife of Standwaitie Bighead, - -- on the eighth day of Feby., 1905[sic]; that there was born to her on said date a female child; that said child is now living and is said to have been named Lizzie, - - - - - - - - - - - -.

                                Nancy Bigpond

Witnesses To Mark:
{

    Subscribed and sworn to before me this 15th day of March, - - - - - - 1905.

                            (No signature given)
    My Commission expires Feb. 21, 1907.   Notary Public.

BIRTH AFFIDAVIT.

DEPARTMENT OF THE INTERIOR.
COMMISSION TO THE FIVE CIVILIZED TRIBES.

    IN RE APPLICATION FOR ENROLLMENT, as a citizen of the Creek Nation, of Lizzie Bighead, born on the 8, day of February, 1904

Name of Father: Stanwaitie Bighead   a citizen of the Creek   Nation.
Name of Mother: Millie Bighead   a citizen of the Creek   Nation.

                  Postoffice   Mounds

AFFIDAVIT OF MOTHER.
                              Child Present
UNITED STATES OF AMERICA, Indian Territory, }
    Western   DISTRICT.

    I, Millie Bighead, on oath state that I am 35 years of age and a citizen by blood, of the Creek Nation; that I am the lawful wife of Stanwaitie Bighead, who is a citizen, by blood, of the Creek Nation; that a female child was born to me on the 8 day of February, 1904, that said child has been named Lizzie Bighead, and was living March 4, 1905.

                                Her
                         Millie x Bighead
                             mark

Applications for Enrollment of Creek Newborn
Act of 1905   Volume II

Witnesses To Mark:
{ Davis Shelby
{ Jesse McDermott

Subscribed and sworn to before me this 25, day of April , 1905.

(Seal)   Edw C Griesel
                                                    Notary Public.

AFFIDAVIT OF ATTENDING ~~PHYSICIAN OR MID-WIFE~~.
Father

UNITED STATES OF AMERICA, Indian Territory, }
      Western   DISTRICT. }

   I, Stanwaitie Bighead , a ----- , on oath state that I attended on Mrs. Millie Bighead my wife ~~of~~ *(blank)* on the 8 day of Feb. ,1904; that there was born to her on said date a female child; that said child was living March 5, 1905, and is said to have been named Lizzie Bighead .   His
                                                    Stanwaitie x Bigpond
Witnesses To Mark: mark
{ Davis Shelby
{ Jesse McDermott

Subscribed and sworn to before me this 25 day of April , 1905.

(Seal)   Edw C Griesel
                                                    Notary Public.

BA-161B.
DEPARTMENT OF THE INTERIOR,
COMMISSION TO THE FIVE CIVILIZED TRIBES.
MUSKOGEE, INDIAN TERRITORY, March 9, 1905.

-ooOoo-

   In the matter of the application for the enrollment of Paul Bowers as a citizen by blood of the Creek Nation.

   FRED BOWERS, being duly sworn, testified as follows:

EXAMINATION BY COMMISSION:
Q What is your name? A Fred Bowers.
Q How old are you? A 37

Applications for Enrollment of Creek Newborn
Act of 1905   Volume II

Q What is your postoffice address? A Tallahassee.

Witness is identified as Fred Bowers on Creek Indian card, Field Number 107, and his name is contained in the partial list of citizens by blood of the Creek Nation, approved by the Secretary of the Interior March 13, 1902, Roll Number 391.

Q Have you a child named Paul Bowers? A Yes, sir.
Q When was Paul Bowers born? A In October sometime; do not know the date exactly.
Q What year? A 1901, I think.
Q Is Paul living? A Yes, sir.
Q What is the name of his mother? A Ida Bowers.
Q Is she a citizen of the Creek Nation? A No, Cherokee.
Q She is a citizen of the Cherokee Nation, is she? A Yes, sir.
Q Has Paul Bowers ever been enrolled as a citizen of any Nation? A Yes, sir--Cherokee.
Q Has he gotten his land? A Yes, sir.
Q If it is found that Paul Bowers has citizenship rights in both the Cherokee and Creek Nation, do you desire to have him enrolled as a Cherokee or Creek? A Creek.
Q If it is found that Paul Bowers is enrolled and has recived his allotment of land in the Cherokee Nation, do you desire to relinquish that allotment and have him enrolled as a Creek? A Yes.

Zera Ellen Parrish, being sworn on her oath states that as a stenographer to the Commission to the Five Civilized Tribes she reported the above case and that this is a full, true and correct transcript of her stenographic notes in same.

Zera Ellen Parrish

Subscribed and sworn to before me this 13th day of March, 1905.

Edw C Griesel
Notary Public.

BA-161-B
DEPARTMENT OF THE INTERIOR,
COMMISSION TO THE FIVE CIVILIZED TRIBES.

Muskogee, Indian Territory, March 9, 1905.

In the matter of the application for the enrollment of Paul Bowers as a Creek.

Fred Bowers, being duly sworn, testified as follows:

EXAMINATION BY THE COMMISSION:
Q What is your name? A Fred Bowers.

Applications for Enrollment of Creek Newborn
Act of 1905 Volume II

Q You have testified here before about Paul Bowers, have you not? A Yes sir.
Q You stated that he was enrolled as a Cherokee? A Yes sir.
Q You want to elect to have him enrolled as a Creek? A Yes sir.
Q Have you changed your mind about it? A Yes sir.
Q You are now decided that, if he is entitled to enrollment in either of these Nations, you elect the Cherokee for him? A Yes sir.
Q You elect to have him enrolled as a Cherokee? A Yes sir.
Q Did you talk with your wife about this? A Yes sir.
Q What did she have to say about it? A Let his enrollment be in the Cherokee Nation. We have done filed for him.

INDIAN TERRITORY, Western District.

I, J. Y. Miller, a stenographer to the Commission to the Five Civilized Tribes, do hereby certify that the above and foregoing is a true and complete translation of my notes as same appear in my stenographic report of this case.

J Y Miller

Sworn to and subscribed before me
this the 19 day of April, 1905.
My Com. expires Apr. 11, 1909   Zera E Parrish
                                           Notary Public.

NC-95

Muskogee, Indian Territory, September 14, 1903.

Clerk in Charge,
    Cherokee Enrollment Division.

Dear Sir:

March 9, 1905, application was made to the Commission to the Five Civilized Tribes for enrollment as a citizen by blood of the Creek Nation of Paul Bowers, born October, 1901, a child of Fred Bowers, a citizen by blood of the Creek Nation, and Ida Bowers, a citizen of the Cherokee Nation. From the testimony of the father, it appears that said Paul Bowers is probably enrolled as a citizen of the Cherokee Nation.

You are requested to advise this Office whether or not said Paul Bowers is enrolled as a citizen of the Cherokee Nation, and if so, the date of the approval of his enrollment by the Secretary of the Interior and his number on the approved roll.

Respectfully,

Acting Commissioner.

Applications for Enrollment of Creek Newborn
Act of 1905   Volume II

Muskogee, Indian Territory, September 21, 1905.

Chief Clerk Cherokee Enrollment Division,
Muskogee, Indian Territory.

Sir:

Receipt is acknowledged of your letter of Sept 13, 1905, (Cher.D. 2510) in which you ask to be advised as to whether or not the records of the Creek Enrollment Division show Fred Bowers a citizen by blood of the Creek Nation and who is the father of Paul Bowers, N.C.95, possesses *(illegible, smudged)* right to enrollment as a citizen of the Cherokee Nation.

You also ask the present post office address of Fred Bowers.

In reply you are advised that it does not appear from the records of this office that said Fred Bowers possesses any right to enrollment as a citizen of the Cherokee Nation: His name appears on Creek Indian card field number 107 and on the partial list of citizens by blood approved by the Secretary of the Interior March 13, 1902.

It appears from said card that said Fred Bowers was listed for enrollment April 5, 1899; that he was then thirty one years of age; that he was the child of Lewis Bowers, deceased, a white man, and Rebecca Bowers, deceased, a half blood Creek Indian.

You are further advised that the present post office address of Fred Bowers is Wagoner, Indian Territory.

Respectfully,

Acting Commissioner.

NC 95,

Muskogee, Indian Territory, February 11, 1907.

Ida Bowers,
c/o Fred Bowers,
Tallahassee, Indian Territory.

Dear Madam:

There is herewith enclosed one copy of the decision of the Commissioner to the Five Civilized Tribes in the matter of the application for the enrollment of your minor child, Paul Bowers, as a citizen of the Creek Nation, denying said application.

The decision, with a copy of the proceedings had in the case, is this day transmitted to the Secretary of the Interior for his review and decision. The final decision

Applications for Enrollment of Creek Newborn
Act of 1905 Volume II

of the Secretary will be made known to you as soon as the Commissioner is informed of the same.

Respectfully,

Commissioner.

Register.
LM-64.

NC 95.

Muskogee, Indian Territory, February 11, 1907.

M. L. Mott,
    Attorney for Creek Nation,
        Muskogee, Indian Territory.

Dear Sir:

    There is herewith enclosed one copy of the decision of the Commissioner to the Five Civilized Tribes in the matter of the application for the enrollment of Paul Bowers, as a citizen of the Creek Nation, denying said application.

    The decision, with a copy of the proceedings had in the case, is this day transmitted to the Secretary of the Interior for his review and decision. The final decision of the Secretary will be made known to you as soon as the Commissioner is informed of the same.

Respectfully,

Commissioner.

LM-65.

NC 95.

Muskogee, Indian Territory, February 11, 1907.

The Honorable,
    The Secretary of the Interior.

Sir:

    There is herewith transmitted the record of proceedings had in the matter of the application for the enrollment of Paul Bowers, as a citizen of the Creek Nation, including the decision of the Commissioner to the Five Civilized Tribes, denying said application.

Respectfully,

Commissioner.

Applications for Enrollment of Creek Newborn
Act of 1905   Volume II

LM-66.

Through the Commissioner
of Indian Affairs.

N.C.95 F.H.W.
A.G.
DEPARTMENT OF THE INTERIOR,
COMMISSIONER TO THE FIVE CIVILIZED TRIBES.

In the matter of the application for the enrollment of Paul Bowers, as a citizen by blood of the Creek Nation.

DECISION.

The record in this case shows that an application was filed on March 9, 1905, for the enrollment of Paul Bowers as a citizen by blood of the Creek Nation, under the provisions of the Act of Congress approved March 3, 1905. Further proceedings were had on the date of the original application.

The evidence and the records of this office show that Paul Bowers is the child of Fred Bowers and Ida Bowers. The said Fred Bowers is identified on a partial schedule of citizens by blood of the Creek Nation approved by the Secretary of the Interior March 13, 1902, opposite roll No. 391. The said Ida Bowers is identified on a partial schedule of citizens by blood of the Cherokee Nation, approved by the Secretary of the Interior December 9, 1902, opposite roll No. 12547.

It further appears from the records of this office that an application was filed on July 1, 1902, in affidavit form, executed by the mother, Ida Bowers, for the enrollment of Paul W. Bowers as a citizen by blood of the Cherokee Nation and the name of the said Paul W. Bowers appears on a partial schedule of citizens by blood of the Cherokee Nation, approved by the Secretary of the Interior December 9, 1902, opposite roll No. 12545.

It also appears from the records of this office that represented by his mother, said Ida Bowers, the said Paul W. Bowers was allowed to select an allotment in the Cherokee Nation on June 30, 1904.

It appears from the evidence and the records of this office that the said applicant, Paul Bowers, and the said Paul W. Bowers are one and the same person.

It further appears in evidence that on March 9, 1905, the father of the said applicant executed a birth affidavit and expressed a desire to have the said Paul Bowers enrolled as a citizen by blood of the Creek Nation but subsequently on the same date, being duly sworn he appeared again before the Commissioner and testified that he and the mother desired to have said applicant enrolled as a citizen of the Cherokee Nation.

Considering the fact that an application was made for the enrollment of said Paul Bowers as a citizen by blood of the Cherokee Nation; that he was duly enrolled as a citizen of said Nation; that an allotment was made for him in said Nation upon the personal application of the mother of the said applicant and that the final election was for the enrollment of said applicant as a citizen by blood of the Cherokee Nation, I am of the

Applications for Enrollment of Creek Newborn
Act of 1905 Volume II

opinion that the enrollment of said Paul Bowers as a citizen by blood of the Cherokee Nation should be allowed to stand, in view of the provisions of the Act of Congress approved June 28, 1898 (30 Stats., 495) which provides in part as follows:

> "The several tribes may, by agreement, determine the right of persons who for any reason may claim citizenship in two or more tribes, and to allotment of lands and distribution of moneys belonging to such tribe; but if no such agreement be made, then such claimant shall be entitled to such rights in one tribe only, and may elect in which tribe he will take such right; but if he fail or refuse to make such selection in due time, he shall be enrolled in the tribe with whom he has resided, and there be given such allotment and distributions, and not elsewhere."

It is therefore, ordered and adjudged that there is no authority of law for the enrollment of the said Paul Bowers as a citizen by blood of the Creek Nation, and the application for his enrollment as such is accordingly denied.

(Name Illegible) Commissioner

Muskogee, Indian Territory,
    FEB 2- 1907

Refer in reply to the following:
    Land 15075-1907.

COPY

DEPARTMENT OF THE INTERIOR,
OFFICE OF INDIAN AFFAIRS,
WASHINGTON.

February 27 1907.

The Honorable,
    The Secretary of the Interior.

Sir:

    I Have[sic] the honor to invite your attention to the record of the Commissioner to the Five Civilized Tribes, in the matter of the application for the enrollment of Paul Bowers as a citizen by blood of the Creek Nation.

    The Commissioner reports that the record in the case shows that an application was filed on March 19, 1905 for the enrollment of the applicant under the provisions of the act of Congress approved March 3, 1905, and that further proceedings were had on the same day.

    He also says that the evidence in the case and the records of his office show that Paul Bowers is the child of Fred and Ida Bowers; that Fred Bowers is identified on a partial schedule of citizens by blood of the Creek Nation approved by the Department on March 13, 1902, opposite roll No. 391; that Ida Bowers is identified on a partial schedule

Applications for Enrollment of Creek Newborn
Act of 1905   Volume II

of citizens by blood of the Cherokee Nation approved by the Department on December 9, 1902, opposite No. 12547; that an application was filed on July 1, 1902, in affidavit form, executed by the mother, Ida Bowers, for the enrollment of Paul W. Bowers as a citizen by blood of the Cherokee Nation; that the name of Paul W. Bowers appears on the partial schedule of citizens by blood of the Cherokee Nation approved by the Department on December 9, 1902, opposite No. 12548; that it also appears from the records of the Commissioner's office that represented by his mother, Ida Bowers, Paul W. Bowers was allowed to select an d lotment[sic] in the Cherokee Nation on June 30, 1904, and that the applicant, Paul Bowers and Paul W. Bowers is one and the same person.

The Commissioner further says that it appears in evidence that on March 9, 1905, the father of the applicant executed a birth affidavit and expressed a desire to have Paul Bowers enrolled as a citizen by blood of the Creek Nation, but on the same day, being duly sworn, he appeared again before the Commissioner and testified that he and the mother desired to have the applicant enrolled as a citizen of the Cherokee Nation.

Considering the fact that the application was made for the enrollment of Paul Bowers as a citizen by blood of the Cherokee Nation; that an allotment was made for him in the nation on the personal application of the mother, and that the final election was for his enrollment as a citizen by blood of the Cherokee Nation, the Commissioner arrived at the opinion that the enrollment of Paul Bowers as a citizen by blood of the Cherokee Nation should be allowed to stand, and on February 2, 1907, he so ordered.

Paul W. Bowers has already been enrolled and allotted as a citizen of the Cherokee Nation. Under the law his parents have authority to elect in which nation he should be enrolled. Having so elected and the allotment having been made to him, it is not believed that the Government should permit persons who may have rights in two nations, after once having elected in which nation they shall be enrolled, to change their minds and institute a reinvestigation of their status, and receive an allotment in another nation. I believe the enrollment of Paul W. Bowers in the Cherokee Nation should be allowed to stand, and that the application for his enrollment as a citizen of the Creek Nation should be denied, and it is so recommended.

Very respectfully,

C. F. Larrabee,

EBH-Y.   Acting Commissioner.

Applications for Enrollment of Creek Newborn
Act of 1905   Volume II

DEPARTMENT OF THE INTERIOR, J.P.
WASHINGTON. O.K.

LRS   I.T.D.

5706, 5722, 5792, 5794-1907.
5814, 5816, 5828, 5830-1907.
5832, 5838, 5840, 5856-1907.
5862, 5868, 5872, 5874-1907.
5882, 5884, 5966-1907.   March 2, 1907.

DIRECT.

Commissioner to the Five Civilized Tribes.
  Muskogee, Indian Territory.

Sir:

Your decisions in the following Creek citizenship cases adverse to the applicants are hereby affirmed.   Copies of Indian Office letters submitting your reports and recommending that the decisions be affirmed are enclosed.

	Date of your
Title of Case:	Letter of Transmittal.
Wester Walker,	January 11, 1907.
Julia Cornelius, et al,	January 28, 1907.
Paul Bowers,	February 11, 1907.
Moses Vaughan (Freedman),	February 11, 1907.
Charles Clark,	February 9, 1907.
Johny Carwile[sic] (Freedman),	February 9, 1907.
Jack and Alice Bell (Freedman),	February 9, 1907.
Yar-mah-lee, et al. (deceased),	February 9, 1907.
Mary Burl (Freedman),	February 11, 1907.
Annie McClelland and Mitchell Cox,	February 9, 1907.
Alvin Smith (deceased) (Freedman),	February 9, 1907.
Isaac and Ethel Grayson (Freedman),	February 9, 1907.
William B. Self et al.	February 11, 1907.
Annie Morgan (Freedman),	February 9, 1907.
Bonnie Griffin (Freedman),	February 11, 1907.
Mose James (Freedman),	February 9, 1907.
Dan Campbell (Freedman),	January 25, 1907.
Josie Wofford,	February 9, 1907.
Daniel Gray, deceased,	February 11, 1907.

A copy hereof and all the papers in the above mentioned cases have been sent to the Indian Office.

Applications for Enrollment of Creek Newborn
Act of 1905   Volume II

Respectfully,

(Signed) James E. Wilson,

Assistant Secretary.

19 inc. and 38 inc.
for Ind. Of.

AFMc
3-2-07.

NC 95

Muskogee, Indian Territory, March 11, 1907.

Fred Bowers,
    Tallahasse[sic], Indian Territory.

Dear Sir:

You are hereby advised that the Secretary of the Interior under date of Marxh 2, 1907, affirmed the decision of the Commissioner to the Five Civilized Tribes, denying the application for the enrollment of your minor child, Paul Bowers, as a citizen by blood of the Creek Nation.

Respectfully,

Commissioner.

BA- 39.

DEPARTMENT OF THE INTERIOR,
COMMISSION TO THE FIVE CIVILIZED TRIBES.
MUSKOGEE, INDIAN TERRITORY, March 14, 1905.

-ooOoo-

In the matter of the application for the enrollment of your Peter Hendrickson , as a citizen of the Creek Nation.

Mary HENDRICKSON, being duly sworn, testified as follows:

EXAMINATION BY COMMISSION:

Q What is your name? A Mary Hendrickson.
Q How old are you? A 29.

Applications for Enrollment of Creek Newborn
Act of 1905   Volume II

Q What is your postoffice address? A Clive now, but it soon will be Bristow.
Q Were you ever married before you married Hendrickson? A Yes, sir.
Q What was your first husband's name? A Stevens.

  Witness is identified as Mary Stevens on Creek Indian Card, Field Number 1051, and her name is contained in the partial list of citizen[sic] by blood of the Creek Nation, approved by the Secretary of the Interior March 13, 1902, Roll Number 3397.

Q Have you a child named Peter Hendrickson? A Yes, sir.
Q Is he living? A Ye ,[sic] sir, this is him.
Q How old is he? A About three years old.
Q When was he born? A May 2nd---I do not remember.
Q Was he born in 1902? A Yes, sir.
Q Did you ever call him any other name besides Peter? A I call him Jack sometimes. His full name is Peter Jackson Hendrickson.
Q And he is living? A Yes, sir.

  Child is present and appears to be bout[sic] the age indicated.

  Zera Ellen Parrish, being duly sworn on her oath states that as stenographer to the Commission to the Five Civilized Tribes she reported the above case and that his[sic] is a full, true and correct transcript of her stenograph-ic notes as taken in same.

            Zera Ellen Parrish

Subscribed and sworn to before me this 17 day of March, 1905.

            Edw C Griesel
              Notary Public.

                  NC 96.

          Muskogee, Indian Territory, May 18, 1905.

Joseph Hendrickson,
    Bristow, Indian Territory.

Dear Sir:

  In the matter of the application for the enrollment of your minor child, Elijah Hendrickson, as a citizen of the Creek Nation, you are advised that the Commission requires the affidavit of the midwife or physician in attendance at the birth of said child, and of two disinterested witnesses as to the birth of said child.

Applications for Enrollment of Creek Newborn
Act of 1905 Volume II

There are herewith enclosed three blank forms of birth affidavits, and in executing same care should be exercised to see that all blanks are properly filled, all names written in full and in the event that either of the persons signing the affidavits is unable to write, signatures by mark must be attested by two witnesses. Each affidavit must be executed before a Notary Public and the notarial seal and signature of the officer must be attached to each separate affidavit.

Respectfully.

BC. Chairman.

NC. 96.

Muskogee, Indian Territory, July 12, 1905.

Mary Hendrickson,
    Bristow, Indian Territory.

Dear Madam:

In the matter of the application for the enrollment of your minor child, Elijah Hendrickson, as a citizen of the Creek Nation, you are advised that this office requires the affidavit of the midwife or physician in attendance at the birth of said child, and of two disinterested witnesses same.

There are herewith enclosed three blank forms of birth affidavits, and in executing same care should be exercised to see that all blanks are properly filled, all names written in full and in the event that either of the persons signing the affidavits is unable to write, signatures by mark must be attested by two witnesses. Each affidavit must be executed before a Notary Public and the notarial seal and signature of the officer must be attached to each separate affidavit.

Respectfully.

BC. Commissioner.

BIRTH AFFIDAVIT.

DEPARTMENT OF THE INTERIOR.
COMMISSION TO THE FIVE CIVILIZED TRIBES.

IN RE APPLICATION FOR ENROLLMENT, as a citizen of the Creek Nation, of Elijah Hendrickson, born on the 6th day of May, 1904

Name of Father:	Joseph Hendrickson	a citizen of the *(blank)*	Nation.
Name of Mother:	Mary Hendrickson	a citizen of the Creek	Nation.

Applications for Enrollment of Creek Newborn
Act of 1905 Volume II

Postoffice   Bristow, I.T.

AFFIDAVIT OF MOTHER.

UNITED STATES OF AMERICA, Indian Territory,
Western   DISTRICT.

I, Mary Hendrickson, on oath state that I am 29 years of age and a citizen by Birth, of the Creek Nation; that I am the lawful wife of Joseph Hendrickson, who is a citizen, by *(blank)* of the *(blank)* Nation; that a male child was born to me on 6th day of May, 1904, that said child has been named Elijah Hendrickson, and was living March 4, 1905.

                          her
                  Mary x Hendrickson
Witnesses To Mark: mark
  P H Johnson
  Albert Ewers

Subscribed and sworn to before me this 20th day of July, 1905.

                  H. F. Johnson
                      Notary Public.

AFFIDAVIT OF ATTENDING PHYSICIAN OR MID-WIFE.

UNITED STATES OF AMERICA, Indian Territory,
Western District   DISTRICT.

I, Joicie Carlile, a neighbor woman, on oath state that I attended on Mrs. Mary Hendrickson, wife of Joseph Hendrickson on the 6th day of May, 1904; that there was born to her on said date a male child; that said child was living March 4, 1905, and is said to have been named Elijah Hendrickson.

                  Joicie Carlile
Witnesses To Mark:

Subscribed and sworn to before me this 2^{d} day of August, 1905.

                  H.F. Johnson
                      Notary Public.

Applications for Enrollment of Creek Newborn
Act of 1905 Volume II

neighbor woman
AFFIDAVIT OF ATTENDING <s>PHYSICIAN OR MID-WIFE</s>.

UNITED STATES OF AMERICA, Indian Territory, ⎱
   Western District   DISTRICT. ⎰

I, Bessie Barney, a neighbor woman, on oath state that I attended on Mrs. Mary Hendrickson, wife of Joseph Hendrickson on the 6th day of May, 1904; that there was born to her on said date a male child; that said child was living March 4, 1905, and is said to have been named Elijah Hendrickson.

             her
           Bessie x Barney
Witnesses To Mark: mark
  ⎰ Homer L Johnson
  ⎱ P H Johnson

Subscribed and sworn to before me this 23^{d} day of July, 1905.

My commission expires Jan 9-1907 H. F. Johnson
                Notary Public.

H.F. JOHNSON, PREST.   L.D. GROOM, CASHIER   G.C. BROWN, ASST. CASH.

No. 6062.

The First National Bank
OF BRISTOW

Bristow, Ind Ter   July, 20.   190 5

United States of America Indian Territory.
   Western District,

I Lizzie Erly on oath state that I am personally and well acquainted with Mary Henderson[sic] a citizen of the Creeknation[sic] and know her to be the mother of a child named Elija Hendrickson born about May 6, 1904.

            Lizzie Earley[sic]

Subscribed and sworn to before me this 20th day of July 1905.

           H.F. Johnson
My commission expires Jan 9-1907   Notary Public

Applications for Enrollment of Creek Newborn
Act of 1905 Volume II

I.D.

REFER IN REPLY TO THE FOLLOWING:
NC-96.

DEPARTMENT OF THE INTERIOR,
COMMISSIONER TO THE FIVE CIVILIZED TRIBES.

Muskogee, Indian Territory, 1905.

Mary Hendrickson,
     Bristow, Indian Territory.

Dear Madam:

    In the matter of the application for the enrollment of your minor child Peter Hendrickson as a citizen by blood of the Creek Nation you are requested to furnish this office with the affidavit of the physician, who attended at the birth of said child, or one disinterested witness showing whether or not said Peter Hendrickson was living March 4, 1905.

    This matter should receive your prompt attention.

Respectfully,

Bristow IT Oct 20-1905   *(Name Illegible)* Commissioner.

To Commissioner

    Mrs Hendrickson thinks that the Physicians[sic] certificate is already in file – Inclosed[sic] find certificate to fact that child was alive March 4-1905 and is still living as per above letter.

H.F. Johnson
Bristow
IT

BIRTH AFFIDAVIT.

DEPARTMENT OF THE INTERIOR.
COMMISSION TO THE FIVE CIVILIZED TRIBES.

    IN RE APPLICATION FOR ENROLLMENT, as a citizen of the Creek Nation Nation, of Peter Hendrickson , born on the 2^d day of May , 1902

Name of Father: Joseph Hendrickson   a citizen of the *(blank)* Nation.
Name of Mother: Mary Hendrickson   a citizen of the Creek Nation.

Postoffice   Bristow Indian Ter

Applications for Enrollment of Creek Newborn
Act of 1905   Volume II

AFFIDAVIT OF MOTHER.

UNITED STATES OF AMERICA, Indian Territory, ⎱
    Western   DISTRICT. ⎰

    I, Mary Hendrickson, on oath state that I am 29 years of age and a citizen by Birth, of the Creek Nation Nation; that I am the lawful wife of Joseph Hendrickson , who is a citizen, by ----- of the ----- Nation; that a male child was born to me on 2^d day of May , 1902, that said child has been named Peter Hendrickson , and was living March 4, 1905.

                                            Mary Hendrickson

Witnesses To Mark:
  ⎰ Albert Ewers
  ⎱ L.D. Groom

    Subscribed and sworn to before me this 20 day of October , 1905.

                                            H. F. Johnson
                                                   Notary Public.
My commission expires Jan 9-1907.

AFFIDAVIT OF ATTENDING PHYSICIAN OR MID-WIFE.

UNITED STATES OF AMERICA, Indian Territory, ⎱
    Western   DISTRICT. ⎰

    I, Nannie Lagow , a witness , on oath state that I ~~attended on Mrs.   , wife of   on the   day of   , 1   ; that there was born to her on said date a~~ *(blank)* ~~child~~; I personally know the boy Peter Hendrickson mentioned above and that that ^ said child was living March 4, 1905, and is ~~said to have been named~~ *(blank)* . living at this date.

                                          her
                                   Nannie x Lagow
Witnesses To Mark: mark
  ⎰ Albert Ewers
  ⎱ L.D. Groom

    Subscribed and sworn to before me this 20 day of Oct, 1905.

                                            H.F. Johnson
                                                Notary Public.
My commission expires Jan. 9-1907.

Applications for Enrollment of Creek Newborn
Act of 1905 Volume II

BIRTH AFFIDAVIT.

DEPARTMENT OF THE INTERIOR.
COMMISSION TO THE FIVE CIVILIZED TRIBES.

IN RE APPLICATION FOR ENROLLMENT, as a citizen of the Creek Nation, of Peter Hendrickson, born on the 2^d day of May, 1902

Name of Father: Joseph Hendrickson   a citizen of the ------   Nation.
Name of Mother: Mary Hendrickson   a citizen of the Creek Nation Nation.

Postoffice   Bristow IT

AFFIDAVIT OF MOTHER.

UNITED STATES OF AMERICA, Indian Territory,
    Western   DISTRICT.

I, Mary Hendrickson, on oath state that I am 29 years of age and a citizen by birth, of the Creek Nation; that I am the lawful wife of Joseph Hendrickson, who is a citizen, by ----- of the ----- Nation; that a male child was born to me on 2^d day of May, 1902, that said child has been named Peter Hendrickson, and is now living.

Mary Hendrickson

Witnesses To Mark:
  Albert Ewers
  L.D. Groom

Subscribed and sworn to before me this 27th day of October, 1905.

H. F. Johnson
Notary Public.

AFFIDAVIT OF ATTENDING PHYSICIAN OR MID-WIFE.

UNITED STATES OF AMERICA, Indian Territory,
    ~~West~~   DISTRICT.

I, George S Turner, a Physician, on oath state that I attended on Mrs. Mary Hendrickson, wife of Joseph Hendrickson on the 2^d day of May, 1902; that there was born to her on said date a male child; that said child is now living and is said to have been named Peter Hendrickson.

GS Turner M.D.

Witnesses To Mark:

Applications for Enrollment of Creek Newborn
Act of 1905   Volume II

Subscribed and sworn to before me this 25 day of Oct, 1905.

(Name Illegible)
Notary Public.

BIRTH AFFIDAVIT.

DEPARTMENT OF THE INTERIOR,
COMMISSION TO THE FIVE CIVILIZED TRIBES.

IN RE APPLICATION FOR ENROLLMENT, as a citizen of the Creek Nation, of Peter Hendrickson , born on the 2 day of May , 1902

Name of Father: Joseph Hendrickson   a citizen of the United States ~~Nation~~.
Name of Mother: Mary Hendrickson   a citizen of the Creek Nation Nation.

Postoffice   Krebs I.T.

AFFIDAVIT OF MOTHER.

UNITED STATES OF AMERICA, Indian Territory, }
    Central   DISTRICT.

I, Mary Hendrickson , on oath state that I am 27 years of age and a citizen by blood, of the Creek Nation; that I am the lawful wife of Joseph Hendrickson , who is a citizen, by birth of the United States ~~Nation~~; that a male child was born to me on the 2^d day of May , 1902, that said child has been named Peter Hendrickson , and is now living.

                    Mary Hendrickson   x
Witnesses To Mark:
 { Will Oglesby
   Harry Oglesby

Subscribed and sworn to before me this 7 *day of* June, *19*02.

                    W. J. Oglesby
                    Notary Public.

Applications for Enrollment of Creek Newborn
Act of 1905 Volume II

AFFIDAVIT OF ATTENDING PHYSICIAN OR MID-WIFE.

UNITED STATES OF AMERICA, Indian Territory,
Central DISTRICT.

I, G S Turner , a Physician , on oath state that I attended on Mrs. Mary Hendrickson , wife of Joe Hendrickson on the 2 day of May , 1902; that there was born to her on said date a male child; that said child is now living and is said to have been named Peter Hendrickson .

G S Turner M.D.

Witnesses To Mark:
{

Subscribed and sworn to before me this 7 *day of* June , *190*2.

W.J. Oglesby
Notary Public.

BIRTH AFFIDAVIT.

DEPARTMENT OF THE INTERIOR.
COMMISSION TO THE FIVE CIVILIZED TRIBES.

IN RE APPLICATION FOR ENROLLMENT, as a citizen of the CREEK Nation, of Elijah Hendrickson , born on the 6" day of May , 1904

Name of Father: Joseph Hendrickson   a citizen of the   U.S.   ~~Nation~~.
Name of Mother: Mary Hendrickson   a citizen of the   Creek   Nation.

Postoffice   Bristow, Ind Ter

AFFIDAVIT OF MOTHER.

UNITED STATES OF AMERICA, Indian Territory,
Western DISTRICT.

I, Mary Hendrickson, on oath state that I am 29 years of age and a citizen by blood, of the Creek Nation; that I am the lawful wife of Joseph Hendrickson , who is a citizen, by ----- of the United States ~~Nation~~; that a male child was born to me on 6" day of May , 1904, that said child has been named Elijah Hendrickson , and is now living.

her
Mary x Hendrickson
mark

Witnesses To Mark:
{ Edward Merrick
  H.G. Hains

Applications for Enrollment of Creek Newborn
Act of 1905   Volume II

Subscribed and sworn to before me this 14th day of March , 1905.

Edward Merrick
Notary Public.

Father
AFFIDAVIT OF <s>ATTENDING PHYSICIAN OR MID-WIFE</s>.

UNITED STATES OF AMERICA, Indian Territory,
    WESTERN   DISTRICT.

I, Joseph Hendrickson , <s>a</s>, on oath state that I attended on Mrs. Mary Hendrickson , my wife <s>of</s> on the 6th day of May , 1904; that there was born to her on said date a male child; that said child is now living and is <s>said to have been</s> named Elijah Hendrickson .

Joseph Hendrickson[sic]

Witnesses To Mark:
{

Subscribed and sworn to before me this 14" day of March, 1905.

Edward Merrick
Notary Public.

DEPARTMENT OF THE INTERIOR,
COMMISSIONER TO THE FIVE CIVILIZED TRIBES.

REFER IN REPLY TO THE FOLLOWING:

N.C. 97.

Muskogee, Indian Territory, August 4, 1905.

James L. Grayson,
    Boynton, Indian Territory.

Dear Sir:

You are hereby advised that on **July 28, 1905** , the Secretary of the Interior approved the enrollment of your minor child, **Pearl Grayson** , as a citizen by blood of the **Creek** Nation, and that the name of said child appears upon the roll of new born citizens of the **Creek** Nation as Number **61** .

The child is now entitled to an allotment, and application therefor should be made without delay at the Land Office for the Nation in which the prospective allotment is located.

An entire allotment for said child must be selected at the time of the original application.

Applications for Enrollment of Creek Newborn
Act of 1905 Volume II

Respectively,

Commissioner.

BIRTH AFFIDAVIT.

DEPARTMENT OF THE INTERIOR.
COMMISSION TO THE FIVE CIVILIZED TRIBES.

IN RE APPLICATION FOR ENROLLMENT, as a citizen of the CREEK Nation, of Pearl Grayson, born on the 11th day of December, 1903

Name of Father: James L. Grayson   a citizen of the   Creek   Nation.
Name of Mother: Matilda Grayson   a citizen of the   US   Nation.

Postoffice   Boynton Ind Ter

AFFIDAVIT OF ~~MOTHER~~. Father

UNITED STATES OF AMERICA, Indian Territory,
     WESTERN   DISTRICT.

I, James L Grayson, on oath state that I am 38 years of age and a citizen by blood, of the Creek Nation; that I am the lawful husband ~~wife~~ of Matilda Grayson, who is a citizen, by ----- of the United States Nation; that a female child was born to ~~me~~ her on 11th day of December, 1903, that said child has been named Pearl Grayson, and is now living.

                               James L. Grayson

Witnesses To Mark:
{

Subscribed and sworn to before me this 14th day of March, 1905.

                               Edward Merrick
                               Notary Public.

AFFIDAVIT OF ATTENDING PHYSICIAN OR MID-WIFE.

UNITED STATES OF AMERICA, Indian Territory,
     WESTERN   DISTRICT.

I, Dr. R. H. Waterford, a physician, on oath state that I attended on Mrs. Matilda Grayson, wife of James L. Grayson on the 11 day of December, 1903; that there was born to her on said date a female child; that said child is now living and is said to have been named Pearl Grayson.

Applications for Enrollment of Creek Newborn
Act of 1905   Volume II

                                          R H Waterford M.D.

Witnesses To Mark:
{

Subscribed and sworn to before me this 14 day of March, 1905.

                                                  Edward Merrick
                                                  Notary Public.

BIRTH AFFIDAVIT.
DEPARTMENT OF THE INTERIOR.
COMMISSION TO THE FIVE CIVILIZED TRIBES.

      IN RE APPLICATION FOR ENROLLMENT, as a citizen of the CREEK Nation, of Pearl Grayson, born on the 11 day of December, 1903

Name of Father: James L. Grayson   a citizen of the   Creek   Nation.
Name of Mother: Matilda Grayson   a citizen of the   US   Nation.

                              Postoffice   Boynton Ind Ter

AFFIDAVIT OF MOTHER.

UNITED STATES OF AMERICA, Indian Territory, ⎫
       WESTERN   DISTRICT. ⎭

      I, Matilda Grayson, on oath state that I am 26 years of age and a citizen by -----, of the United States ~~Nation~~; that I am the lawful wife of James L Grayson, who is a citizen, by blood of the Creek Nation; that a female child was born to me on 11th day of December, 1903, that said child has been named Pearl Grayson, and is now living.

                                                Matilda Grayson

Witnesses To Mark:
{

Subscribed and sworn to before me this 14th day of March, 1905.

                                                Edward Merrick
                                                Notary Public.

Applications for Enrollment of Creek Newborn
Act of 1905   Volume II

NC 98.

Muskogee, Indian Territory, May 18, 1905.

Billie Bruner,
    Okmulgee, Indian Territory.

Dear Sir:

    In the matter of the application for the enrollment of your minor child, Richard Douglas Bruner, as a citizen of the Creek Nation, you are advised that the Commission requires the affidavit of the midwife or physician in attendance at the birth of said child, and if no midwife was present, the Commission requires the affidavits of two disinterested witnesses as to the birth of said child.

    There are herewith enclosed two blank forms of birth affidavits, and in executing same care should be exercised to see that all blanks are properly filled, all names written in full and in the event that the persons signing the affidavits are unable to write, signatures by mark must be attested by two witnesses. Each affidavit must be executed before a Notary Public and the notarial seal and signature of the officer must be attached to each separate affidavit.

Respectfully,

BC.   Chairman.

DEPARTMENT OF THE INTERIOR,
COMMISSIONER TO THE FIVE CIVILIZED TRIBES.

REFER IN REPLY TO THE FOLLOWING:
N.C. 98.

Muskogee, Indian Territory, **August 4, 1905.**

Billie Bruner,
    Okmulgee, Indian Territory.

Dear Sir:

    You are hereby advised that on **July 28, 1905**, the Secretary of the Interior approved the enrollment of your minor child, **Richard Douglas Bruner**, as a citizen by blood of the **Creek** Nation, and that the name of said child appears upon the roll of new born citizens of the **Creek** Nation as Number **62**.

    The child is now entitled to an allotment, and application therefor should be made without delay at the Land Office for the Nation in which the prospective allotment is located.

    An entire allotment for said child must be selected at the time of the original application.

Applications for Enrollment of Creek Newborn
Act of 1905   Volume II

Respectively,

Commissioner.

BIRTH AFFIDAVIT.

DEPARTMENT OF THE INTERIOR.
COMMISSION TO THE FIVE CIVILIZED TRIBES.

IN RE APPLICATION FOR ENROLLMENT, as a citizen of the   C R E E K   Nation, of Richard Douglas Bruner , born on the eight day of January , 1904

Name of Father: Billie Bruner   a citizen of the C R E E K   Nation.
Name of Mother: Adaline Bruner   a citizen of the C R E E K   Nation.

Postoffice   Okmulgee, I.T.

AFFIDAVIT OF MOTHER.

UNITED STATES OF AMERICA, Indian Territory,
WESTERN   DISTRICT.

I, Adaline Bruner , on oath state that I am thirty nine years of age and a citizen by blood , of the C R E E K Nation; that I am the lawful wife of Billie Bruner , who is a citizen, by blood of the   C R E E K   Nation; that a male child was born to me on eight day of January , 1904 , that said child has been named Richard Douglas Bruner , and was living March 4, 1905.

Adaline Bruner

Witnesses To Mark:

Subscribed and sworn to before me this 7th day of June - - - - - - , 1905.

My Commission expires Feb. 21, 1907   R.S. Barton
                                                                    Notary Public.

AFFIDAVIT OF ATTENDING PHYSICIAN OR MID-WIFE.

UNITED STATES OF AMERICA, Indian Territory,
WESTERN   DISTRICT.

I, Malinda Anderson , a acting midwife , on oath state that I attended on Mrs. Adaline Bruner , wife of Billie Bruner on the eight   day of January , 1904 ; that there

Applications for Enrollment of Creek Newborn
Act of 1905   Volume II

was born to her on said date a male child; that said child was living March 4, 1905, and is said to have been named Richard Douglas Bruner .

Malinda Anderson

Witnesses To Mark:
{

Subscribed and sworn to before me this 7th day of June , 1905.

My Commission expires Feb. 21, 1907   R.S. Barton
Notary Public.

BIRTH AFFIDAVIT.

DEPARTMENT OF THE INTERIOR.
COMMISSION TO THE FIVE CIVILIZED TRIBES.

IN RE APPLICATION FOR ENROLLMENT, as a citizen of the CREEK Nation, of Richard Douglas Bruner , born on the 8 day of January , 1904

Name of Father: Billy Bruner   a citizen of the   Creek   Nation.
Name of Mother: Adaline Bruner   a citizen of the   Creek   Nation.

Postoffice   Okmulgee

Child Present

AFFIDAVIT OF MOTHER.

UNITED STATES OF AMERICA, Indian Territory,⎱
        WESTERN   DISTRICT. ⎰

I, Adaline Bruner , on oath state that I am 39 years of age and a citizen by blood, of the Creek   Nation; that I am the lawful wife of Billy Bruner   , who is a citizen, by blood of the Creek   Nation; that a male   child was born to me on 8 day of January, 1904, that said child has been named Richard Douglas Bruner , and is now living.

Adaline Bruner

Witnesses To Mark:
{

Subscribed and sworn to before me this 14 day of March , 1905.

Edw C Griesel
Notary Public.

Applications for Enrollment of Creek Newborn
Act of 1905   Volume II

AFFIDAVIT OF ATTENDING PHYSICIAN OR MID-WIFE.

UNITED STATES OF AMERICA, Indian Territory, }
   WESTERN   DISTRICT. }

                      husband of Adaline Bruner

I, Billy Bruner, a—, on oath state that I attended on Mrs. Adaline Bruner, wife of myself on the 8 day of January, 1904 ; that there was born to her on said date a male child; that said child is now living and is said to have been named Richard Douglas Bruner.

                                  Billy Bruner

Witnesses To Mark:
{

    Subscribed and sworn to before me this 14 day of March, 1905.

                                    Edw C Griesel
                                    Notary Public.

                                    BA04CO & 4CO 1/2B.

                    Muskogee, Indian Territory, April 18, 1905.

W. G. Cooper,
    Notary Public. Public,
        Broken Arrow, Indian Territory.

Dear Sir:

    The Commission is in receipt of your letter of April 10, 1905, in which you state that it has been impossible to secure the evidence of Mrs. Annie Kelly, mid-wife, who waited on Mrs. Nettie Castillo at the birth of her child, Mabelle Castillo. You ask what is to be done in said case.

    In reply you are advised that the affidavits of Nettie and Walter Castillo, relative to the birth of their child, Mabelle Castillo, have been filed with the Commission are considered as an application for the enrollment of your minor child, you are advised that the Commission requires further evidence as to the birth of said child. of said Mabelle Castillo as a citizen of the Creek Nation.

    There is herewith enclosed a printed circular containing information relative to the enrollment of children born since May 25, 1901, to citizens of the Creek Nation. You are further advised that the parents of said Mabelle Castillo should use the utmost diligence in seeing that the regulations therein set forth are complied with in every respect.

Applications for Enrollment of Creek Newborn
Act of 1905   Volume II

Respectfully,

Circular.   Chairman.

NC 99.

Muskogee, Indian Territory, May 18, 1905.

George C. Castello,
    Broken Arrow, Indian Territory.

Dear Sir:

    In the matter of the application for the enrollment of your minor child, Mabel Castello, as a citizen of the Creek Nation, you are advised that the Commission requires the affidavits of two disinterested witnesses as to the birth of said child.

    There are herewith enclosed two blank forms of birth affidavits, and in executing same care should be exercised to see that all blanks are properly filled, all names written in full and in the event that the persons signing the affidavits are unable to write, signatures by mark must be attested by two witnesses. Each affidavit must be executed before a Notary Public and the notarial seal and signature of the officer must be attached to each separate affidavit.

Respectfully,

BC.   Chairman.

NC 99.

Muskogee, Indian Territory June 6, 1905.

Nettie Castello,
    Broken Arrow, Indian Territory.

Dear Madam:

    In the matter of the application for the enrollment of your minor child, Mable Castello, as a citizen of the Creek Nation, you are advised that the Commission requires your affidavit relative to its birth.

    There is herewith enclosed a blank form of birth affidavit, and in executing same care should be exercised to see that all blanks are properly filled, all names written in full and in the event that you are unable to write, signature by mark must be attested by two witnesses. The affidavit must be executed before a Notary Public and the notarial seal and signature of the officer must be attached to the affidavit.

Applications for Enrollment of Creek Newborn
Act of 1905 Volume II

Respectfully,

1 BA

Commissioner in Charge.

NC 99.

Muskogee, Indian Territory, June 22, 1905.

Nettie Castello,
    Broken Arrow, Indian Territory.

Dear Madam:

    There are on file with the Commission affidavits relative to the birth of your minor child, Mabel Castello, in which the family name is given as Castello and Castillo.

    You are requested to advise the Commission as to the correct name of said child.

Respectfully,

Chairman.

NC 99.

Muskogee, Indian Territory, June 22, 1905.

W. C. Cooper,
    Coweta, Indian Territory.

Dear Sir:

    The Commission is in receipt of your letter of June 13, 1905, enclosing affidavits in the matter of the application for the enrollment of your minor child, you are advised that the Commission requires further evidence as to the birth of said child. of Mabel Castello. You state that it is impossible to secure the affidavit of the midwife or physician in attendance at the birth of said child who was in attendance at the birth of said child, and you ask how to proceed in the matter.

    In reply you are advised that if it is impossible to secure the affidavit of the midwife, the Commission desires the affidavits of two disinterested witnesses relative to the birth of said child. Your attention is called to the fact that in the affidavit on file with the Commission, the family name is given as Castello, and in the affidavit sent by you the name is given as Castillo. This discrepancy in the names should be corrected.

Applications for Enrollment of Creek Newborn
Act of 1905 Volume II

Respectfully,

2 BA   Chairman.

W.G. Cooper,
    Real Estate Dealer,
        Notary Public.

Broken Arrow, I.T., June 27, 1905.

Commission to the five tribes,

    Gentlemen:

        I herewithhand you another affidavit in the application of Mabel Castillo for enrollment at your request had two disinterested witness[sic] to make affidavit as to the birth of the child, as it was impossible to get the midwifes[sic] affidavit. There was a mistake made by myself in spelling the name in the former papers I spelled it Castello and should have been spelled <u>Castillo.</u>

Yours Resp.

(Signed) W.G. Cooper

BIRTH AFFIDAVIT.
DEPARTMENT OF THE INTERIOR.
COMMISSION TO THE FIVE CIVILIZED TRIBES.

    IN RE APPLICATION FOR ENROLLMENT, as a citizen of the Creek Nation, of Mable Castillo , born on the 23 day of Sept. , 1903

Name of Father: G. C. Castillo   a citizen of the United States Nation.
Name of Mother: Nettie Castillo   a citizen of the Creek Nation.

Postoffice   Broken Arrow, I.T.

AFFIDAVIT OF MOTHER.

UNITED STATES OF AMERICA, Indian Territory,
    Western   DISTRICT.

    I, Nettie Castillo , on oath state that I am *(blank)* years of age and a citizen by Blood, of the Creek Nation; that I am the lawful wife of G C Castillo , who is a citizen, by *(blank)* of the United States ~~Nation~~; that a Female child was born to me

Applications for Enrollment of Creek Newborn
Act of 1905   Volume II

on 23 day of September , 1903 , that said child has been named Mable Castillo , and was living March 4, 1905.

Nettie Castillo

Witnesses To Mark:
{

Subscribed and sworn to before me this 26 day of June , 1905.

W G Cooper

Com Exp <u>Oct 25</u> 1906   Notary Public.

AFFIDAVIT OF ATTENDING PHYSICIAN OR MID-WIFE.

UNITED STATES OF AMERICA, Indian Territory, ⎤
      Western   DISTRICT. ⎦

(No other name given) we know Mable Castillo to be the We ~~I~~, Fred Bukey and   , ~~a~~ , on oath state that ~~I attended on Mrs.~~ , ~~wife of~~ child of Mrs. Nettie Castillo wife of G C Castillo and on the 23 day of September , 1903 ; that there was born to her on said date a Female child; that said child was living March 4, 1905, and is said to have been named Mable Castillo.

Fred Bukey
L.E. Smalley

Witnesses To Mark:
{

Subscribed and sworn to before me this 26 day of June, 1905.

W G Cooper
Notary Public.

BIRTH AFFIDAVIT.

DEPARTMENT OF THE INTERIOR.

COMMISSION TO THE FIVE CIVILIZED TRIBES.

IN RE APPLICATION FOR ENROLLMENT, as a citizen of the CREEK Nation, of Mabel Castello , born on the 23 day of Sept., 1903

Name of Father: Geo. C. Castello	a citizen of the U. S. Nation.
Name of Mother: Nettie "	a citizen of the Creek Nation.

Postoffice   Broken Arrow

Applications for Enrollment of Creek Newborn
Act of 1905   Volume II

AFFIDAVIT OF ~~MOTHER~~.

UNITED STATES OF AMERICA, Indian Territory,
WESTERN   DISTRICT.

    I, Geo. C. Castello , on oath state that I am 29 years of age and a citizen by ----- , of the   U. S.   Nation; that I am the lawful ~~wife~~ hus of Nettie Castello , who is a citizen, by   blood   of the   Creek   Nation; that a   female   child was born to me on 23   day of Sept. , 1903, that said child has been named   Mabel Castello   , and is now living.

Geo C Castillo

Witnesses To Mark:
{

    Subscribed and sworn to before me this 10 day of March, 1905.

Edw C Griesel
Notary Public.

BIRTH AFFIDAVIT.

DEPARTMENT OF THE INTERIOR.
COMMISSION TO THE FIVE CIVILIZED TRIBES.

    IN RE APPLICATION FOR ENROLLMENT, as a citizen of the CREEK Nation, of Mabel Castello , born on the 23 day of Sept. , 1903

| Name of Father: | Geo C. Castillo | a citizen of the | U.S. | Nation. |
| Name of Mother: | Nettie   " | a citizen of the | Creek | Nation. |

Postoffice   Broken Arrow

AFFIDAVIT OF MOTHER.

UNITED STATES OF AMERICA, Indian Territory,
WESTERN   DISTRICT.

    I, Nettie Castello , on oath state that I am 27 years of age and a citizen by blood, of the Creek   Nation; that I am the lawful wife of Geo C Castello , who is a citizen, by ----- of the U S Nation; that a female   child was born to me on 23^d day of Sept , 1903 , that said child has been named Mabel Castello , and is now living.

Nettie Castillo

Witnesses To Mark:
{

Applications for Enrollment of Creek Newborn
Act of 1905   Volume II

Subscribed and sworn to before me this 11th day of Mar , 1905.

          My Com   J McDermott
          Ex July 25" 1907   Notary Public.

BIRTH AFFIDAVIT.

DEPARTMENT OF THE INTERIOR.
COMMISSION TO THE FIVE CIVILIZED TRIBES.

IN RE APPLICATION FOR ENROLLMENT, as a citizen of the Creek Nation, of Mable Castillo , born on the 23 day of Sept. , 1903

Name of Father: G. C. Castillo   a citizen of the United States Nation.
Name of Mother: Nettie Castillo   a citizen of the Creek Nation.

          Postoffice   *(blank)*

AFFIDAVIT OF MOTHER.

UNITED STATES OF AMERICA, Indian Territory, ⎱
     Western   DISTRICT. ⎰

I, Nettie Castillo , on oath state that I am 28 years of age and a citizen by Blood, of the Creek Nation; that I am the lawful wife of G. C. Castillo , who is a citizen, by *(blank)* of the United States Nation; that a Female child was born to me on 23 day of September , 1903 , that said child has been named Mable Castillo , and was living March 4, 1905.

                                   Nettie Castillo

Witnesses To Mark:
  {

Subscribed and sworn to before me this 26 day of June , 1905.

                                  W G Cooper
               Com Exp Oct <u>25 1906</u>   Notary Public.

AFFIDAVIT OF ATTENDING PHYSICIAN OR MID-WIFE.

UNITED STATES OF AMERICA, Indian Territory, ⎱
     Western   DISTRICT. ⎰

              (No other name given) we know Mable Castillo to be the We ~~I~~, Fred Bukey and , ~~a~~ , on oath state that ~~I attended on Mrs.~~ , ~~wife of~~ child of Mrs. Nettie Castillo wife of G C Castillo and on the 23 day of September , 1903 ;

Applications for Enrollment of Creek Newborn
Act of 1905 Volume II

that there was born to her on said date a Female child; that said child was living March 4, 1905, and is said to have been named Mable Castillo.

Witnesses To Mark:
{

Fred Bukey
(Illegible) Smalley

Subscribed and sworn to before me this 26 day of June, 1905.

W G Cooper
Notary Public.

AFFIDAVIT OF ATTENDING PHYSICIAN OR MID-WIFE.

UNITED STATES OF AMERICA, Indian Territory, }
Western DISTRICT.

I, R. S. Plumlee , a Physician , on oath state that I attended on Mrs. Nettie Castillo , wife of G.C. Castillo on the 15th day ~~day of~~ of birth of , ; ~~that there was born to her on said date~~ a female child; that said child was living March 4, 1905, and is said to have been named Mabel Castillo. and affirm to best of my knowledge that said child was daughter of Nettie Castillo

R.S. Plumlee, M.D.

Witnesses To Mark:
{

Subscribed and sworn to before me this 20 day of May, 1905.

Com Ex. Oct 25, 1906

W G Cooper
Notary Public.

BIRTH AFFIDAVIT.

DEPARTMENT OF THE INTERIOR.
COMMISSION TO THE FIVE CIVILIZED TRIBES.

IN RE APPLICATION FOR ENROLLMENT, as a citizen of the Creek Nation, of Mable Castillo , born on the 23 day of Sept. , 1903

Name of Father:	G. C. Castillo	a citizen of the United States Nation.
Name of Mother:	Nettie Castillo	a citizen of the Creek Nation.

Postoffice Broken Arrow

Applications for Enrollment of Creek Newborn
Act of 1905   Volume II

AFFIDAVIT OF MOTHER.

UNITED STATES OF AMERICA, Indian Territory, }
Western   DISTRICT.

I, Nettie Castillo , on oath state that I am 28 years of age and a citizen by Blood, of the Creek Nation; that I am the lawful wife of G. C. Castillo , who is a citizen, ~~by~~ *(blank)* of the United States Nation; that a Female child was born to me on 23 day of September , 1903 , that said child has been named Mable Castillo , and was living March 4, 1905.

Nettie Castillo

Witnesses To Mark:
{

Subscribed and sworn to before me this 13 day of June , 1905.

W. G. Cooper

Com Ex 10/25._ 1906   Notary Public.

AFFIDAVIT OF ATTENDING PHYSICIAN OR MID-WIFE.

UNITED STATES OF AMERICA, Indian Territory, }
Western   DISTRICT.

I, R. S. Plumlee , a physician , on oath state that I attended on Mrs. Nettie Castello , wife of George C. Castello on or about 12th day of October , 1903; that there was in her case ~~born to her on said date~~ a female child; that said child was living March 4, 1905, and is said to have been named Mabel Castello. Said child to best of my knowledge and belief was child of Nettie Castillo.

R.S. Plumlee, M.D.

Witnesses To Mark: ~~R.S. Plumlee~~
{
Subscribed and sworn to before me this 13 day of June, 1905.

W G Cooper
Notary Public.

Applications for Enrollment of Creek Newborn
Act of 1905 Volume II

DEPARTMENT OF THE INTERIOR,
COMMISSIONER TO THE FIVE CIVILIZED TRIBES.

REFER IN REPLY TO THE FOLLOWING:

N.C. 100.

Muskogee, Indian Territory, **August 4, 1905.**

Hettie E. Brian,
    Care of Charlie Brian,
        Morris, Indian Territory.
Dear Madam:

    You are hereby advised that on **July 28, 1905**, the Secretary of the Interior approved the enrollment of your minor child, **Mary Ellen**, as a citizen by blood of the **Creek** Nation, and that the name of said child appears upon the roll of new born citizens of the **Creek** Nation as Number **64**.

    The child is now entitled to an allotment, and application therefor should be made without delay at the Land Office for the Nation in which the prospective allotment is located.

    An entire allotment for said child must be selected at the time of the original application.

        Respectively,

                Commissioner.

DEPARTMENT OF THE INTERIOR,
COMMISSIONER TO THE FIVE CIVILIZED TRIBES.

REFER IN REPLY TO THE FOLLOWING:

N.C. 100.

Muskogee, Indian Territory, **August 4, 1905.**

Hettie E. Brian,
    Care of Charlie Brian,
        Morris, Indian Territory.
Dear Madam:

    You are hereby advised that on **July 28, 1905**, the Secretary of the Interior approved the enrollment of your minor child, **John William Brian**, as a citizen by blood of the **Creek** Nation, and that the name of said child appears upon the roll of new born citizens of the **Creek** Nation as Number **63**.

    The child is now entitled to an allotment, and application therefor should be made without delay at the Land Office for the Nation in which the prospective allotment is located.

    An entire allotment for said child must be selected at the time of the original application.

Applications for Enrollment of Creek Newborn
Act of 1905   Volume II

Respectively,

Commissioner.

(Both affidavits below typed as given)

United States of America,
State of Missouri, Lawrence County.

J.J. Chamblis, of lawful age, being first duly sworn,on his oath states; That on July 3Ist.,I903,he was a practising physician located at the Town of Morris Indian Territory,and that he was the attending physician at the birth of a boy child to Hettie E. Brian,formerly Hettie E. Ashley,and Charley M. Brian-her husband; on the 3Ist.,day of July 1903.

J J Chambliss M.D.

Subscribed and sworn to before me this 6 day of Apr. I905.

My Com. Ex. Jan 1908   John B Williams
                            Notary Public.

United States of America,
   Indian Territory,
Western Judicial District.

J.H.Adcock, of lawful age, being first duly sworn on his oath states: That on February 14th. 1905 he was a practicing Physician located at the town of Morris, Indian Territory, and that he was the attending Physician at the birth of a girl child to Hettie E.Brian, formerly Hettie E.Ashley and Charley M. Brian, her husband on the 14th day of February, 1905.

J. H. Adcock

Subscribed and sworn to before me this 12th. day of April 1905

AE Bowers
Notary Public.

My commission expires July 22nd.1908.

Applications for Enrollment of Creek Newborn
Act of 1905   Volume II

BIRTH AFFIDAVIT.

DEPARTMENT OF THE INTERIOR.
COMMISSION TO THE FIVE CIVILIZED TRIBES.

IN RE APPLICATION FOR ENROLLMENT, as a citizen of the CREEK Nation, of John William Briyan, born on the 31 day of July, 1903

Name of Father: Charlie Briyan	a citizen of the U. S.	Nation.
Name of Mother: Hettie E. "	a citizen of the Creek	Nation.

Postoffice   Morris, I.T.

(Child Present) HGH

AFFIDAVIT OF MOTHER.

UNITED STATES OF AMERICA, Indian Territory,
    WESTERN   DISTRICT.

I, Hettie E. Briyan, on oath state that I am 21 years of age and a citizen by blood, of the Creek Nation; that I am the lawful wife of Charlie Bryan, who is a citizen, by ----- of the U. S. Nation; that a male child was born to me on 31 day of July, 1903, that said child has been named John William Briyan, and is now living.

Hettie E Brian

Witnesses To Mark:

Subscribed and sworn to before me this 9 day of March, 1905.

Edw C Griesel
Notary Public.

BIRTH AFFIDAVIT.

DEPARTMENT OF THE INTERIOR.
COMMISSION TO THE FIVE CIVILIZED TRIBES.

IN RE APPLICATION FOR ENROLLMENT, as a citizen of the CREEK Nation, of Mary Ellen Briyan, born on the 14 day of Feb., 1905

Name of Father:	Charlie Briyan	a citizen of the U. S.	Nation.
Name of Mother:	Hettie E. "	a citizen of the Creek	Nation.

Postoffice   Morris, I.T.

Applications for Enrollment of Creek Newborn
Act of 1905   Volume II

(Child Present) HGH

AFFIDAVIT OF MOTHER.

UNITED STATES OF AMERICA, Indian Territory, }
WESTERN DISTRICT.

    I, Hettie E. Bryan, on oath state that I am 21 years of age and a citizen by blood, of the Creek Nation; that I am the lawful wife of Charlie Bryan, who is a citizen, by -- --- of the U. S. Nation; that a *(blank)* child was born to me on 14 day of Feb, 1905, that said child has been named Mary Ellen Briyan, and is now living.

                          Hettie E Brian

Witnesses To Mark:
{

    Subscribed and sworn to before me this 9 day of March, 1905.

                          Edw C Griesel
                          Notary Public.

DEPARTMENT OF THE INTERIOR,
COMMISSIONER TO THE FIVE CIVILIZED TRIBES.

REFER IN REPLY TO THE FOLLOWING:
N.C. 101.

                 Muskogee, Indian Territory, **August 4, 1905.**

Walter J. Escoe,
    Oktaha, Indian Territory.

Dear Sir:

    You are hereby advised that on **July 28, 1905**, the Secretary of the Interior approved the enrollment of your minor child, **William Albert Escoe**, as a citizen by blood of the **Creek** Nation, and that the name of said child appears upon the roll of new born citizens of the **Creek** Nation as Number **65**.

    The child is now entitled to an allotment, and application therefor should be made without delay at the Land Office for the Nation in which the prospective allotment is located.

    An entire allotment for said child must be selected at the time of the original application.

                        Respectively,

                            Commissioner.

Applications for Enrollment of Creek Newborn
Act of 1905 Volume II

BIRTH AFFIDAVIT.

DEPARTMENT OF THE INTERIOR.
COMMISSION TO THE FIVE CIVILIZED TRIBES.

IN RE APPLICATION FOR ENROLLMENT, as a citizen of the Creek Nation, of William Albert Escoe, born on the 3rd day of Jan., 1904

Name of Father:	Walter J. Escoe	a citizen of the	Creek	Nation.
Name of Mother:	Sarah M Escoe	a citizen of the	Creek	Nation.

Postoffice   Oktaha, I.T.

AFFIDAVIT OF MOTHER.

UNITED STATES OF AMERICA, Indian Territory,
Western   DISTRICT.

I, Sarah M. Escoe, on oath state that I am 24 years of age and a citizen by blood, of the Creek Na. Nation; that I am the lawful wife of Walter J. Escoe, who is a citizen, by blood of the Creek Na. Nation; that a male child was born to me on 3rd day of Jan, 1904, that said child has been named William Albert Escoe, and is now living.

Sarah M Escoe

Witnesses To Mark:
{ A.H. Hall
  A E Campbell

Subscribed and sworn to before me this 17 day of March, 1905.

W. A. Cain
Notary Public.

AFFIDAVIT OF ATTENDING PHYSICIAN OR MID-WIFE.

UNITED STATES OF AMERICA, Indian Territory,
Western   DISTRICT.

I, Dr. A.J. Snelson, a Physician, on oath state that I attended on Mrs. Sarah M. Esco[sic], wife of Walter J Escoe on the 3rd day of January, 1904; that there was born to her on said date a male child; that said child is now living and is said to have been named William Albert Escoe.

A.J. Snelson M.D.

Witnesses To Mark:
{

Applications for Enrollment of Creek Newborn
Act of 1905   Volume II

Subscribed and sworn to before me this 17th day of March, 1905.

W M *(Illegible)*
Notary Public.

Com Expires Feb 24 – 1907

BIRTH AFFIDAVIT.

DEPARTMENT OF THE INTERIOR.
COMMISSION TO THE FIVE CIVILIZED TRIBES.

IN RE APPLICATION FOR ENROLLMENT, as a citizen of the CREEK Nation, of William Albert Escoe , born on the 3 day of Jan. , 1904

Name of Father:	Walter J. Escoe	a citizen of the	Creek	Nation.
Name of Mother:	Sarah M "	a citizen of the	"	Nation.

Postoffice   Oktaha

AFFIDAVIT OF ~~MOTHER~~. father

UNITED STATES OF AMERICA, Indian Territory, ⎫
 WESTERN   DISTRICT. ⎭

I, Walter J. Escoe , on oath state that I am 25 years of age and a citizen by blood, of the Creek Nation; that I am the lawful ~~wife~~ husband of Sarah M. Escoe , who is a citizen, by blood of the Creek Nation; that a male child was born to me on 3 day of Jan , 1904 , that said child has been named William Albert Escoe , and was living March 4, 1905.

Walter J Escoe

Witnesses To Mark:
{

Subscribed and sworn to before me this 14 day of March, 1905.

Edw C Griesel
Notary Public.

Applications for Enrollment of Creek Newborn
Act of 1905 Volume II

NC 102.

Muskogee, Indian Territory, May 17, 1905.

Joe Barnett,
    Bixby, Indian Territory.

Dear Sir:

    In the matter of the application for the enrollment of your minor child, Jensey Barnett, as a citizen of the Creek Nation, you are advised that the Commission requires the affidavit of the midwife or physician in attendance at the birth of said child.

    There is herewith enclosed a blank form of birth affidavit, and in executing same care should be exercised to see that all blanks are properly filled, all names written in full and in the event that the person signing the affidavit is unable to write, signature by mark must be attested by two witnesses. Each affidavit must be executed before a Notary Public and the notarial seal and signature of the officer must be attached to each separate affidavit.

                        Respectfully,

BC.   Chairman.

BIRTH AFFIDAVIT.

DEPARTMENT OF THE INTERIOR.
COMMISSION TO THE FIVE CIVILIZED TRIBES.

    IN RE APPLICATION FOR ENROLLMENT, as a citizen of the CREEK Nation, of Jincy Barnett, born on the 13 day of May, 1903

Name of Father: Joe Barnett   a citizen of the   Creek   Nation.
Name of Mother: Wanney "   a citizen of the   "   Nation.

                      Postoffice   Bixby

Child Present

AFFIDAVIT OF MOTHER.

UNITED STATES OF AMERICA, Indian Territory,
    WESTERN   DISTRICT.

    I, Wanney Barnett, on oath state that I am 24 years of age and a citizen by blood, of the Creek Nation; that I am the lawful wife of Joe Barnett, who is a citizen, by blood of the Creek Nation; that a female child was born to me on 13 day of May, 1903, that said child has been named Jincy Barnett, and was living March 4, 1905.

Applications for Enrollment of Creek Newborn
Act of 1905   Volume II

Her
Wanney x Barnett
mark

Witnesses To Mark:
{ J McDermott
{ EC Griesel

Subscribed and sworn to before me this 14 day of March , 1905.

Edw C Griesel
Notary Public.

AFFIDAVIT OF ATTENDING PHYSICIAN OR MID-WIFE.

UNITED STATES OF AMERICA, Indian Territory, }
     Western   DISTRICT.

I, Joe Barnett , am , ~~on oath state that I attended on Mrs~~. husband , ~~wife~~ of Wanney Barnett on the 13 day of May , 1903 ; that there was born to her on said date a female child; that said child was living March 4, 1905, and is said to have been named Jincy Barnett .

His
Joe x Barnett
mark

Witnesses To Mark:
{ J McDermott
{ EC Griesel

Subscribed and sworn to before me this 14 day of March, 1905.

Edw C Griesel
Notary Public.

BIRTH AFFIDAVIT.

DEPARTMENT OF THE INTERIOR.
COMMISSION TO THE FIVE CIVILIZED TRIBES.

IN RE APPLICATION FOR ENROLLMENT, as a citizen of the Creek Nation, of Jansie Barnett, born on the 13th day of May , 1903

Name of Father: Joe Barnett   a citizen of the   Creek   Nation.
Name of Mother: Wanney Barnett   a citizen of the   Creek   Nation.

Postoffice   Bixby, Ind. Ter.

Applications for Enrollment of Creek Newborn
Act of 1905 Volume II

AFFIDAVIT OF MOTHER.

UNITED STATES OF AMERICA, Indian Territory,
    Western   DISTRICT.

    I, Wannie Barnett , on oath state that I am about 24 years of age and a citizen by blood , of the Creek Nation; that I am the lawful wife of Joe Barnett , who is a citizen, by blood of the Creek Nation; that a female child was born to me on 13th day of May , 1903, that said child has been named Jansie Barnett , and was living March 4, 1905.

                                      Wanney Barnett

Witnesses To Mark:
- Henry McCoy Bixby I.T.
- Job *(Illegible)* Bixby IT

Subscribed and sworn to before me this 15th day of March , 1905.

                                      Francis R Brennan
                                             Notary Public.

AFFIDAVIT OF ATTENDING PHYSICIAN OR MID-WIFE.

UNITED STATES OF AMERICA, Indian Territory,
    Western   DISTRICT.

    I, Jackson Beaver , a Physician , on oath state that I attended on Mrs. Wannie Barnett , wife of Joe Barnett on the 13th day of May , 1903 ; that there was born to her on said date a female child; that said child was living March 4, 1905, and is said to have been named Jansie Barnett .

                                      his
                                Jackson x Beaver

Witnesses To Mark: mark
- Henry McCoy Bixby I.T.
- Job *(Illegible)* Bixby IT

Subscribed and sworn to before me this 15th day of March , 1905.

                                      Francis R Brennan
                                        Notary Public.

BIRTH AFFIDAVIT.

DEPARTMENT OF THE INTERIOR.
COMMISSION TO THE FIVE CIVILIZED TRIBES.

    IN RE APPLICATION FOR ENROLLMENT, as a citizen of the Creek Nation, of Jensey Barnett, born on the 13th day of May , 1903

Applications for Enrollment of Creek Newborn
Act of 1905   Volume II

Name of Father: Joseph Barnett   a citizen of the   Creek   Nation.
Name of Mother: Wanney Barnett   a citizen of the   Creek   Nation.

Postoffice   Bixby, Ind. Ter.

AFFIDAVIT OF MOTHER.

UNITED STATES OF AMERICA, Indian Territory, }
    Western   DISTRICT.

I, Wanney Barnett, on oath state that I am 25 years of age and a citizen by blood, of the Creek Nation; that I am the lawful wife of Joseph Barnett, who is a citizen, by blood of the Creek Nation; that a female child was born to me on 13th day of May, 1903, that said child has been named Jensey Barnett, and was living March 4, 1905.

           her
         Wanney x Barnett
Witnesses To Mark: mark
{ Henry McCoy
{ Willie Fox

Subscribed and sworn to before me this 19th day of June, 1903[sic]

(Name Illegible)
Notary Public.
My Commission Expires July 2nd, 1906.

AFFIDAVIT OF ATTENDING PHYSICIAN OR MID-WIFE.

UNITED STATES OF AMERICA, Indian Territory, }
    Western   DISTRICT.

I, Eliza Techarna Beaver, a Creek Indian acting as midwife, on oath state that I attended on Mrs. Wanney Barnett, wife of Joseph Barnett on the 13th day of May, 1903; that there was born to her on said date a female child; that said child was living March 4, 1905, and is said to have been named Jensey Barnett.

          her
       Eliza x Techarna Beaver
Witnesses To Mark: mark
{ Henry McCoy
{ Willie Fox

Subscribed and sworn to before me this 19th day of June, 1905.

(Name Illegible)
Notary Public.
My Commission Expires July 2nd, 1906.

Applications for Enrollment of Creek Newborn
Act of 1905   Volume II

COMMISSIONERS:
TAMS BIXBY,
THOMAS B. NEEDLES,
C.R. BRECKINBRIDGE.

DEPARTMENT OF THE INTERIOR,
COMMISSIONER TO THE FIVE CIVILIZED TRIBES.

REFER IN REPLY TO THE FOLLOWING:

WM. O. BEALL
Secretary

ADDRESS ONLY THE
COMMISSION TO THE FIVE CIVILIZED TRIBES.

Sapula IT
April 26, 1905

Commission to Five Tribes
    Muskogee, IT

Gentleman

    There is enclosed herewith application for the enrollment of Jensey Barnett, Creek infant, father Joe Barnett, mother Wannie Barnett born May 13, 1903. It appears that application was made for the enrollment of this child by the parents who made to the Commission affidavits on March 15, 1905 the name of the child being given in said affidavits as <u>Jennie</u>   The enclosed application is for the purpose of correcting the name to Jensey Barnett.

                      Respectfully,

                      Tams Bixby

HGH

COMMISSIONERS:
TAMS BIXBY,
THOMAS B. NEEDLES,
C.R. BRECKINBRIDGE.

DEPARTMENT OF THE INTERIOR,
COMMISSIONER TO THE FIVE CIVILIZED TRIBES.

REFER IN REPLY TO THE FOLLOWING:

WM. O. BEALL
Secretary

ADDRESS ONLY THE
COMMISSION TO THE FIVE CIVILIZED TRIBES.

Muskogee, Indian Territory, March 18, 1905.

Joe Barnett,
    Bixby, Indian Territory.

Dear Sir:

    The Commission is in receipt of your letter of March 15, enclosing birth affidavit in the matter of the enrollment of Jennie Barnett, as a citizen of the Creek Nation. You ask to be advised when the Secretary of the Interior approves the roll.

    In reply you are advised that said affidavit has been filed with the records of the commission. When final action is had in the matter, you will be duly advised.

Applications for Enrollment of Creek Newborn
Act of 1905   Volume II

                              Respectfully,

Name of child should be Jensey Barnett

                              Tams Bixby

                                   Chairman.

BIRTH AFFIDAVIT.

DEPARTMENT OF THE INTERIOR.
COMMISSION TO THE FIVE CIVILIZED TRIBES.

IN RE APPLICATION FOR ENROLLMENT, as a citizen of the Creek Nation, of Jensey Barnett, born on the 13 day of May , 1903

Name of Father: Joe Barnett   a citizen of the   Creek   Nation.
(Ouchee)
Name of Mother: Wanney Barnett   a citizen of the   Creek   Nation.
(Ouchee)
                              Postoffice   Bixby

AFFIDAVIT OF MOTHER.

UNITED STATES OF AMERICA, Indian Territory, }   Child Present
        Western   DISTRICT.

I, Wanney Barnett , on oath state that I am 24 years of age and a citizen by blood, of the Creek Nation; that I am the lawful wife of Joe Barnett , who is a citizen, by blood of the Creek Nation; that a female child was born to me on 13 day of May , 1903, that said child has been named Jensey Barnett , and was living March 4, 1905.

                              Wanney Barnett
Witnesses To Mark:
  { David Shelby
  { Jesse McDermott

   Subscribed and sworn to before me this 25 day of April , 1905.

      (Seal)   Edw C Griesel
                                       Notary Public.

Applications for Enrollment of Creek Newborn
Act of 1905   Volume II

AFFIDAVIT OF ATTENDING ~~PHYSICIAN OR MID-WIFE~~.

UNITED STATES OF AMERICA, Indian Territory, }
  Western   DISTRICT.

    I, Joe Barnett, ~~a~~ *(blank)*, on oath state that I attended on Mrs. Wannie Barnett, my wife of *(blank)* on the 13 day of May, 1903; that there was born to her on said date a female child; that said child was living March 4, 1905, and is said to have been named Jensey Barnett.

                                            his
                                     Joe x Barnett
Witnesses To Mark: mark
  { David Shelby
    Jesse McDermott

    Subscribed and sworn to before me this 25 day of April, 1905.

(Seal)   Edw C Griesel
                                    Notary Public.

DEPARTMENT OF THE INTERIOR,
COMMISSIONER TO THE FIVE CIVILIZED TRIBES.

REFER IN REPLY TO THE FOLLOWING:
N.C. 103.

                              Muskogee, Indian Territory, **August 4, 1905.**

Johnson E. Tiger,
    Wetumka[sic], Indian Territory.

Dear Sir:

    You are hereby advised that on **July 28, 1905**, the Secretary of the Interior approved the enrollment of your minor child, **Ethan Allen H. Tiger**, as a citizen by blood of the **Creek** Nation, and that the name of said child appears upon the roll of new born citizens of the **Creek** Nation as Number **66**.

    The child is now entitled to an allotment, and application therefor should be made without delay at the Land Office for the Nation in which the prospective allotment is located.

    An entire allotment for said child must be selected at the time of the original application.

                                   Respectively,

                                                  Commissioner.

Applications for Enrollment of Creek Newborn
Act of 1905   Volume II

BIRTH AFFIDAVIT.

DEPARTMENT OF THE INTERIOR.
COMMISSION TO THE FIVE CIVILIZED TRIBES.

IN RE APPLICATION FOR ENROLLMENT, as a citizen of the CREEK Nation, of Ethan Allen H. Tiger, born on the 30 day of June, 1903

Name of Father: Johnson E. Tiger   a citizen of the   Creek   Nation.
Name of Mother: Lena E.   "   a citizen of the   "   Nation.

Postoffice   Wetumka[sic], I.T.

AFFIDAVIT OF ~~MOTHER~~. father

UNITED STATES OF AMERICA, Indian Territory,
WESTERN DISTRICT.

I, Johnson E. Tiger, on oath state that I am 30 years of age and a citizen by blood, of the Creek Nation; that I am the lawful ~~wife~~ husb of Lena E. Tiger, who is a citizen, by blood of the Creek Nation; that a male child was born to me on 30" day of June, 1903, that said child has been named Ethan Allen H. Tiger, and is now living.

Johnson E. Tiger

Witnesses To Mark:

Subscribed and sworn to before me this 9 day of March, 1905.

Edw C Griesel
Notary Public.

DEPARTMENT OF THE INTERIOR,
COMMISSION TO THE FIVE CIVILIZED TRIBES.

IN RE APPLICATION FOR ENROLLMENT, as a citizen of the Creek Nation, of E.A.H. Tiger, born on the 30 day of June, 1903

Name of Father: John E. Tiger   a citizen of the   Creek   Nation.
Name of Mother: Lena E. Tiger   a citizen of the   Creek   Nation.

Post Office: Wetumka[sic], I.T.

Applications for Enrollment of Creek Newborn
Act of 1905   Volume II

AFFIDAVIT OF MOTHER.

UNITED STATES OF AMERICA, Indian Territory, }
   (blank)   DISTRICT.

    I, Lena E. Tiger , on oath state that I am 31 years of age and a citizen by blood, of the Creek Nation; that I am the lawful wife of John E. Tiger , who is a citizen, by blood of the Creek Nation; that a male child was born to me on 30 day of June , 1903 , that said child has been named Ethan Allen H. Tiger , and is now living.

                                  Lena E Tiger

Witnesses To Mark:
{

    Subscribed and sworn to before me this 8 day of Mar, 1905.

    my com ex. 7-1-1906   Jas A. *(Illegible)*
                                                  Notary Public.

AFFIDAVIT OF ATTENDING PHYSICIAN OR MID-WIFE.

UNITED STATES OF AMERICA, Indian Territory, }
      Western   DISTRICT.

    I, Thomas J Cagle , a Physician , on oath state that I attended on Mrs. Lena E Tiger , wife of Johnson E Tiger on the 30 day of June , 1903 ; that there was born to her on said date a male child; that said child is now living and is said to have been named Ethan Allen Hitchcock Tiger.

                                  Thomas J Cagle

Witnesses To Mark:
{

    Subscribed and sworn to before me this 7th day of March, 1905.

    My Com Ex. July 1- 1906   Nat Williams
                                                  Notary Public.

DEPARTMENT OF THE INTERIOR, COMMISSIONER TO THE FIVE CIVILIZED TRIBES.	REFER IN REPLY TO THE FOLLOWING: N.C. 104.

                            Muskogee, Indian Territory, **August 4, 1905.**

Robert O. Burton,
        Canadian, Indian Territory.

Applications for Enrollment of Creek Newborn
Act of 1905 Volume II

Dear Sir:

You are hereby advised that on **July 28, 1905**, the Secretary of the Interior approved the enrollment of your minor child, **Ethel V. Burton**, as a citizen by blood of the **Creek** Nation, and that the name of said child appears upon the roll of new born citizens of the **Creek** Nation as Number **67**.

The child is now entitled to an allotment, and application therefor should be made without delay at the Land Office for the Nation in which the prospective allotment is located.

An entire allotment for said child must be selected at the time of the original application.

Respectively,

Commissioner.

BIRTH AFFIDAVIT.

DEPARTMENT OF THE INTERIOR.
COMMISSION TO THE FIVE CIVILIZED TRIBES.

IN RE APPLICATION FOR ENROLLMENT, as a citizen of the CREEK Nation, of Ethel V. Burton, born on the 29 day of June , 1902

Name of Father: Robert O. Burton	a citizen of the	Creek Nation.
Name of Mother: Mollie E. "	a citizen of the	U. S. Nation.

Postoffice Canadian, I.T.

AFFIDAVIT OF ~~MOTHER~~. father

UNITED STATES OF AMERICA, Indian Territory, ⎫
    WESTERN   DISTRICT. ⎬

I, Robert O. Burton , on oath state that I am 29 years of age and a citizen by blood, of the Creek Nation; that I am the lawful ~~wife~~ husb of Mollie E. Burton , who is a citizen, by ----- of the U. S. ~~Nation~~; that a female child was born to me on 29 day of June , 1902 , that said child has been named Ethel V. Burton , and is now living.

R O Burton

Witnesses To Mark:

Applications for Enrollment of Creek Newborn
Act of 1905 Volume II

Subscribed and sworn to before me this 9 day of March, 1905.

Edw C Griesel
Notary Public.

BIRTH AFFIDAVIT.

DEPARTMENT OF THE INTERIOR.
COMMISSION TO THE FIVE CIVILIZED TRIBES.

IN RE APPLICATION FOR ENROLLMENT, as a citizen of the Creek Nation, of Ethel Victoria Burton, born on the 29 day of June, 1902

Name of Father: Robert Owen Burton   a citizen of the   Creek   Nation. Tuckabatche[sic] Town
Name of Mother: Mollie E. Burton   a citizen of the United States Nation.

Postoffice   Canadian, Ind. Ter.

AFFIDAVIT OF MOTHER.

UNITED STATES OF AMERICA, Indian Territory, }   Child is Present
    Western   DISTRICT.

I, Mollie E. Burton, on oath state that I am 34 years of age and a citizen ~~by~~ *(blank)*, of the United States ~~Nation~~; that I am the lawful wife of Robert Owen Burton, who is a citizen, by blood of the Creek Nation; that a female child was born to me on 29 day of June, 1902, that said child has been named Ethel Victoria Burton, and was living March 4, 1905.

Mollie E. Burton

Witnesses To Mark:
{

Subscribed and sworn to before me this 3 day of April, 1905.

Drennan C Skaggs
Notary Public.

AFFIDAVIT OF ATTENDING PHYSICIAN OR MID-WIFE.

UNITED STATES OF AMERICA, Indian Territory, }
    Western   DISTRICT.

I, R. M. Counterman, a physician, on oath state that I attended on Mrs. Mollie E. Burton, wife of R.O. Burton on the 29 day of June, 1902; that there was born to

Applications for Enrollment of Creek Newborn
Act of 1905   Volume II

her on said date a female child; that said child was living March 4, 1905, and is said to have been named *(blank)* .

R.M. Counterman M.D.

Witnesses To Mark:
{

    Subscribed and sworn to before me this 5 day of April, 1905.

Revel Haskell, Jr.
Notary Public.

BIRTH AFFIDAVIT.

DEPARTMENT OF THE INTERIOR.
COMMISSION TO THE FIVE CIVILIZED TRIBES.

IN RE APPLICATION FOR ENROLLMENT, as a citizen of the CREEK Nation, of Wynema O. Burton , born on the 17 day of April   , 1904

Name of Father: Robert O. Burton	a citizen of the	Creek	Nation.
Name of Mother: Mollie E. "	a citizen of the	U. S.	Nation.

Postoffice   Canadian, I.T.

AFFIDAVIT OF <s>MOTHER</s>. father

UNITED STATES OF AMERICA, Indian Territory, }
    WESTERN   DISTRICT.

    I, Robert O. Burton , on oath state that I am 29 years of age and a citizen by blood, of the Creek   Nation; that I am the lawful <s>wife</s> husb of Mollie E. Burton , who is a citizen, by ----- of the U. S. Nation; that a female child was born to <s>me</s> her on 17 day of April , 1904 , that said child has been named Wynema O. Burton, and is now living.

R O Burton

Witnesses To Mark:
{

    Subscribed and sworn to before me this 9 day of March, 1905.

Edw C Griesel
Notary Public.

Applications for Enrollment of Creek Newborn
Act of 1905 Volume II

BIRTH AFFIDAVIT.

DEPARTMENT OF THE INTERIOR.
COMMISSION TO THE FIVE CIVILIZED TRIBES.

IN RE APPLICATION FOR ENROLLMENT, as a citizen of the Creek Nation, of Wynema Owen Burton, born on the 17 day of April , 1904

Name of Father: Robert Owen Burton   a citizen of the   Creek   Nation. Tuckabatche[sic] Town
Name of Mother: Mollie E. Burton   a citizen of the United States Nation.

Postoffice   Canadian, Ind. Ter.

AFFIDAVIT OF MOTHER.

UNITED STATES OF AMERICA, Indian Territory, }   Child is Present
    Western   DISTRICT.

I, Mollie E. Burton , on oath state that I am 34 years of age and a citizen ~~by~~ (blank) , of the United States ~~Nation~~; that I am the lawful wife of Robert Owen Burton, who is a citizen, by blood of the Creek Nation; that a female child was born to me on 17 day of April , 1904 , that said child has been named Wynema Owen Burton , and was living March 4, 1905.

                                        Mollie E. Burton
Witnesses To Mark:
{

Subscribed and sworn to before me this 3 day of April , 1905.

                                        Drennan C Skaggs
                                        Notary Public.

AFFIDAVIT OF ATTENDING PHYSICIAN OR MID-WIFE.

UNITED STATES OF AMERICA, Indian Territory, }
    Western   DISTRICT.

I, R. M. Counterman , a Physician , on oath state that I attended on Mrs. Mollie E. Burton , wife of R.O. Burton on the 17 day of April , 1904 ; that there was born to her on said date a Female child; that said child was living March 4, 1905, and is said to have been named Wynema Owen Burton .

                                        R.M. Counterman M.D.
Witnesses To Mark:
{

Applications for Enrollment of Creek Newborn
Act of 1905   Volume II

Subscribed and sworn to before me this 5 day of April, 1905.

Revel Haskell, Jr.
Notary Public.

NC 105.

Muskogee, Indian Territory, May 18, 1905.

C. H. Wilson,
    Canadian, Indian Territory.

Dear Sir:

    In the matter of the application for the enrollment of your minor child, Oleta Wilson, as a citizen of the Creek Nation, you are advised that the Commission requires the affidavits of the mother of said child and of the midwife or physician in attendance at the birth of said child.

    There is herewith enclosed a blank form of birth affidavit, and in executing same care should be exercised to see that all blanks are properly filled, all names written in full and in the event that either of the persons signing the affidavit is unable to write, signatures by mark must be attested by two witnesses. Each affidavit must be executed before a Notary Public and the notarial seal and signature of the officer must be attached to each separate affidavit.

Respectfully,

BC.   Chairman.

DEPARTMENT OF THE INTERIOR,
COMMISSIONER TO THE FIVE CIVILIZED TRIBES.

REFER IN REPLY TO THE FOLLOWING:
N.C. 105.

Muskogee, Indian Territory, August 4, 1905.

Lydia Wilson,
    Care of C. H. Wilson,
        Canadian, Indian Territory.

Dear Madam:

    You are hereby advised that on **July 28, 1905**, the Secretary of the Interior approved the enrollment of your minor child, **Oleta Wilson**, as a citizen by blood of the **Creek** Nation, and that the name of said child appears upon the roll of new born citizens of the **Creek** Nation as Number **69**.

Applications for Enrollment of Creek Newborn
Act of 1905   Volume II

The child is now entitled to an allotment, and application therefor should be made without delay at the Land Office for the Nation in which the prospective allotment is located.

An entire allotment for said child must be selected at the time of the original application.

Respectively,

Commissioner.

BIRTH AFFIDAVIT.

DEPARTMENT OF THE INTERIOR.
COMMISSION TO THE FIVE CIVILIZED TRIBES.

IN RE APPLICATION FOR ENROLLMENT, as a citizen of the CREEK Nation, of Oleta Wilson, born on the 3 day of Aug, 1902

Name of Father: C. H. Wilson   a citizen of the U.S.   Nation.
Name of Mother: Lydia   "   a citizen of the   Creek   Nation.

Postoffice   Canadian, I.T.

AFFIDAVIT OF ~~MOTHER~~. father

UNITED STATES OF AMERICA, Indian Territory,
    WESTERN   DISTRICT.

I, C. H. Wilson, on oath state that I am 28 years of age and a citizen by ----- , of the U. S.   Nation; that I am the lawful ~~wife~~ husb of Lydia Wilson , who is a citizen, by blood of the Creek   Nation; that a female   child was born to me on 3 day of Aug, 1902 , that said child has been named Oleta Wilson , and is now living.

C H Wilson

Witnesses To Mark:
{

Subscribed and sworn to before me this 9 day of March, 1905.

Edw C Griesel
Notary Public.

Applications for Enrollment of Creek Newborn
Act of 1905   Volume II

BIRTH AFFIDAVIT.

DEPARTMENT OF THE INTERIOR.
COMMISSION TO THE FIVE CIVILIZED TRIBES.

IN RE APPLICATION FOR ENROLLMENT, as a citizen of the Creek Nation, of Oleta Wilson, born on the 4 day of Aug , 1902

Name of Father: C. H. Wilson   a citizen of the United States Nation.
Name of Mother: Lydia Belle Wilson (Burton)   a citizen of the   Creek   Nation.

Postoffice   Melette, Ind. Ter.

AFFIDAVIT OF MOTHER.
Child present

UNITED STATES OF AMERICA, Indian Territory, }
     Western   DISTRICT.

I, Lydia Belle Wilson, on oath state that I am 24 years of age and a citizen by blood , of the Creek Nation; that I am the lawful wife of C. H. Wilson , who is a citizen, by *(blank)* of the United States Nation; that a female child was born to me on 4 day of April , 1902 , that said child has been named Oleta Wilson , and was living March 4, 1905.

                                          Lydia Belle Wilson
Witnesses To Mark:
{

Subscribed and sworn to before me this 3 day of April , 1905.

                                          Drennan C Skaggs
                                          Notary Public.

AFFIDAVIT OF ATTENDING PHYSICIAN OR MID-WIFE.

UNITED STATES OF AMERICA, Indian Territory, }
     Western   DISTRICT.

I, Louis Bagly , a Physician , on oath state that I attended on Mrs. Lydia Belle Wilson , wife of C. H. Wilson on the 4th day of Aug , 1902 ; that there was born to her on said date a female child; that said child was living March 4, 1905, and is said to have been named Oleta Wilson .

                                          Louis Bagly
Witnesses To Mark:
{

Applications for Enrollment of Creek Newborn
Act of 1905   Volume II

Subscribed and sworn to before me this 4th day of April, 1905.

                                              Chas. H. Collins
                                              Notary Public.

DEPARTMENT OF THE INTERIOR,
COMMISSIONER TO THE FIVE CIVILIZED TRIBES.

REFER IN REPLY TO THE FOLLOWING:
N.C. 106.

Muskogee, Indian Territory, **August 4, 1905.**

Stephen Smith,
    Haskell, Indian Territory.

Dear Sir:

    You are hereby advised that on **July 28, 1905**, the Secretary of the Interior approved the enrollment of your minor child, **Terry Steven Smith**, as a citizen by blood of the **Creek** Nation, and that the name of said child appears upon the roll of new born citizens of the **Creek** Nation as Number **70**.

    The child is now entitled to an allotment, and application therefor should be made without delay at the Land Office for the Nation in which the prospective allotment is located.

    An entire allotment for said child must be selected at the time of the original application.

                                      Respectively,

                                                      Commissioner.

BIRTH AFFIDAVIT.

DEPARTMENT OF THE INTERIOR.
COMMISSION TO THE FIVE CIVILIZED TRIBES.

    IN RE APPLICATION FOR ENROLLMENT, as a citizen of the CREEK Nation, of Terry Steven Smith, born on the 27 day of Oct, 1903.

Name of Father: Steven Smith	a citizen of the Creek	Nation.
Name of Mother: Emma "	a citizen of the U. S.	Nation.

                                    Postoffice   Haskell

Applications for Enrollment of Creek Newborn
Act of 1905 Volume II

(Child present)

AFFIDAVIT OF MOTHER.

UNITED STATES OF AMERICA, Indian Territory, }
   WESTERN   DISTRICT.

    I, Emma Smith , on oath state that I am 29 years of age and a citizen by ----- , of the U. S. Nation; that I am the lawful wife of Steven Smith , who is a citizen, by blood of the Creek Nation; that a male child was born to me on 27 day of Oct. , 1903 , that said child has been named Terry Steven Smith , and is now living.

                                          Emma Smith

Witnesses To Mark:
{

    Subscribed and sworn to before me this 14 day of March , 1905.

                                           Edw C Griesel
                                                Notary Public.

                              father
AFFIDAVIT OF ~~ATTENDING PHYSICIAN OR MID-WIFE~~.

UNITED STATES OF AMERICA, Indian Territory, }
   WESTERN   DISTRICT.

                                                      husband

    I, Steven Smith , a m , ~~on oath state that I attended on Mrs. , wife~~ of Emma Smith on the 27 day of Oct. , 1903; that there was born to her on said date a male child; that said child is now living and is said to have been named Terry Steven Smith .

                                          Stephen Smith

Witnesses To Mark:
{

    Subscribed and sworn to before me this 14 day of March, 1905.

                                           Edw C Griesel
                                              Notary Public.

AFFIDAVIT OF ATTENDING PHYSICIAN OR MID-WIFE.

UNITED STATES OF AMERICA, Indian Territory, }
    Western   DISTRICT.

    I, W. C. Mitchell , a Physician , on oath state that I attended on Mrs. Emma Smith , wife of Stephen Smith on the 27th day of October , 1903 ; that there was born

Applications for Enrollment of Creek Newborn
Act of 1905   Volume II

to her on said date a male child; that said child is now living and is said to have been named Terry Stephen Smith .

W.C. Mitchell

Witnesses To Mark:
{

Subscribed and sworn to before me this 21st day of March, 1905.

(Name Illegible)
Notary Public.

Acquaintance
AFFIDAVIT OF ~~ATTENDING PHYSICIAN OR MID-WIFE~~.

UNITED STATES OF AMERICA, Indian Territory,
   Western Judicial   **DISTRICT.**

acquaintance
   I, L. Cheek + M J Cheek   , an acquaintances , on oath state that I ~~attended on~~ Mrs. Winnie Wolf , wife of John Wolf on the 18 day of May , 1904 ; that there was born to her on said date a male child; that said child was living March 4, 1905, and is said to have been named Jim Wolf .

L Cheek
M J Cheek

Witnesses To Mark:
{

Subscribed and sworn to before me this 25 day of November, 1905.

Tripper Dunn
Notary Public.

   my Commission Expires Aug. 19" 1908

DEPARTMENT OF THE INTERIOR,
COMMISSIONER TO THE FIVE CIVILIZED TRIBES.
MUSKOGEE, I. T. July 3, 1905.

   In the matter of the application for the enrollment as a citizen of the Seminole Nation, under the Act of March 3, 1905, of Jim Wolf.

JOHN WOLF, being first duly sworn, testified as follows:

BY THE COMMISSIONER:

Q What is your name? A John Wolf.
Q What is your age: A I am 49.
Q What is your post office? A Little.

Applications for Enrollment of Creek Newborn
Act of 1905   Volume II

Q Little, Indian Territory. A Yes.
Q You come here you say in the matter of the enrollment of your child, Jim Wolf, as a Seminole? A Yes.
Q If[sic] your child, Jim Wolf, living now? A Yes.
Q Are you a citizen of any tribe of Indians? A Why, I am a citizen of the Wichitas.
Q Are you a citizen by blood of the Wichita tribe? A No, not blood
Q What kind of a citizen are you? A Creek.
Q You are a Creek Indian by blood? A Yes, just adopted by the Wichitas.
Q Has your child, Jim Wolf, any Wichita blood? A No Wichita blood at all.
Q Who is the mother of your child? A Minnie Wolf, a Seminole.
Q Winnie or Minnie are one and the same are they? A Yes.
Q Do you know under what name she has taken her land? A Yes as Seminole.
Q What name did she take her land under, Winney? A Yes, Winney Cornelius.
Q You desire to have your child, Jim Wolf enrolled as a citizen of the Senimole Nation? A Yes.
Q And you relinquish for said child, any and all right, title and interest he may have to enrollment and tribal property in the Wichita tribe of Indians, if he is enrolled as a citizen of the Seminole Nation? A Yes.
Q You understand you are giving up all his right as a Wichita? A Yes.

Witness excused.

Lola Mann, being first duly sworn, states that the above and foregoing is a full, true and correct transcript of her stenographic noes, taken in said case on said date.

Lola Mann

Subscribed and sworn to before me this 23rd day of July, 1905.

Walter W Chappell
Notary Public.

DEPARTMENT OF THE INTERIOR.
COMMISSIONER TO THE FIVE CIVILIZED TRIBES,
Muskogee, Indian Territory,
September 26, 1905.

Sem. NB 105.

In the matter of the application for the enrollment of Jim Wolf as a citizen of the Seminole Nation under the Act of March 3, 1905.

John Wolf sworn interpreter.

Winey Wolf being duly sworn through John Wolf, sworn interpreter, testifies as follows:

Applications for Enrollment of Creek Newborn
Act of 1905   Volume II

Q[sic]   Examination by Commissioner.

Q. What is your name? A. Winey Wolf.
Q. How old are you? A. She don't know exactly. She was born a little after the war broke out.
Q. What is your post office? A. Little, Indian Territory.
Q. You are here to see about the enrollment of your child Jim Wolf? A. Yes.
Q. When was Jim Wolf born? Two years and over.
Q. What year would that make it? A. He was born in 1904.
Q. What month? A. 18th of May.
Q. Is this Jim Wolf you have with you? A. Yes.
   (Child apparently about two years old with mother.)
Q. Is your child a full blood Creek? A. Yes.
Q. She dosn't[sic] mean that, does she? What tribe do you belong to? A Seminole.
Q Then your child is both Creek and Seminole blood is he? A. Yes.
Q. Then you didn't mean that your child was a full blood Creek Indian? A. No, she says it is not full blood Creek, but half Creek.
Q. Half Creek and half Seminole? A. Yes.
Q. What is your husband's name? A. John Wolf.
Q. He is the father of Jim Wolf is he? A. Yes.
Q. What tribe does your husband John Wolf belong to? A. Adopted Wichata[sic].
Q. What Indian tribe does he belong to by blood? A. His blood is Creek, Muskogee. Mother lived in creek Nation ? He was just adopted into Wichita tribe.
Q. In which tribe do you desire to have your child Jim Wolf enrolled A. Wants him enrolled in the Seminole Country.
Q. Do you relinquish any rights, interests or title this child may have in the lands and tribal property of the Wichitas in the event the child is enrolled as a citizen of the Seminole Nation. A. Yes.

Ella Bailey being duly sworn states that as stenographer to the Commissioner to the Five Civilized Tribes Five Civilized Tribes, that the above and foregoing is a full, true and correct transcript of her stenographic notes taken on the 18th day of September 1905 in the above case.

                                          Ella Bailey

Subscribed and sworn to before me this the *(illegible)* day of September 1905.

                                Walter W Chappell
                                Notary Public.

NC 107.   JLDe.

DEPARTMENT OF THE INTERIOR,
COMMISSIONER TO THE FIVE CIVILIZED TRIBES.

In the matter of the application for the enrollment of Jim Wolf, as a citizen by blood of the Creek Nation.

Applications for Enrollment of Creek Newborn
Act of 1905   Volume II

DECISION.

The record in this case shows that on December 22, 1905, application was made, in affidavit form, for the enrollment of Jim Wolf, as a citizen by blood of the Creek Nation.

The testimony taken on July 3, 1906, and on September 26, 1906, in the matter of the application for the enrollment of Jim Wolf, as a citizen of the Seminole Nation, under the Act of Congress approved March 3, 1905, is attached hereto and made a part of the record herein.

It appears from the evidence filed in this cause and from the records in the possession of this office that said Jim Wolf was born May 18, 1904, and is the child of John Wolf, who was born of Creek parents, but was adopted into the Wichita tribe, and Minnie Wolf, identified as Winey Cornelius, under which name she appears upon the approved roll of citizens of the Seminole Nation, opposite roll number 1101, and it does not appear from the evidence nor from said records that either of said parents is a member of or an applicant for membership in the Creek Nation.

An examination of the records of this office shows that application has been made for the enrollment of the said Jim Wolf, as a citizen of the Seminole Nation, and that his name has been placed upon a partial schedule of new born citizens of said Seminole Nation, which partial schedule is soon to be forwarded to the Secretary of the Interior for appropriate action.

It appearing that there is no authority of law for the enrollment of said Jim Wolf, as a citizen by blood of the Creek Nation, it is ordered and adjudged that the said Jim Wolf is not entitled to enrollment as such, and said application is accordingly denied.

Muskogee, Indian Territory,   *(Name Illegible)*   Commissioner.
JAN 18 1907

N.C. 107.

Muskogee, Indian Territory, June 22, 1906.

John Wolf,
    Little, Indian Territory.

Dear Sir:

In the matter of the application for the enrollment of your minor child, Jim Wolf, as a citizen by blood of the Creek Nation, you are advised that it is required that you furnish this office with the affidavits of Minnie Wolf, the mother of said child and of the midwife in attendance at his birth. For this purpose there is inclosed[sic] blank form of birth affidavit. Said affidavit should show the name of the child, the names of its parents, the date of its birth and whether or not it was living March 4, 1906[sic].

You are requested to furnish information which will enable this office to identify you and Minnie Wolf, the mother of said child, on its roll of citizens of the Creek Nation.

This matter should receive your prompt attention.

Applications for Enrollment of Creek Newborn
Act of 1905 Volume II

Respectfully,

RA   Commissioner.

REFER IN REPLY TO THE FOLLOWING:

Sem NB-105

DEPARTMENT OF THE INTERIOR,
COMMISSIONER TO THE FIVE CIVILIZED TRIBES.

Muskogee, Indian Territory, January 10, 1907.

Chief Clerk,
    Creek Enrollment Division.

Dear Sir:

    You are hereby advised that Jim Wolf, son of John Wolf a Wichita Indian, and Winey Wolf, formerly Cornelius, a Seminole, is an applicant for enrollment as a new born citizen of the Seminole Nation under the Act of Congress approved March 3, 1905 and his name has been placed upon a schedule of such citizens which is now being prepared for forwarding to the Secretary of the Interior.

    You will be notified when his enrollment is approved by the Department.

Respectfully,

(Name Illegible)   Commissioner

NC 107.

Muskogee, Indian Territory, January 19, 1907.

Minnie Wolf,
    c/o John Wolf,
        Little, Indian Territory.

Dear Madam:

    There is herewith enclosed one copy of the statement and order of the Commissioner to the Five Civilized Tribes, dated January 18, 1907, dismissing the application for the enrollment of your minor child, Jim Wolf, as a citizen of the Creek Nation.

Respectfully,

Register.   Commissioner.
LM-30.

Applications for Enrollment of Creek Newborn
Act of 1905 Volume II

REFER IN REPLY TO THE FOLLOWING:
Sem NB-105.

DEPARTMENT OF THE INTERIOR,
COMMISSIONER TO THE FIVE CIVILIZED TRIBES.

Muskogee, Indian Territory, March 2, 1907.

Chief Clerk,
    Creek Enrollment Division.

Dear Sir:

    You are hereby advised that on February 12, 1907, the Secretary of the Interior approved the enrollment of Jim Wolf as New Born Citizen of the Seminole Nation, under the Act of Congress approved March 3, 1905.

    Respectfully,

    (Name Illegible) Commissioner.

N C 107

COPY

Dawes Commission,

    Please write to me at Little I. T.

    (Signed) John H. Wolf

CERTIFICATE OF TRUE COPY.

United States of America, ⎫
  Indian Territory,   ⎬ ss.
  Western District.   ⎭
    I, **R. P. HARRISON**, Clerk of the United States Court in the Western District, Indian Territory, do hereby certify that the instrument hereto attached is a full, true and correct copy of a Marriage License *as the same appears from the records of my office.*

    WITNESS my hand and seal of said Court at   Muskogee
    in said Territory, this 24" day of June   A. D. 1905

By   John Harlan   R. P. Harrison
        Deputy Clerk   *Clerk and Ex-Officio Recorder.*

Book   H   page 835

Applications for Enrollment of Creek Newborn
Act of 1905 Volume II

MARRIAGE LICENSE.

United States of America ⎫
   Indian Territory   ⎬ ss.
Northern Western District   ⎭   No. 268

To Any Person Authorized by Law to Solemnize Marriage – Greeting:

You are Hereby Commanded to Solemnize the Rite and Publish the Banns of Matrimony between Mr. James O. Callahan *of* Muskogee *in the Indian Territory, aged* 42 *years and Miss* Bettie Hardin *of* Muskogee *in the Indian Territory aged* 26 *years according to law, and do you officially sign and return this license to the parties herein named.*

    Witness my hand and official seal ~~at Muskogee Indian Territory~~ *this* 4th *day of* October *A. D.* ~~190~~ 1899

                                               Jas A. Winston
                                          Clerk of the U S Court

By   -----   Deputy

CERTIFICATE OF MARRIAGE

United States of America ⎫
   Indian Territory   ⎬ ss.
Northern Western District   ⎭

    I, Sam G. Thompson *, a Minister of the Gospel, DO HEREBY CERTIFY that on the* 5" *day of* Oct *A D* ~~190~~ 1899 *did duly and according to law as commanded in the foregoing License, solemnize the Rite and Publish the Banns of Matrimony between the parties therein named.*

    WITNESS my hand this 5" *day of* Oct *A. D.* ~~190~~ 1899

    My credentials are recorded in the office of the Clerk of the United States Court, Indian Territory, Western District Book   D , page   211

                                             Sam G. Thompson
                                           A Minister of the Gospel

Note   This license and certificate of marriage must be returned to the office of the Clerk of the United States court in the Western District Indian Territory from whence it was issued within sixty days from the date thereof of the party to whom the license was issued will be liable in the amount of the one hundred dollars ($100.00)

Applications for Enrollment of Creek Newborn
Act of 1905 Volume II

Filed and duly recorded, this 7" day of Oct. 1899.
Book H page 335   Jas. A. Winston Clerk U.S. Court.

BIRTH AFFIDAVIT.

DEPARTMENT OF THE INTERIOR.
COMMISSION TO THE FIVE CIVILIZED TRIBES.

IN RE APPLICATION FOR ENROLLMENT, as a citizen of the Creek Nation, of Mary Elizabeth Callahan , born on the 8th day of Feby , 1902

Name of Father: James O. Callahan   a citizen of the Creek Nation.
Name of Mother: Mary E. Callahan   a citizen of the United States ~~Nation~~.

Postoffice   Muskogee, Ind. Ty.

AFFIDAVIT OF MOTHER.

UNITED STATES OF AMERICA, Indian Territory,
  Western   DISTRICT.

I, Mary E. Callahan , on oath state that I am 32 years of age and a citizen by ~~marriage~~ ----- , of the ~~Creek~~ U.S. Nation; that I am the lawful wife of James O. Callahan , who is a citizen, by blood of the Creek Nation; that a Female child was born to me on 8th day of Feby , 1902 , that said child has been named Mary Elizabeth Callahan , and is now living.

                                         Mary E. Callahan
Witnesses To Mark:
{

Subscribed and sworn to before me this 10 day of Mch , 1905.

                                         W T Wisdom
                                         Notary Public.

AFFIDAVIT OF ATTENDING PHYSICIAN OR MID-WIFE.

UNITED STATES OF AMERICA, Indian Territory,
  (blank)   DISTRICT.

I, N.C. Rogers , a physician , on oath state that I attended on Mrs. Mary E. Callahan , wife of J. O. Callahan on the 8th day of Feby , 1902 ; that there was born to her on said date a female child; that said child is now living and is said to have been named Mary Elizabeth Callahan .

                                         N.C. Rogers

Applications for Enrollment of Creek Newborn
Act of 1905 Volume II

Witnesses To Mark:
{

Subscribed and sworn to before me this 10 day of Mch, 1905.

W T Wisdom
Notary Public.

BIRTH AFFIDAVIT.

DEPARTMENT OF THE INTERIOR.
COMMISSION TO THE FIVE CIVILIZED TRIBES.

IN RE APPLICATION FOR ENROLLMENT, as a citizen of the Creek Nation, of Etta Sibyl Callahan , born on the 23rd day of April , 1904

Name of Father: James O. Callahan   a citizen of the Creek Nation.
Name of Mother: Mary E. Callahan   a citizen of the United States Nation.

Postoffice   Muskogee, I.T.

AFFIDAVIT OF MOTHER.

UNITED STATES OF AMERICA, Indian Territory, }
    Western   DISTRICT.

I, Mary E. Callahan , on oath state that I am 32 years of age and a citizen ~~by~~ of ~~marriage~~ , of the ~~Creek~~ U.S. Nation; that I am the lawful wife of James O. Callahan , who is a citizen, by blood of the Creek Nation; that a Female child was born to me on 23rd day of April , 1904 , that said child has been named Etta Sibyl , and is now living.

Mary E. Callahan

Witnesses To Mark:
{

Subscribed and sworn to before me this 10 day of Mch , 1905.

W T Wisdom
Notary Public.

Applications for Enrollment of Creek Newborn
Act of 1905 Volume II

AFFIDAVIT OF ATTENDING PHYSICIAN OR MID-WIFE.

UNITED STATES OF AMERICA, Indian Territory, ⎫
   (blank)   DISTRICT.   ⎬

I, N.C. Rogers , a physician , on oath state that I attended on Mrs. Mary E. Callahan , wife of J. O. Callahan on the 23^d day of April , 1904 ; that there was born to her on said date a *(blank)* child; that said child is now living and is said to have been named Etta Sibyl Callahan .

N.C. Rogers

Witnesses To Mark:
{

Subscribed and sworn to before me this 10 day of Mch, 1905.

W T Wisdom
Notary Public.

NC 109.

Muskogee, Indian Territory, May 17, 1905.

Miller Bruner,
   Haskell, Indian Territory.

Dear Sir:
   In the matter of the application for the enrollment of your minor child, Mineffie Bruner, as a citizen of the Creek Nation, you are advised that the Commission requires the affidavit of the midwife or physician in attendance at the birth of said child.

   There is herewith enclosed a blank form of birth affidavit, and in executing same care should be exercised to see that all blanks are properly filled, all names written in full and in the event that the person signing the affidavit is unable to write, signature by mark must be attested by two witnesses. Each affidavit must be executed before a Notary Public and the notarial seal and signature of the officer must be attached to each separate affidavit.

Respectfully,

BC.   Chairman.

Applications for Enrollment of Creek Newborn
Act of 1905   Volume II

DEPARTMENT OF THE INTERIOR,
COMMISSIONER TO THE FIVE CIVILIZED TRIBES.

REFER IN REPLY TO THE FOLLOWING:

N.C. 109.

Muskogee, Indian Territory, **August 4, 1905.**

Miller Bruner,
    Haskell, Indian Territory.

Dear Sir:

    You are hereby advised that on **July 28, 1905** , the Secretary of the Interior approved the enrollment of your minor child, **Ella Bruner** , as a citizen by blood of the **Creek** Nation, and that the name of said child appears upon the roll of new born citizens of the **Creek** Nation as Number **73** .

    The child is now entitled to an allotment, and application therefor should be made without delay at the Land Office for the Nation in which the prospective allotment is located.

    An entire allotment for said child must be selected at the time of the original application.

        Respectively,

                Commissioner.

BIRTH AFFIDAVIT.

DEPARTMENT OF THE INTERIOR.
COMMISSION TO THE FIVE CIVILIZED TRIBES.

    IN RE APPLICATION FOR ENROLLMENT, as a citizen of the CREEK Nation, of Mineffie Bruner, born on the 25 day of March , 1904

Name of Father: Miller Bruner   a citizen of the   Creek   Nation.
Name of Mother: Lucy   "   a citizen of the   "   Nation.

        Postoffice   Haskell, I.T.

AFFIDAVIT OF ~~MOTHER~~.
        father

UNITED STATES OF AMERICA, Indian Territory,
    WESTERN   DISTRICT.

    I, Miller Bruner , on oath state that I am 55 years of age and a citizen by blood , of the Creek Nation; that I am the lawful ~~wife~~ husb of Lucy Bruner , who is a citizen, by blood of the Creek Nation; that a female child was born to me on 25 day of March , 1904 , that said child has been named Mineffie Bruner , and is now living.

Applications for Enrollment of Creek Newborn
Act of 1905   Volume II

                                          Miller Bruner

Witnesses To Mark:
{

    Subscribed and sworn to before me this 9 day of March , 1905.

                                     Edw C Griesel
                                     Notary Public.

Child Present Gi

AFFIDAVIT OF ATTENDING ~~PHYSICIAN OR MID-WIFE~~.

UNITED STATES OF AMERICA, Indian Territory,
    WESTERN   DISTRICT.

    I, Lucy Bruner , ~~a~~ Mother , on oath state ~~that I attended on Mrs.~~ *(blank)* , ~~wife of~~ on the 25 day of March , 1904 ; that there was born to her on said date a female child; that said child is now living and is said to have been named Mineffie Bruner .

                                     Her
                                Lucy x Bruner
Witnesses To Mark: mark
{ J McDermott
{ EC Griesel

    Subscribed and sworn to before me this 13 day of March, 1905.

    (Seal)   Edw C Griesel
                                  Notary Public.

BIRTH AFFIDAVIT.

                      DEPARTMENT OF THE INTERIOR.
           COMMISSION TO THE FIVE CIVILIZED TRIBES.

    IN RE APPLICATION FOR ENROLLMENT, as a citizen of the Creek Nation, of Mineffie Bruner, born on the 25 day of March , 1904

Name of Father: Miller Bruner   a citizen of the   Creek   Nation.
Name of Mother: Lucy Bruner   a citizen of the   Creek   Nation.

                        Postoffice   Haskell, I.T.

Applications for Enrollment of Creek Newborn
Act of 1905   Volume II

AFFIDAVIT OF MOTHER.

UNITED STATES OF AMERICA, Indian Territory, }
   Western   DISTRICT.

    I, Lucy Bruner   , on oath state that I am ~~55~~ 31 years of age and a citizen by Blood , of the Creek Nation; that I am the lawful wife of Miller Bruner , who is a citizen, by Blood of the Creek Nation; that a female   child was born to me on 25 day of March , 1904, that said child has been named Mineffie Bruner , and was living March 4, 1905.

                                                her
                                      Lucy x Bruner
Witnesses To Mark: mark
  { Isom Peters
    Joe Colbert

    Subscribed and sworn to before me this 23rd day of May , 1905.

                                      Ralph Dresback
                                        Notary Public.

AFFIDAVIT OF ATTENDING PHYSICIAN OR MID-WIFE.

UNITED STATES OF AMERICA, Indian Territory, }
   Western   DISTRICT.

    I, Louisa Peters , a midwife   , on oath state that I attended on Mrs. Lucy Bruner, wife of Miller Bruner on the 25 day of March , 1904 ; that there was born to her on said date a female child; that said child was living March 4, 1905, and is said to have been named Mineffie Bruner .

                                                her
                                    Louisa x Peters
Witnesses To Mark: mark
  { Isom Peters
    Joe Colbert

    Subscribed and sworn to before me this 23 day of May, 1905.

                                      Ralph Dresback
                                        Notary Public.

Applications for Enrollment of Creek Newborn
Act of 1905   Volume II

BIRTH AFFIDAVIT.

DEPARTMENT OF THE INTERIOR.
COMMISSION TO THE FIVE CIVILIZED TRIBES.

IN RE APPLICATION FOR ENROLLMENT, as a citizen of the CREEK Nation, of Ella Bruner, born on the 14" day of March, 1902
Name of Father: Miller Bruner   a citizen of the   Creek   Nation.
Name of Mother: Lucy   "   a citizen of the   "   Nation.

Postoffice   Haskell I.T.

AFFIDAVIT OF MOTHER.

UNITED STATES OF AMERICA, Indian Territory,
    WESTERN   DISTRICT.

I, Miller Bruner, on oath state that I am 55 years of age and a citizen by blood, of the Creek Nation; that I am the lawful ~~wife~~ hus of Lucy Bruner, who is a citizen, by blood of the Creek Nation; that a female child was born to me on 14 day of March, 1902, that said child has been named Ella Bruner, and ~~is now living~~. died Sept. 1903.

                           Miller Bruner

Witnesses To Mark:
{

Subscribed and sworn to before me this 9 day of March, 1905.

                         Edw C Griesel
                             Notary Public.

N.C. 109   JLD
DEPARTMENT OF THE INTERIOR,
COMMISSIONER TO THE FIVE CIVILIZED TRIBES.

In the matter of the application for the enrollment of Ella Bruner, deceased, as a citizen by blood of the Creek Nation.

                . . . .

STATEMENT AND ORDER.

The record in this case shows that on March 9, 1905, application was made, in affidavit form, for the enrollment of Ella Bruner, deceased, as a citizen by blood of the Creek Nation, under the provisions of the act of Congress approved March 3, 1905.

Applications for Enrollment of Creek Newborn
Act of 1905   Volume II

It appears that the affidavit filed in this matter that said Ella Bruner, deceased, was born March 14, 1902, and died in September 1903.

The act of Congress approved March 3, 1905, (33 Stats., 1048), provides:

"That the Commission to the Five Civilized Tribes is authorized for sixty days after the date of the approval of this act to receive and consider applications for enrollment, of children, <u>born subsequent to May twenty-fifth, nineteen hundred and one, and prior to March fourth, nineteen hundred and five, and living on said latter date, to citizens of the</u> Creek tribe of Indians whose enrollment has been approved by the Secretary of the Interior prior to the approval of this act; and to enroll and make allotments to such children."

It is, therefore, ordered that the application for the enrollment of said Ella Bruner, deceased, as a citizen by blood of the Creek Nation, be, and the same is, hereby dismissed.

(Name Illegible) Commissioner.

Muskogee, Indian Territory.
JAN 4 1907

Cr NC-110

DEPARTMENT OF THE INTERIOR,
COMMISSION TO THE FIVE CIVILIZED TRIBES.

Muskogee, Indian Territory, May 29, 1905.

In the matter of the application for the enrollment of Lydia C. Anderson as a Creek Freedman.

Emma Anderson, being duly sworn, testified as follows:

EXAMINATION BY THE COMMISSION:
Q What is your name? A Emma Anderson.
Q How old are you? A 33 years old.
Q What is your postoffice? A Haskell.
Q Are you a citizen of the Creek Nation? A Yes sir.
Q Have you a child named Lydia C. Anderson? A Yes sir.
Q Do you call her Lydia C. Anderson or just Lydia Anderson? A Lydia C Anderson.
Q When was this child born? A October /6[sic], 1903. There was a mistake in the first affidavit; it was 1904.
Q Is that child living? A Yes sir.
Q How old will it be next October? A Two years old.

Solomon Anderson, being duly sworn, testified as follows:

Applications for Enrollment of Creek Newborn
Act of 1905   Volume II

EXAMINATION BY THE COMMISSION:
Q What is your name? A Solomon Anderson.
Q How old are you? A 35 years old.
Q What is your postoffice address? A Haskell. I am a citizen by blood of the Creek Nation. I am the father of Lydia C. Anderson. The child was born October /6[sic], 1903; it will be two years old next October. They made a mistake in the first affidavit when they had the child was born in 1904.

INDIAN TERRITORY, Western District.
I, J. Y. Miller, a stenographer to the Commission to the Five Civilized Tribes, do hereby certify that the above and foregoing is a true and complete translation of my notes as same appear in my stenographic report of this case.

JY Miller

Sworn to and subscribed before me
this the 17 day of June, 1905.

Edw C Griesel
Notary Public.

BIRTH AFFIDAVIT.
DEPARTMENT OF THE INTERIOR.
COMMISSION TO THE FIVE CIVILIZED TRIBES.

IN RE APPLICATION FOR ENROLLMENT, as a citizen of the Creek Nation, of Lydia C. Anderson, born on the 16" day of Oct, 1904

Name of Father: Solomon Anderson   a citizen of the   Creek   Nation.
Name of Mother: Emma   "   a citizen of the   "   Nation.

Postoffice   Haskell, I.T.

AFFIDAVIT OF MOTHER.
Child Present Gr
UNITED STATES OF AMERICA, Indian Territory,
    Western   DISTRICT.
        Emma
I, ~~Solomon~~ Anderson, on oath state that I am 32 years of age and a citizen by blood, of the Creek Nation; that I am the lawful wife of Solomon Anderson, who is a citizen, by blood of the Creek Nation; that a female child was born to me on 16 day of Oct, 1904, that said child has been named Lydia C. Anderson, and is now living.

Emma Anderson

Applications for Enrollment of Creek Newborn
Act of 1905 Volume II

Witnesses To Mark:
{

    Subscribed and sworn to before me this 14 day of March , 1905.

                        Edw C Griesel
                            Notary Public.

BIRTH AFFIDAVIT.

DEPARTMENT OF THE INTERIOR.
COMMISSION TO THE FIVE CIVILIZED TRIBES.

    IN RE APPLICATION FOR ENROLLMENT, as a citizen of the CREEK Nation, of Lydia C. Anderson , born on the 16 day of Oct , 1904

Name of Father: Solomon Anderson   a citizen of the   Creek   Nation.
Name of Mother: Emma   "   a citizen of the   "   Nation.

                    Postoffice   Haskell, I.T.

                    AFFIDAVIT OF MOTHER. father

UNITED STATES OF AMERICA, Indian Territory, }
    WESTERN   DISTRICT.

    I, Solomon Anderson , on oath state that I am 35 years of age and a citizen by blood, of the Creek   Nation; that I am the lawful wife husb of Emma Anderson , who is a citizen, by blood of the Creek   Nation; that a female   child was born to me on 16 day of Oct   , 1904 , that said child has been named   Lydia C. Anderson , and is now living.

                        Solomon Anderson
Witnesses To Mark:
{

    Subscribed and sworn to before me this 9 day of March, 1905.

                        Edw C Griesel
                          Notary Public.

Applications for Enrollment of Creek Newborn
Act of 1905 Volume II

BIRTH AFFIDAVIT.

DEPARTMENT OF THE INTERIOR.
COMMISSION TO THE FIVE CIVILIZED TRIBES.

IN RE APPLICATION FOR ENROLLMENT, as a citizen of the Creek Nation, of Lydia Anderson, born on the 16 day of October, 19o3[sic]

Name of Father:	Solomon Anderson	a citizen of the Creek	Nation.
Name of Mother:	Emma Anderson	a citizen of the Creek	Nation.

Postoffice   Haskell, Ind.Ter.

AFFIDAVIT OF MOTHER.

UNITED STATES OF AMERICA, Indian Territory,
Western DISTRICT.

I, Emma Anderson, on oath state that I am 33 years of age and a citizen by Birth, of the Creek Nation; that I am the lawful wife of Solomon Anderson, who is a citizen, by Birth of the Creek Nation; that a female child was born to me on 16th day of October, 19o3[sic], that said child has been named Lydia Anderson, and was living March 4, 1905.

Emma Anderson

Witnesses To Mark:
{ Robt W Hamilton
{ Toney E. Proctor

Subscribed and sworn to before me this 22nd day of May, 1905.

(Name Illegible)
Notary Public.

AFFIDAVIT OF ATTENDING PHYSICIAN OR MID-WIFE.

UNITED STATES OF AMERICA, Indian Territory,
Western DISTRICT.

I, Mary Dann, a Midwife, on oath state that I attended on Mrs. Emma Anderson, wife of Solomon Anderson on the 16th day of October, 19o3[sic]; that there was born to her on said date a female child; that said child was living March 4, 1905, and is said to have been named Lydia Anderson.

her
Mary Dann x
mark

Applications for Enrollment of Creek Newborn
Act of 1905   Volume II

Witnesses To Mark:
  { Robt W Hamilton
  { Toney E Proctor

Subscribed and sworn to before me this 22nd day of May, 1905.

(Name Illegible)
Notary Public.

NC 110.

Muskogee, Indian Territory, May 17, 1905.

Solomon Anderson,
  Haskell, Indian Territory.

Dear Sir:

In the matter of the application for the enrollment of your minor child, Lydia Anderson, as a citizen of the Creek Nation, you are advised the Commission requires the affidavit of the midwife or physician in attendance at the birth of said child.

There is herewith enclosed a blank form of birth affidavit, and in executing same care should be exercised to see that all blanks are properly filled, all names written in full and in the event that the person signing the affidavit is unable to write, signature by mark must be attested by two witnesses. Each affidavit must be executed before a Notary Public and the notarial seal and signature of the officer must be attached to each separate affidavit.

Respectfully,

Chairman.

BC.

NC 110.

Muskogee, Indian Territory, May 25, 1905.

Emma Anderson,
  Haskell, Indian Territory.

Dear Madam,
  In the matter of the application for the enrollment of your minor child, Lydia Anderson, there are on file with the Commission affidavits containing conflicting dates of birth.

Applications for Enrollment of Creek Newborn
Act of 1905   Volume II

You are advised that you are required to appear before the Commission at its office in Muskogee, Indian Territory, at an early date for the purpose of being examined under oath.

Respectfully,

Chairman.

BIRTH AFFIDAVIT.

DEPARTMENT OF THE INTERIOR.
COMMISSION TO THE FIVE CIVILIZED TRIBES.

IN RE APPLICATION FOR ENROLLMENT, as a citizen of the CREEK Nation, of Oliver R. Smith, born on the 21 day of Jan, 1904

Name of Father:	Enoch Smith	a citizen of the U.S.	Nation.
Name of Mother:	Janie "	a citizen of the Creek	Nation.

Postoffice   Redfork I.T.

(Child present) HGH

AFFIDAVIT OF MOTHER.

UNITED STATES OF AMERICA, Indian Territory, }
   WESTERN   DISTRICT. }

I, Janie Smith, on oath state that I am 25 years of age and a citizen by blood, of the Creek Nation; that I am the lawful wife of Enoch Smith, who is a citizen, by ----- of the U. S. Nation; that a *(blank)* child was born to me on 21 day of Jan, 1904, that said child has been named Oliver R. Smith, and is now living.

Janie Smith

Witnesses To Mark:
{

Subscribed and sworn to before me this 9 day of March, 1905.

Edw C Griesel
Notary Public.

Applications for Enrollment of Creek Newborn
Act of 1905 Volume II

BIRTH AFFIDAVIT.

DEPARTMENT OF THE INTERIOR.
COMMISSION TO THE FIVE CIVILIZED TRIBES.

IN RE APPLICATION FOR ENROLLMENT, as a citizen of the Creek Nation, of Oliver Russell Smith , born on the 21st day of January , 1904

Name of Father: Enoch O. Smith   a citizen of the   U.S.   Nation.
Name of Mother: Janie Smith   a citizen of the   Creek   Nation.

                    Postoffice   Red Fork Ind. Ter.

AFFIDAVIT OF MOTHER.

UNITED STATES OF AMERICA, Indian Territory,
    Western   DISTRICT.

I, Janie Smith , on oath state that I am 26 years of age and a citizen by blood , of the Creek Nation; that I am the lawful wife of Enoch O. Smith , who is a citizen, by birth of the U. S. Nation; that a male child was born to me on 21st day of January , 1904 , that said child has been named Oliver Russell Smith , and was living March 4, 1905.

                                     Janie Smith

Witnesses To Mark:
{

    Subscribed and sworn to before me this 29th day of May , 1905.

                                  Allen Henry
My commission expires October 19, 1907   Notary Public.

AFFIDAVIT OF ATTENDING PHYSICIAN OR MID-WIFE.

UNITED STATES OF AMERICA, Indian Territory,
    Western   DISTRICT.

I, Lizzie Denney , a Mid-Wife , on oath state that I attended on Mrs. Janie Smith , wife of Enoch O. Smith on the 21st day of January , 1904 ; that there was born to her on said date a male child; that said child was living March 4, 1905, and is said to have been named Oliver Russell Smith .

                                   Lizzie Denney

Witnesses To Mark:
{

Applications for Enrollment of Creek Newborn
Act of 1905   Volume II

Subscribed and sworn to before me this 14th day of June, 1905.

My commission expires October 19, 1907   Allen Henry
                                                                            Notary Public.

NC 111.

Muskogee, Indian Territory, May 17, 1905.

Enox Smith,
    Redfork, Indian Territory.

Dear Sir:

    In the matter of the application for the enrollment of your minor child Oliver R. Smith, as a citizen of the Creek Nation, you are advised that the Commission requires the affidavit of the midwife or physician in attendance at the birth of said child.

    There is herewith enclosed a blank form of birth affidavit, and in executing same care should be exercised to see that all blanks are properly filled, all names written in full and in the event that the person signing the affidavit is unable to write, signature by mark must be attested by two witnesses. Each affidavit must be executed before a Notary Public and the notarial seal and signature of the officer must be attached to each separate affidavit.

                      Respectfully,

BC.   Chairman.

NC 112.

Muskogee, Indian Territory, May 17, 1905.

James M. Ishmael,
    Jenks, Indian Territory.

Dear Sir:

    In the matter of the application for the enrollment of your minor children, James L. and Eva J. Ishmael, as citizens of the Creek Nation, you are hereby advised that the Commission requires the affidavit of the midwife or physician in attendance at the birth of said children.

    There are herewith enclosed two blank forms of birth affidavits, and in executing same care should be exercised to see that all blanks are properly filled, all names written

Applications for Enrollment of Creek Newborn
Act of 1905   Volume II

in full and in the event that the persons signing the affidavits are unable to write, signature by mark must be attested by two witnesses. Each affidavit must be executed before a Notary Public and the notarial seal and signature of the officer must be attached to each separate affidavit.

Respectfully,

BC.   Chairman.

BIRTH AFFIDAVIT.

DEPARTMENT OF THE INTERIOR.
COMMISSION TO THE FIVE CIVILIZED TRIBES.

IN RE APPLICATION FOR ENROLLMENT, as a citizen of the CREEK Nation, of James L. Ishmael, born on the 19 day of Sept., 1904

Name of Father: James M. Ishmael   a citizen of the   Creek   Nation.
Name of Mother: Maude   "   a citizen of the   U S   Nation.

Postoffice   Jenks, I.T.

(Child present) HGH

AFFIDAVIT OF <s>MOTHER</s>. father

UNITED STATES OF AMERICA, Indian Territory, ⎫
      WESTERN   DISTRICT. ⎭

    I, James M. Ishmael, on oath state that I am 24 years of age and a citizen by blood, of the Creek Nation; that I am the lawful <s>wife</s> hus of Maude Ishmael, who is a citizen, by ----- of the U S Nation; that a *(blank)* child was born to me on 19 day of Sept, 1904, that said child has been named James L. Ishmael, and is now living.

James M. Ishmael

Witnesses To Mark:
   {

    Subscribed and sworn to before me this 9 day of March, 1905.

Edw C Griesel
Notary Public.

Applications for Enrollment of Creek Newborn
Act of 1905 Volume II

BIRTH AFFIDAVIT.

DEPARTMENT OF THE INTERIOR.
COMMISSION TO THE FIVE CIVILIZED TRIBES.

IN RE APPLICATION FOR ENROLLMENT, as a citizen of the CREEK Nation, of James L. Ishmael, born on the 19 day of Sept., 1904

Name of Father: James M. Ishmael	a citizen of the	Creek	Nation.
Name of Mother: Maude "	a citizen of the	U S	Nation.

Postoffice Jenks, I.T.

(Child present) HGH

AFFIDAVIT OF MOTHER.

UNITED STATES OF AMERICA, Indian Territory,
    WESTERN   DISTRICT.

    I, Maude Ishmael, on oath state that I am 21 years of age and a citizen by -----, of the U. S. Nation; that I am the lawful wife of James M. Ishmael, who is a citizen, by blood of the Creek Nation; that a *(blank)* child was born to me on 19 day of Sept., 1904, that said child has been named James L. Ishmael, and is now living.

                                               Maude Ishmael

Witnesses To Mark:

    Subscribed and sworn to before me this 9 day of March, 1905.

                                        Edw C Griesel
                                              Notary Public.

BIRTH AFFIDAVIT.

DEPARTMENT OF THE INTERIOR.
COMMISSION TO THE FIVE CIVILIZED TRIBES.

IN RE APPLICATION FOR ENROLLMENT, as a citizen of the CREEK Nation, of Eva J. Ishmael, born on the 2 day of Jan., 1903

Name of Father: James M. Ishmael	a citizen of the	Creek	Nation.
Name of Mother: Maude "	a citizen of the	U S	Nation.

Postoffice Jenks, I.T.

Applications for Enrollment of Creek Newborn
Act of 1905 Volume II

(Child present) HGH

AFFIDAVIT OF ~~MOTHER~~. father

UNITED STATES OF AMERICA, Indian Territory,
WESTERN DISTRICT.

  I, James M. Ishmael , on oath state that I am 24 years of age and a citizen by blood , of the Creek Nation; that I am the lawful ~~wife~~ husb of Maude Ishmael , who is a citizen, by ----- of the U. S. Nation; that a female child was born to me on 2 day of Jan , 1903 , that said child has been named Eva J. Ishmael , and is now living.

           James M. Ishmael

Witnesses To Mark:
{

  Subscribed and sworn to before me this 9 day of March, 1905.

           Edw C Griesel
            Notary Public.

BIRTH AFFIDAVIT.

DEPARTMENT OF THE INTERIOR.
COMMISSION TO THE FIVE CIVILIZED TRIBES.

  IN RE APPLICATION FOR ENROLLMENT, as a citizen of the CREEK Nation, of Eva J. Ishmael , born on the 2 day of Jan. , 1903

Name of Father: James M. Ishmael	a citizen of the	Creek Nation.
Name of Mother: Maude "	a citizen of the	U S Nation.

       Postoffice Jenks, I.T.

(Child present) HGH

AFFIDAVIT OF MOTHER.

UNITED STATES OF AMERICA, Indian Territory,
WESTERN DISTRICT.

  I, Maude Ishmael, on oath state that I am 21 years of age and a citizen by ----- , of the U. S. Nation; that I am the lawful wife of James M. Ishmael , who is a citizen, by blood of the Creek Nation; that a female child was born to me on 2 day of Jan. , 1903 , that said child has been named Eva J. Ishmael , and is now living.

           Maude Ishmael

Witnesses To Mark:
{

Applications for Enrollment of Creek Newborn
Act of 1905 Volume II

Subscribed and sworn to before me this 9 day of March , 1905.

            Edw C Griesel
            Notary Public.

BIRTH AFFIDAVIT.

DEPARTMENT OF THE INTERIOR.
COMMISSION TO THE FIVE CIVILIZED TRIBES.

IN RE APPLICATION FOR ENROLLMENT, as a citizen of the Creek Nation, of Eva J. Ishmael , born on the 2 day of January , 1903

Name of Father: James M. Ishmael	a citizen of the	Creek	Nation.
Name of Mother: Maude Ishmael	a citizen of the	-----	Nation.

        Postoffice   Jenks, Ind Ter

AFFIDAVIT OF MOTHER.

UNITED STATES OF AMERICA, Indian Territory, ⎫
  Western   DISTRICT. ⎭

  I, Maude Ishmael, on oath state that I am 21 years of age and a citizen by ----- , of the ----- Nation; that I am the lawful wife of James M. Ishmael , who is a citizen, by Blood of the Creek Nation; that a female child was born to me on 12[sic] day of January , 1903 , that said child has been named Eva J. Ishmael , and was living March 4, 1905.

            Maude Ishmael

Witnesses To Mark:

{

Subscribed and sworn to before me this 22 day of May , 1905.

            Wm P. Rook
            Notary Public.

AFFIDAVIT OF ATTENDING PHYSICIAN OR MID-WIFE.

UNITED STATES OF AMERICA, Indian Territory, ⎫
  Western   DISTRICT. ⎭

  I, Mary J Covey , a midwife , on oath state that I attended on Mrs. Maude Ishmael , wife of James M Ishmael on the 2 day of January , 1903 ; that there was born to her on said date a female child; that said child was living March 4, 1905, and is said to have been named *(blank)* .

Applications for Enrollment of Creek Newborn
Act of 1905   Volume II

Mary J Covey

Witnesses To Mark:
{

Subscribed and sworn to before me this 22 day of May, 1905.

Wm P Rook
Notary Public.

BIRTH AFFIDAVIT.

DEPARTMENT OF THE INTERIOR.
COMMISSION TO THE FIVE CIVILIZED TRIBES.

IN RE APPLICATION FOR ENROLLMENT, as a citizen of the Creek Nation, of   James L. Ishmael , born on the 19 day of Sept , 1904

Name of Father: James M. Ishmael	a citizen of the	Creek	Nation.
Name of Mother: Maud Ishmael	a citizen of the	-----	Nation.

Postoffice   Jenks, Ind Ter

AFFIDAVIT OF MOTHER.

UNITED STATES OF AMERICA, Indian Territory, ⎫
    Western   DISTRICT. ⎭

    I, Maude Ishmael, on oath state that I am 21 years of age and a citizen by ----- , of the ----- Nation; that I am the lawful wife of James M. Ishmael , who is a citizen, by Blood of the Creek   Nation; that a   male   child was born to me on 19th day of September , 1904 , that said child has been named   James L. Ishmael , and was living March 4, 1905.

Maude Ishmael

Witnesses To Mark:
{

Subscribed and sworn to before me this 22nd day of May , 1905.

Wm P. Rook
Notary Public.

Applications for Enrollment of Creek Newborn
Act of 1905 Volume II

AFFIDAVIT OF ATTENDING PHYSICIAN OR MID-WIFE.

UNITED STATES OF AMERICA, Indian Territory,}
Western DISTRICT.

I, Mary J Covey , a midwife , on oath state that I attended on Mrs. Maude Ishmael , wife of James M Ishmael on the 19th day of September , 1904 ; that there was born to her on said date a male child; that said child was living March 4, 1905, and is said to have been named James L Ishmael .

Mary J Covey

Witnesses To Mark:
{

Subscribed and sworn to before me this 22 day of May, 1905.

Wm P Rook
Notary Public.

BIRTH AFFIDAVIT.

DEPARTMENT OF THE INTERIOR.
COMMISSION TO THE FIVE CIVILIZED TRIBES.

IN RE APPLICATION FOR ENROLLMENT, as a citizen of the CREEK Nation, of Loney Martin, born on the 13 day of March , 1902

Name of Father: Johnson Martin   a citizen of the   Creek   Nation.
Name of Mother: Susanna   "   a citizen of the   "   Nation.

Postoffice   Weer

AFFIDAVIT OF ~~MOTHER~~. father

UNITED STATES OF AMERICA, Indian Territory,}
WESTERN DISTRICT.

I, Johnson Martin, on oath state that I am 6 years of age and a citizen by blood , of the Creek Nation; that I am the lawful ~~wife~~ hus of Susanna Martin , who is a citizen, by blood of the Creek Nation; that a female child was born to me on 13 day of March , 1902 , that said child has been named Loney Martin , and is now living.

Johnson Martin

Witnesses To Mark:
{

Applications for Enrollment of Creek Newborn
Act of 1905 Volume II

Subscribed and sworn to before me this 10 day of March, 1905.

Edw C Griesel
Notary Public.

BIRTH AFFIDAVIT.

DEPARTMENT OF THE INTERIOR.
COMMISSION TO THE FIVE CIVILIZED TRIBES.

IN RE APPLICATION FOR ENROLLMENT, as a citizen of the Creek Nation, of Lonie Martin, born on the 13th day of March, 1902

Name of Father:	Johnson Martin	a citizen of the	Creek Nation.
Name of Mother:	Susana Martin	a citizen of the	Creek Nation.

Postoffice   Weer I T

AFFIDAVIT OF MOTHER.

UNITED STATES OF AMERICA, Indian Territory,
Western DISTRICT.

I, Susana Martin, on oath state that I am 19 years of age and a citizen by Blood, of the Creek Nation; that I am the lawful wife of Johnson Martin, who is a citizen, by Blood of the Creek Nation; that a Female child was born to me on 13th day of March, 1902, that said child has been named Lonie Martin, and was living March 4, 1905.

Susana Martin

Witnesses To Mark:

Subscribed and sworn to before me this 5th day of April, 1905.

James S. Day
Notary Public.

AFFIDAVIT OF ATTENDING PHYSICIAN OR MID-WIFE.

UNITED STATES OF AMERICA, Indian Territory,
Western DISTRICT.

I, Jennie Berryhill, a midwife, on oath state that I attended on Mrs. Susana Martin, wife of Johnson Martin on the 13th day of March, 1902; that there was born to her on said date a Female child; that said child was living March 4, 1905, and is said to have been named Lonie Martin.

Applications for Enrollment of Creek Newborn
Act of 1905 Volume II

                                          her
                               Mrs. Jennie x Berryhill

Witnesses To Mark: mark
{ I F Johnson
  Mitchell *(Illegible)*

Subscribed and sworn to before me this 5th day of April, 1905.

                                James S Day
My Commission Expires   Notary Public.
        March 10th 1907

BIRTH AFFIDAVIT.

DEPARTMENT OF THE INTERIOR.
COMMISSION TO THE FIVE CIVILIZED TRIBES.

IN RE APPLICATION FOR ENROLLMENT, as a citizen of the CREEK Nation, of John Martin, born on the 16 day of March, 1904

Name of Father: Johnson Martin   a citizen of the   Creek   Nation.
Name of Mother: Susanna "   a citizen of the   "   Nation.

                        Postoffice   Weer, I.T.

                AFFIDAVIT OF ~~MOTHER.~~ father

UNITED STATES OF AMERICA, Indian Territory, }
     WESTERN   DISTRICT.

    I, Johnson Martin, on oath state that I am 26 years of age and a citizen by blood, of the Creek Nation; that I am the lawful ~~wife~~ hus of Susanna Martin, who is a citizen, by blood of the Creek Nation; that a male child was born to me on 16 day of March, 1904, that said child has been named John Martin, and ~~is now living~~. died Dec. 16-1904

                                  Johnson Martin

Witnesses To Mark:
{
  Subscribed and sworn to before me this 10 day of March, 1905.

                                Edw C Griesel
                                Notary Public.

Applications for Enrollment of Creek Newborn
Act of 1905 Volume II

NC 113   JLD

DEPARTMENT OF THE INTERIOR,
COMMISSIONER TO THE FIVE CIVILIZED TRIBES.

....

In the matter of the application for the enrollment of John Martin, deceased, as a citizen by blood of the Creek Nation.

///////////////

STATEMENT AND ORDER.

The record in this case shows that on March 10, 1905, application was made, in affidavit form, for the enrollment of John Martin, deceased, as a citizen by blood of the Creek Nation, under the provisions of the act of Congress approved March 3, 1905.

It appears that the affidavit filed in this matter that said John Martin, deceased, was born March 16, 1904, and died December 16, 1904.

The act of Congress approved March 3, 1905, (33 Stats., 1048), provides:

"That the Commission to the Five Civilized Tribes is authorized for sixty days after the date of the approval of this act to receive and consider applications for enrollments, <u>of children, born subsequent to May twenty-fifth, nineteen hundred and one, and prior to March fourth, nineteen hundred and five, and living on said latter date,</u> to citizens of the Creek tribe of Indians whose enrollment has been approved by the Secretary of the Interior prior to the approval of this act; and to enroll and make allotments to such children."

It is, therefore, ordered that the application for the enrollment of   as a citizen by blood of the Creek Nation be, and the same is, hereby dismissed.

                                                            (Name Illegible) Commissioner.

Muskogee, Indian Territory.
JAN 4 1907

                                                                        NC 113.
Muskogee, Indian Territory, May 18, 1905.

Johnson Martin,
    Weer, Indian Territory.

Dear Sir:

In the matter of the application for the enrollment of your minor child, Lovey Martin, as a citizen of the Creek Nation, you are advised that the Commission requires the affidavit of the midwife or physician in attendance at the birth of said child.

There is herewith enclosed a blank form of birth affidavit, and in executing same care should be exercised to see that all blanks are properly filled, all names written in full

Applications for Enrollment of Creek Newborn
Act of 1905   Volume II

and in the event that the person signing the affidavit is unable to write, signature by mark must be attested by two witnesses. Each affidavit must be executed before a Notary Public and the notarial seal and signature of the officer must be attached to each separate affidavit.

                Respectfully,

BC.   Chairman.

DEPARTMENT OF THE INTERIOR,
COMMISSIONER TO THE FIVE CIVILIZED TRIBES.

REFER IN REPLY TO THE FOLLOWING:
N.C. 113.

                Muskogee, Indian Territory, **August 4, 1905.**

Johnson Martin,
    Weer, Indian Territory.

Dear Sir:

    You are hereby advised that on **July 28, 1905**, the Secretary of the Interior approved the enrollment of your minor child, **Loney Martin**, as a citizen by blood of the **Creek** Nation, and that the name of said child appears upon the roll of new born citizens of the **Creek** Nation as Number **74**.

    The child is now entitled to an allotment, and application therefor should be made without delay at the Land Office for the Nation in which the prospective allotment is located.

    An entire allotment for said child must be selected at the time of the original application.

                Respectively,

                              Commissioner.

                            NC 114.

                Muskogee, Indian Territory, May 18, 1905.

Benton Callahan,
    Morse, Indian Territory.

Dear Sir:

Applications for Enrollment of Creek Newborn
Act of 1905   Volume II

In the matter of the application for the enrollment of your minor child, Sam Callahan, as a citizen of the Creek Nation, you are advised that the Commission requires your affidavit as to the birth of said child.

There is herewith enclosed a blank form of birth affidavit, and in executing same care should be exercised to see that all blanks are properly filled, all names written in full and in the event that the person signing the affidavit is unable to write, signature by mark must be attested by two witnesses. Each affidavit must be executed before a Notary Public and the notarial seal and signature of the officer must be attached to each separate affidavit.

Respectfully,

BC. Chairman.

Muskogee, Indian Territory,
June 24, 1905.

The Honorable Commission
    to the Five Civilized Tribes,
        Muskogee, Indian Territory.

Gentlemen:-

This certifies that I solemnized the rites of matrimony between S. B. Callahan, Jr., to Miss Secelia Sweeney on the _____ day of _____, 1887, and that I am an ordained minister of the M. E. Church, South.

Respectfully,

Theo. F. Brewer

BIRTH AFFIDAVIT.

DEPARTMENT OF THE INTERIOR.
COMMISSION TO THE FIVE CIVILIZED TRIBES.

IN RE APPLICATION FOR ENROLLMENT, as a citizen of the CREEK Nation, of Sam Callahan, born on the 21 day of Oct, 1902

Name of Father: Benton Callahan	a citizen of the Creek	Nation.
Name of Mother: Cecilia "	a citizen of the U. S.	Nation.

Postoffice   Morse, I.T.

Applications for Enrollment of Creek Newborn
Act of 1905 Volume II

AFFIDAVIT OF MOTHER.

UNITED STATES OF AMERICA, Indian Territory,
WESTERN DISTRICT.

    I, Cecilia Callahan, on oath state that I am 38 years of age and a citizen by -----, of the U. S. Nation; that I am the lawful wife of Benton Callahan, who is a citizen, by blood of the Creek Nation; that a male child was born to me on 21 day of Oct, 1902, that said child has been named Sam Callahan, and is now living.

                                  Cecelia Callahan

Witnesses To Mark:
{

    Subscribed and sworn to before me this 10 day of March, 1905.

                                   Edw C Griesel
                                       Notary Public.

AFFIDAVIT OF ATTENDING PHYSICIAN OR MID-WIFE.

UNITED STATES OF AMERICA, Indian Territory,
    Western DISTRICT.

    I, J.O. Callahan, a physician, on oath state that I attended on Mrs. Cecilia Callahan, wife of Benton Callahan on the 21 day of Oct, 1902 ; that there was born to her on said date a male child; that said child is now living and is said to have been named Sam Callahan.

                                   J.O. Callahan, M.D.

Witnesses To Mark:
{

    Subscribed and sworn to before me this 10 day of March, 1905.

                                   Edw C Griesel
                                     Notary Public.

BIRTH AFFIDAVIT.

DEPARTMENT OF THE INTERIOR.
COMMISSION TO THE FIVE CIVILIZED TRIBES.

    IN RE APPLICATION FOR ENROLLMENT, as a citizen of the Creek Nation, of Sam Callahan, born on the 21 day of Oct, 1902

Applications for Enrollment of Creek Newborn
Act of 1905   Volume II

Name of Father: Benton Callahan   a citizen of the   Creek   Nation.
Name of Mother: Cecilia Callahan   a citizen of the   U. S. A.   Nation.

Postoffice   Morse, I.T.

AFFIDAVIT OF ~~MOTHER~~. father

UNITED STATES OF AMERICA, Indian Territory, }
Western   DISTRICT.

I, Benton Callahan , on oath state that I am 39 years of age and a citizen by Blood , of the Creek Nation; that I am the lawful ~~wife~~ Husband of Cecelia Callahan , who is a citizen, by *(blank)* of the United States ~~Nation~~; that a male child was born to ~~me~~ her on 21 day of Oct , 1902 , that said child has been named Sam Callahan , and is now living.

Benton Callahan

Witnesses To Mark:
{

Subscribed and sworn to before me this 23 day of may, 1905.

My Commission Expires March 5th, 1908   C. C. Eskridge
Notary Public.

BIRTH AFFIDAVIT.
DEPARTMENT OF THE INTERIOR.
COMMISSION TO THE FIVE CIVILIZED TRIBES.

IN RE APPLICATION FOR ENROLLMENT, as a citizen of the CREEK Nation, of Archibald McKinnon , born on the 16 day of March , 1904

Name of Father: R. W. McKinnon   a citizen of the   U. S.   Nation.
Name of Mother: Amanda S. "   a citizen of the   Creek   Nation.

Postoffice   Morris, I.T.

AFFIDAVIT OF MOTHER.

UNITED STATES OF AMERICA, Indian Territory, }
   WESTERN   DISTRICT.

I, Amanda S. McKinnon , on oath state that I am 23 years of age and a citizen by blood , of the Creek Nation; that I am the lawful wife of R W McKinnon , who is a

Applications for Enrollment of Creek Newborn
Act of 1905   Volume II

citizen, by ----- of the U. S. Nation; that a male child was born to me on 16 day of March, 1904 , that said child has been named Archibald McKinnon , and is now living. died Nov. 4-1904

Amanda S. McKinnon

Witnesses To Mark:
{

Subscribed and sworn to before me this 9 day of March , 1905.

Edw C Griesel
Notary Public.

NC 113   JLD
DEPARTMENT OF THE INTERIOR,
COMMISSIONER TO THE FIVE CIVILIZED TRIBES.
....

In the matter of the application for the enrollment of Archibald McKinnon, deceased, as a citizen by blood of the Creek Nation.
....

STATEMENT AND ORDER.

The record in this case shows that on March 9, 1905, application was made, in affidavit form, for the enrollment of Archibald McKinnon, deceased, as a citizen by blood of the Creek Nation, under the provisions of the act of Congress approved March 3, 1905.

It appears that the affidavit filed in this matter that said Archibald McKinnon, deceased, was born March 16, 1904, and died November 4, 1904.

The act of Congress approved March 3, 1905, (33 Stats., 1048), provides:

"That the Commission to the Five Civilized Tribes is authorized for sixty days after the date of the approval of this act to receive and consider applications for enrollment, of children, <u>born subsequent to May twenty-fifth, nineteen hundred and one, and prior to March fourth, nineteen hundred and five, and living on said latter date</u>, to citizens of the Creek tribe of Indians whose enrollment has been approved by the Secretary of the Interior prior to the approval of this act; and to enroll and make allotments to such children."

It is, therefore, ordered that the application for the enrollment of Archibald McKinnon as a citizen by blood of the Creek Nation be, and the same is, hereby dismissed.

(Name Illegible) Commissioner.

Muskogee, Indian Territory.
JAN 4 1907

Applications for Enrollment of Creek Newborn
Act of 1905 Volume II

United States of America,
Indian Territory, Western District.

    W.C. Mitchener, of lawful age, being first duly sworn on his oath states;

    That he is a practising[sic] phisician[sic], located in the town of Okmulgee Indian Territory, and that he attended Mrs. Amanda S. McKinnon, formerly Amanda S. Ashley, during confinement on the 25th., day of July, 1901[sic], at which time a girl child was born.

    He further states, that the said child is now living, and that her name is Lila Bell McKinnon.

                                 W. C. Mitchener MD

Subscribed and sworn to before me this IIth[sic]., day of March, 1905[sic].

                                 (Name Illegible)
                                       Notary Public.
My Commission expires Aug. Ist., 1906.

BIRTH AFFIDAVIT.

DEPARTMENT OF THE INTERIOR.
COMMISSION TO THE FIVE CIVILIZED TRIBES.

    IN RE APPLICATION FOR ENROLLMENT, as a citizen of the CREEK Nation, of Lila Belle McKinnon, born on the 25 day of July, 1901

Name of Father: R. W. McKinnon   a citizen of the U. S.   Nation.
Name of Mother: Amanda S. McKinnon   a citizen of the Creek   Nation.

                          Postoffice   Morris, I.T.

(Child present) HGH

AFFIDAVIT OF MOTHER.

UNITED STATES OF AMERICA, Indian Territory,
    WESTERN   DISTRICT.

    I, Amanda S. McKinnon, on oath state that I am 23 years of age and a citizen by blood, of the Creek Nation; that I am the lawful wife of R W McKinnon, who is a citizen, by ----- of the U. S. Nation; that a female child was born to me on 25 day of July, 1901, that said child has been named Lila Belle McKinnon, and is now living.

                                 Amanda S. McKinnon

Witnesses To Mark:

Applications for Enrollment of Creek Newborn
Act of 1905   Volume II

Subscribed and sworn to before me this 9 day of March, 1905.

                                        Edw C Griesel
                                        Notary Public.

DEPARTMENT OF THE INTERIOR,
COMMISSIONER TO THE FIVE CIVILIZED TRIBES.

REFER IN REPLY TO THE FOLLOWING:
N.C. 116.

                          Muskogee, Indian Territory, **August 4, 1905.**

Daniel B. Smith,
    Haskell, Indian Territory.

Dear Sir:

    You are hereby advised that on **July 28, 1905**, the Secretary of the Interior approved the enrollment of your minor child, **Ruth Smith**, as a citizen by blood of the **Creek** Nation, and that the name of said child appears upon the roll of new born citizens of the **Creek** Nation as Number **76**.

    The child is now entitled to an allotment, and application therefor should be made without delay at the Land Office for the Nation in which the prospective allotment is located.

    An entire allotment for said child must be selected at the time of the original application.

                                Respectively,

                                              Commissioner.

BIRTH AFFIDAVIT.

DEPARTMENT OF THE INTERIOR.
COMMISSION TO THE FIVE CIVILIZED TRIBES.

    IN RE APPLICATION FOR ENROLLMENT, as a citizen of the Creek Nation, of Ruth Smith, born on the 23 day of Dec, 1902.

Name of Father: Daniel B. Smith   a citizen of the   Creek   Nation.
Name of Mother: Mary I.   "   a citizen of the   "   Nation.

                            Postoffice   Haskell, I.T.

Applications for Enrollment of Creek Newborn
Act of 1905 Volume II

Child present Gr

AFFIDAVIT OF MOTHER.

UNITED STATES OF AMERICA, Indian Territory, }
Western   DISTRICT.

I, Mary I. Smith, on oath state that I am 31 years of age and a citizen by blood, of the Creek Nation; that I am the lawful wife of Daniel B Smith, who is a citizen, by blood of the Creek Nation; that a Female child was born to me on 23 day of Dec, 1902, that said child has been named Ruth Smith, and is now living.

Mary I Smith

Witnesses To Mark:

Subscribed and sworn to before me this 17 day of March, 1905.

Edw C Griesel
Notary Public.

AFFIDAVIT OF ATTENDING PHYSICIAN OR MID-WIFE.

UNITED STATES OF AMERICA, Indian Territory, }
Western   DISTRICT.

I, Augusta R. Moore, a Mid Wife, on oath state that I attended on Mrs. Mary I Smith, wife of Daniel Smith on the 23 day of Dec, 1902; that there was born to her on said date a Female child; that said child is now living and is said to have been named Ruth Smith.

Augusta R. Moore

Witnesses To Mark:

Subscribed and sworn to before me this 17 day of March, 1905.

Edw C Griesel
Notary Public.

BIRTH AFFIDAVIT.

DEPARTMENT OF THE INTERIOR.
COMMISSION TO THE FIVE CIVILIZED TRIBES.

IN RE APPLICATION FOR ENROLLMENT, as a citizen of the CREEK Nation, of Ruth Smith, born on the 23 day of Dec, 1902

Applications for Enrollment of Creek Newborn
Act of 1905 Volume II

Name of Father: Daniel B. Smith   a citizen of the Creek Nation.
Name of Mother: Mary I "   a citizen of the " Nation.

Postoffice   Haskell, I.T.

AFFIDAVIT OF ~~MOTHER~~. Father

UNITED STATES OF AMERICA, Indian Territory,
WESTERN DISTRICT.

I, Daniel B. Smith, on oath state that I am 45 years of age and a citizen by blood, of the Creek Nation; that I am the lawful ~~wife~~ hus of Mary I Smith, who is a citizen, by blood of the Creek Nation; that a female child was born to me on 23 day of Dec, 1902, that said child has been named Ruth mith, and is now living.

                      Daniel B Smith

Witnesses To Mark:

Subscribed and sworn to before me this 10 day of March, 1905.

                      Edw C Griesel
                      Notary Public.

DEPARTMENT OF THE INTERIOR,
COMMISSIONER TO THE FIVE CIVILIZED TRIBES.

REFER IN REPLY TO THE FOLLOWING:
N.C. 117.

Muskogee, Indian Territory, **August 4, 1905.**

Mary I. Cable,
     Care of Adam M. Cable,
         Morris, Indian Territory.

Dear Madam:

     You are hereby advised that on **July 28, 1905**, the Secretary of the Interior approved the enrollment of your minor child, **Virgie Plimmer Cable**, as a citizen by blood of the **Creek** Nation, and that the name of said child appears upon the roll of new born citizens of the **Creek** Nation as Number **77**.

     The child is now entitled to an allotment, and application therefor should be made without delay at the Land Office for the Nation in which the prospective allotment is located.

Applications for Enrollment of Creek Newborn
Act of 1905   Volume II

An entire allotment for said child must be selected at the time of the original application.

Respectively,

Commissioner.

BIRTH AFFIDAVIT.

DEPARTMENT OF THE INTERIOR.
COMMISSION TO THE FIVE CIVILIZED TRIBES.

IN RE APPLICATION FOR ENROLLMENT, as a citizen of the CREEK Nation, of Virgie Plimmer Cable, born on the 26 day of Nov., 1904

Name of Father: Adam M. Cable   a citizen of the   U. S.   Nation.
Name of Mother: Mary I. Cable   a citizen of the   Creek   Nation.

Postoffice   Morris, I.T.

(Child present)

AFFIDAVIT OF MOTHER.

UNITED STATES OF AMERICA, Indian Territory, ⎫
    WESTERN   DISTRICT.   ⎭

I, Mary I. Cable, on oath state that I am 29 years of age and a citizen by blood, of the Creek   Nation; that I am the lawful wife of Adam M. Cable, who is a citizen, by ----- of the U. S. Nation; that a female child was born to me on 26 day of Nov., 1904, that said child has been named Virgie Plimmer Cable, and is now living.

Mary I. Cable

Witnesses To Mark:
{

Subscribed and sworn to before me this 9 day of March, 1905.

Edw C Griesel
Notary Public.

AFFIDAVIT OF ATTENDING PHYSICIAN OR MID-WIFE.

UNITED STATES OF AMERICA, Indian Territory, ⎫
    WESTERN   DISTRICT.   ⎭

I, John Lee, a Physician, on oath state that I attended on Mrs. Mary I Cable, wife of Adam M. Cable on the 26 day of Nov, 1904; that there was born to her on

Applications for Enrollment of Creek Newborn
Act of 1905   Volume II

said date a Female child; that said child is now living and is said to have been named Virgie Plimmer Cable .

Dr. John Lee

Witnesses To Mark:
{

Subscribed and sworn to before me this 9 day of March, 1905.

Edw C Griesel
Notary Public.

DEPARTMENT OF THE INTERIOR,
COMMISSIONER TO THE FIVE CIVILIZED TRIBES.

REFER IN REPLY TO THE FOLLOWING:
N.C. 118.

Muskogee, Indian Territory, **August 4, 1905.**

Sarty Cowe,
Wetumka[sic], Indian Territory.

Dear Sir:

You are hereby advised that on **July 28, 1905**, the Secretary of the Interior approved the enrollment of your minor child, **Effa Cowe**, as a citizen by blood of the **Creek** Nation, and that the name of said child appears upon the roll of new born citizens of the **Creek** Nation as Number **78**.

The child is now entitled to an allotment, and application therefor should be made without delay at the Land Office for the Nation in which the prospective allotment is located.

An entire allotment for said child must be selected at the time of the original application.

Respectively,

Commissioner.

BIRTH AFFIDAVIT.

DEPARTMENT OF THE INTERIOR.
COMMISSION TO THE FIVE CIVILIZED TRIBES.

IN RE APPLICATION FOR ENROLLMENT, as a citizen of the Creek Nation, of Effa Cowe, born on the 11 day of February, 1903

Applications for Enrollment of Creek Newborn
Act of 1905 Volume II

Name of Father: Sarty Cowe a citizen of the Creek Nation.
Name of Mother: Melinda Cowe a citizen of the Creek Nation.

Postoffice Wetumka[sic]

AFFIDAVIT OF MOTHER.

UNITED STATES OF AMERICA, Indian Territory,
Western DISTRICT.

I, Melinda Cowe , on oath state that I am about 24 years of age and a citizen by blood, of the Creek Nation; that I am the lawful wife of Sarty Cowe , who is a citizen, by blood of the Creek Nation; that a male child was born to me on 11 day of February , 1903 , that said child has been named Effa Cowe , and is now living.

Melinda Cowe

Witnesses To Mark:
{

Subscribed and sworn to before me this 9th day of March , 1905.

(Name Illegible)
My com ex. 7-1-1906 Notary Public.

AFFIDAVIT OF ATTENDING PHYSICIAN OR MID-WIFE.

UNITED STATES OF AMERICA, Indian Territory,
Western DISTRICT.

I, Winey Scott , a Creek Woman , on oath state that I attended on Mrs. Sarty Cowe , wife of Sarty Cowe on the 11 day of February , 1903 ; that there was born to her on said date a male child; that said child is now living and is said to have been named Effa Cowe .

her
Winey x Scott
Witnesses To Mark mark
(Name Illegible)
Phil D. Dunford

Subscribed and sworn to before me this 9 day of March, 1905.

(Name Illegible)
My com ex. 7-1-1906 Notary Public.

Applications for Enrollment of Creek Newborn
Act of 1905 Volume II

NC 119.

Muskogee, Indian Territory, May 18, 1905.

Sam Porter,
    Nordack, Indian Territory.

Dear Sir:

    In the matter of the application for the enrollment of your minor children, L. Ray and Edith P. Porter, as citizens of the Creek Nation, you are advised that the Commission desires the affidavit of the midwife in the former and in the later the affidavits of two disinterested witnesses as to the birth of said children.

    There are herewith enclosed three blank forms of birth affidavit, and in executing same care should be exercised to see that all blanks are properly filled, all names written in full and in the event that the persons signing the affidavits is[sic] unable to write, signatures by mark must be attested by two witnesses. Each affidavit must be executed before a Notary Public and the notarial seal and signature of the officer must be attached to each separate affidavit.

                            Respectfully,

BC.   Chairman.

NC 119.

Muskogee, Indian Territory, June 30, 1905.

Susan Porter,
    Naudac, Indian Territory.

Dear Madam:

    In the matter of the application for the enrollment of your minor children, L. Roy and Edith P. Porter, as citizens of the Creek Nation, you are advised that the Commission requires the affidavit of the midwife or physician in attendance at the birth of L. Roy Porter, and in the case of Edith P. Porter, the affidavits of two disinterested witnesses, is required.

    There are herewith enclosed three blank forms of birth affidavit, and in executing same care should be exercised to see that all blanks are properly filled, all names written in full and in the event that either of the persons signing the affidavits is unable to write, signature by mark must be attested by two witnesses. Each affidavit must be executed before a Notary Public and the notarial seal and signature of the officer must be attached to each separate affidavit.

                            Respectfully,

LM-6-27-91.   Chairman.

Applications for Enrollment of Creek Newborn
Act of 1905 Volume II

BIRTH AFFIDAVIT.

DEPARTMENT OF THE INTERIOR.
COMMISSION TO THE FIVE CIVILIZED TRIBES.

IN RE APPLICATION FOR ENROLLMENT, as a citizen of the Creek Nation, of Edith P. Porter, born on the 20 day of Oct, 1901

Name of Father: Sam Porter   a citizen of the   U. S.   Nation.
Name of Mother: Susan Porter   a citizen of the   Creek   Nation.
                         Postoffice   Naudack

Child Present

AFFIDAVIT OF MOTHER.

UNITED STATES OF AMERICA, Indian Territory,
    Western   DISTRICT.

I, Susan Porter, on oath state that I am 22 years of age and a citizen by blood, of the Creek Nation; that I am the lawful wife of Sam Porter, who is a citizen, by ----- of the U.S. Nation; that a Female child was born to me on 20 day of Oct, 1901, that said child has been named Edith Porter, and is now living.

                                          Susie Porter

Witnesses To Mark:

Subscribed and sworn to before me this 18 day of March, 1905.

                                          Edw C Griesel
                                              Notary Public.

BIRTH AFFIDAVIT.

DEPARTMENT OF THE INTERIOR.
COMMISSION TO THE FIVE CIVILIZED TRIBES.

IN RE APPLICATION FOR ENROLLMENT, as a citizen of the Creek Nation, of Edith P. Porter, born on the 20" day of October, 1901

Name of Father: Sam Porter   a citizen of the   U. S.   Nation.
Name of Mother: Susan   "   a citizen of the   Creek   Nation.

                             Postoffice   Naudack, I.T.

Applications for Enrollment of Creek Newborn
Act of 1905 Volume II

acquaintance
AFFIDAVIT OF <s>MOTHER</s>.

UNITED STATES OF AMERICA, Indian Territory, ⎱
    Western   DISTRICT. ⎰

I, Bosie Scott, on oath state that I am 45 years of age and a citizen by Blood, of the Creek Nation; that I am acquainted with Susan Porter, a Creek citizen the lawful wife of Sam Porter, who is a citizen, by ----- of the U.S. Nation; that a female child was born to <s>me</s> her on 20" day of October, 1901, that said child is said to have <s>has</s> been named Edith P. Porter, <s>and was living March 4, 1905</s>.

Bosie Scott

Witnesses To Mark:
{

Subscribed and sworn to before me this 11th day of July, 1905.

Thomas F. Turner
Notary Public.

---

acquaintance
AFFIDAVIT OF <s>ATTENDING PHYSICIAN OR MID-WIFE</s>.

UNITED STATES OF AMERICA, Indian Territory, ⎱
    Western   DISTRICT. ⎰

                                                              know

I, T. M. Siler, an acquaintance, on oath state that I <s>attended on</s> Mrs. Susan Porter, wife of Sam Porter on the 20" day of October, 1901; <s>that</s> there was born to her on said date a female child; that said child was living March 4, 1905, and is said to have been named Edith P. Porter.

T M Siler

Witnesses To Mark:
{

Subscribed and sworn to before me this 11th day of July, 1905.

Thos F. Turner
Notary Public.

BIRTH AFFIDAVIT.

DEPARTMENT OF THE INTERIOR.
COMMISSION TO THE FIVE CIVILIZED TRIBES.

IN RE APPLICATION FOR ENROLLMENT, as a citizen of the Creek Nation, of L. Ray Porter, born on the 5 day of Aug, 1903

Applications for Enrollment of Creek Newborn
Act of 1905   Volume II

Name of Father: Sam Porter   a citizen of the   U. S.   Nation.
Name of Mother: Susan   "   a citizen of the   Creek   Nation.

                              Postoffice   Naudack

Child Present

AFFIDAVIT OF MOTHER.

UNITED STATES OF AMERICA, Indian Territory, ⎫
   Western   DISTRICT. ⎭

    I, Susan Porter , on oath state that I am 22 years of age and a citizen by blood , of the Creek Nation; that I am the lawful wife of Sam Porter , who is a citizen, by ----- of the U.S. Nation; that a male child was born to me on 5 day of Aug , 1903 , that said child has been named L. Ray Porter , and is now living.

                              Susie Porter

Witnesses To Mark:
{

    Subscribed and sworn to before me this 18 day of March , 1905.

                              Edw C Griesel
                                  Notary Public.

BIRTH AFFIDAVIT.

DEPARTMENT OF THE INTERIOR.
COMMISSION TO THE FIVE CIVILIZED TRIBES.

    IN RE APPLICATION FOR ENROLLMENT, as a citizen of the Creek Nation, of L. Ray Porter, born on the 5" day of August , 1903

Name of Father: Sam Porter   a citizen of the   U. S.   Nation.
Name of Mother: Susan Porter   a citizen of the   Creek   Nation.

                              Postoffice   Naudack, I.T.

AFFIDAVIT OF ~~MOTHER~~.
                              disinterested party

UNITED STATES OF AMERICA, Indian Territory, ⎫
   Western   DISTRICT. ⎭

    I, Henry Baker, on oath state that I am acquainted with Susan Porter ~~years of age and a citizen~~ by blood , of the Creek Nation; that she is the lawful wife of Sam Porter, who is a citizen, by ----- of the U.S. Nation; that a male child was born to ~~me~~ her on

Applications for Enrollment of Creek Newborn
Act of 1905   Volume II

or about 5" day of August, 1903, that said child has been named L. Ray Porter, and was living March 4, 1905. further I have no interest in this case and am no kin to the parties herein

Henry Baker

Witnesses To Mark:
{ H G Johnston
  R A Robertson

    Subscribed and sworn to before me this 7th day of July, 1905.
    My com exp
    Feb 12 - 1908   E. F. Cooledge
                                            Notary Public.

acquaintance
AFFIDAVIT OF <s>ATTENDING PHYSICIAN OR MID-WIFE</s>.

UNITED STATES OF AMERICA, Indian Territory, ⎫
    Western   DISTRICT.   ⎬
                                 ⎭

    I, Millie Baker, an acquaintance, on oath state that I <s>attended on</s> know Mrs. Susan Porter, wife of Sam Porter & on or about the 5" day of August, 1903; that there was born to her on said date a male child; that said child was living March 4, 1905, and is said to have been named L. Ray Porter. further am no kin to parties herein nor have I any interest in this case.

her
Millie x Baker
mark

Witnesses To Mark:
{ Henry Baker
  H G Johnston

    Subscribed and sworn to before me this 7th day of July, 1905.
    My com exp
    Feb 12 - 1908   E. F. Cooledge
                                            Notary Public.

BIRTH AFFIDAVIT.

DEPARTMENT OF THE INTERIOR.
COMMISSION TO THE FIVE CIVILIZED TRIBES.

    IN RE APPLICATION FOR ENROLLMENT, as a citizen of the Creek Nation, of Edith P. Porter, born on the *(blank)* day of *(blank)*, 1901

Name of Father: Sam. N. Porter   a <s>citizen of the</s> non-citizen   Nation.
Name of Mother: Susan Porter   a citizen of the   Creek   Nation.

Postoffice   Naudack, I.T.

Applications for Enrollment of Creek Newborn
Act of 1905 Volume II

AFFIDAVIT OF MOTHER.

UNITED STATES OF AMERICA, Indian Territory, }
   Western   DISTRICT.

    I, Susan N. Porter, on oath state that I am 22 years of age and a citizen by blood, of the Creek Nation; that I am the lawful wife of Sam N. Porter, who is a ~~citizen by~~ non-citizen ~~of the (blank) Nation~~; that a female child was born to me on 20 day of October, 1901, that said child has been named Edith P. Porter, and was living March 4, 1905.

                                    Susan N Porter

Witnesses To Mark:
   { S. A. Mantooth
   { J L. Schad

    Subscribed and sworn to before me this 13th day of June, 1905.

                                  E E Riley
My commission expires June 18-1908   Notary Public.

United States of America,)
   Indian Territory,   )ss.
Western Judicial District.)

    Aaron Turnbow and Wm. Baker, being by me, the undersigned authority first duly sworn, on their oaths, each separately states, as follows, to-wit:
    I am acquainted with Sam. Porter and with Susan Porter, his wife, and know that she is a Citizen of the Creek Nation, and that lands have been allotted to her in said Nation. I am acquainted with the family of Sam. and Susan Porter, and know that they have one child Edith P. Porter about the age of four years, and one child L. Ray Porter about two years of age. I know that both of the said children are now living. I am not interested in the application made for the enrollment of the said children. I have been acquainted with Mr. and Mrs. Porter and their family for at least five years. And the said Wm. Baker says that is post office address is Naudak, I.T. and the said Aaron Turnbow says that his post office address is Checotah, I.T.; and further affiants sayeth not.

                                  Aaron Turnbow
                                  Wm Baker

Subscribed and sworn to before me his 10 day of June, 1905.

                                  E.E. Riley
                                  Notary Public.

My commission will expire ~~5/26-07~~.
                 June 18-1908

Applications for Enrollment of Creek Newborn
Act of 1905 Volume II

BIRTH AFFIDAVIT.

DEPARTMENT OF THE INTERIOR.
COMMISSION TO THE FIVE CIVILIZED TRIBES.

IN RE APPLICATION FOR ENROLLMENT, as a citizen of the Creek Nation, of L. Ray Porter, born on the 5th day of August, 1903

Name of Father:	Sam. N. Porter	a ~~citizen of the~~ non-citizen	~~Nation.~~
Name of Mother:	Susan Porter	a citizen of the Creek	Nation.

Postoffice   Naudack, I.T.

AFFIDAVIT OF MOTHER.

UNITED STATES OF AMERICA, Indian Territory,
    Western   DISTRICT.

I, Susan N. Porter, on oath state that I am 22 years of age and a citizen by blood, of the Creek Nation; that I am the lawful wife of Sam. N. Porter, who is a ~~citizen by~~ non-citizen ~~of the~~ *(blank)* ~~Nation~~; that a male child was born to me on 5th day of August, 1903, that said child has been named L. Ray Porter, and was living March 4, 1905.

                                          x   Susan N Porter

Witnesses To Mark:
    { S. A. Mantooth
      J L. Schad

Subscribed and sworn to before me this 13th day of June, 1905.

                                     E E Riley
My commission expires June 18-1905[sic]   Notary Public.

BIRTH AFFIDAVIT.

DEPARTMENT OF THE INTERIOR.
COMMISSION TO THE FIVE CIVILIZED TRIBES.

IN RE APPLICATION FOR ENROLLMENT, as a citizen of the Creek Nation, of Elsie B. Jacobs, born on the 3rd day of Sept., 1904

Name of Father:	John A. Jacobs	a citizen of the Creek Nation.
Name of Mother:	Mary Jacobs	a citizen of the United States Nation.

Postoffice   Holdenville, I.T.

Applications for Enrollment of Creek Newborn
Act of 1905   Volume II

AFFIDAVIT OF MOTHER.

UNITED STATES OF AMERICA, Indian Territory,
   Western   DISTRICT.

I, Mary Jacobs , on oath state that I am 30 years of age and a citizen by blood , of the U.S. ~~Nation~~; that I am the lawful wife of John A. Jacobs , who is a citizen, by blood of the Creek Nation; that a Female child was born to me on 3rd day of Sept , 190 , that said child has been named Elsie B. Jacobs , and was living March 4, 1905.

Mary Jacobs

Witnesses To Mark:
{

Subscribed and sworn to before me this 25th day of May , 1905.

My com. ex. May 16-1908   L M Miller
                                                         Notary Public.

AFFIDAVIT OF ATTENDING PHYSICIAN OR MID-WIFE.

UNITED STATES OF AMERICA, Indian Territory,
   Western   DISTRICT.

I, Nellie Ellis , a midwife , on oath state that I attended on Mrs. Mary Jacobs , wife of John A. Jacobs   on the 3rd day of Sept , 1904 ; that there was born to her on said date a Female child; that said child was living March 4, 1905, and is said to have been named Elsie B. Jacobs .

Nellie Ellis

Witnesses To Mark:
{

Subscribed and sworn to before me this 25th day of May , 1905.

My com. ex. May 16" 1908   L M Miller
                                                         Notary Public.

Applications for Enrollment of Creek Newborn
Act of 1905 Volume II

SUPPLEMENTAL PROOF.

DEPARTMENT OF THE INTERIOR,
COMMISSION TO THE FIVE CIVILIZED TRIBES.

IN RE Application for Enrollment, as a citizen of the Creek (or Muskogee) Nation, of Elsey B. Jacobs, born on the 3rd day of September, 1904

Name of Father: John A. Jacobs   a citizen of the   Creek   Nation.
Name of Mother: Mary Jacobs   a citizen of the   U.S.   Nation.

Postoffice   Holdenville, I.T.

AFFIDAVIT OF PARENT.
(To be made if child is now living)

UNITED STATES OF AMERICA,
   Indian Territory,
Western   DISTRICT.

    I, John A. Jacobs, on oath state that I am 33 years of age and a citizen by Blood, of the Creek (or Muskogee) Nation; that I am the Father of Elsey B. Jacobs a Female child who was born on the 3 day of September, 1904, that said child is now living.

                                      John A. Jacobs

Witnesses To Mark:
{

Subscribed and sworn to before me this 9th *day of* March, *190*5.

                               L.M. Miller
                                       Notary Public.

AFFIDAVIT OF ~~PARENT~~.

UNITED STATES OF AMERICA,
   Indian Territory,
Western   DISTRICT.

    I, Sam H. Miller, on oath state that I am 36 years of age and a citizen by Blood, of the Creek (or Muskogee) Nation; that I am the Relative of Elsey B. Jacobs a Female child who was born on the 3 day of September, 1904, that said child ~~died~~ now living on ~~the day of, 190~~.

                                      Sam H. Miller

Witnesses To Mark:
{

Applications for Enrollment of Creek Newborn
Act of 1905 Volume II

Subscribed and sworn to before me this 9th *day of* March, *1905*.

L.M. Miller
Notary Public.

NC 120.
Muskogee, Indian Territory, May 18 1905.

John A. Jacobs,
 Holdenville, Indian Territory.

Dear Sir:

In the matter of the application for the enrollment of your minor child, Elsey B. Jacobs, as a citizen of the Creek Nation, you are advised that the Commission requires the affidavits of the mother and midwife or physician in attendance at the birth of said child.

There is herewith enclosed a blank form of birth affidavit, and in executing same care should be exercised to see that all blanks are properly filled, all names written in full and in the event that either of the persons signing the affidavit is unable to write, signature by mark must be attested by two witnesses. Each affidavit must be executed before a Notary Public and the notarial seal and signature of the officer must be attached to each separate affidavit.

Respectfully,

BC. Chairman.

NC 121.

Muskogee, Indian Territory, May 18, 1905.

Ned Sarty,
 Coweta, Indian Territory. Indian.

Dear Sir:

In the matter of the application for the enrollment of your minor child, Mamie Sarty, as a citizen of the Creek Nation, you are advised that the Commission requires the affidavit of the midwife or physician in attendance at the birth of said child.

There is herewith enclosed a blank form of birth affidavit, and in executing same care should be exercised to see that all blanks are properly filled, all names written in full and in the event that the person signing the affidavit is unable to write, signature by mark

Applications for Enrollment of Creek Newborn
Act of 1905   Volume II

must be attested by two witnesses. Each affidavit must be executed before a Notary Public and the notarial seal and signature of the officer must be attached to each separate affidavit.

          Respectfully,

BC.   Chairman.

BIRTH AFFIDAVIT.

DEPARTMENT OF THE INTERIOR.
COMMISSION TO THE FIVE CIVILIZED TRIBES.

  IN RE APPLICATION FOR ENROLLMENT, as a citizen of the Creek Nation, of Alfred Sarty, born on the 7 day of March, 1904

Name of Father: Ned Sarty	a citizen of the Creek	Nation.
Name of Mother: Eliza Sarty	a citizen of the Creek	Nation.

         Postoffice Coweta

      AFFIDAVIT OF MOTHER.

UNITED STATES OF AMERICA, Indian Territory, ⎱
  Western   DISTRICT. ⎰

  I, Eliza Sarty, on oath state that I am 23 years of age and a citizen by blood, of the Creek Nation; that I am the lawful wife of Ned Sarty, who is a citizen, by blood of the Creek Nation; that a male child was born to me on 7 day of March, 1904, that said child has been named Alfred Sarty, and ~~is now living~~. Died Dec. 5, 1904

           Her
         Eliza x Sarty
Witnesses To Mark: mark
 { Ned Sarty
 { EC Griesel

  Subscribed and sworn to before me this 10 day of March, 1905.

           Edw C Griesel
            Notary Public.

Applications for Enrollment of Creek Newborn
Act of 1905 Volume II

NC 121   JLD

DEPARTMENT OF THE INTERIOR,
COMMISSIONER TO THE FIVE CIVILIZED TRIBES.

....

In the matter of the application for the enrollment of Alfred Sarty, deceased, as a citizen by blood of the Creek Nation.

....

STATEMENT AND ORDER.

The record in this case shows that on March 10, 1905, application was made, in affidavit form, for the enrollment of Alfred Sarty, deceased, as a citizen by blood of the Creek Nation, under the provisions of the act of Congress approved March 3, 1905.

It appears from the affidavit filed in this matter that said Alfred Sarty, deceased, was born March 7, 1904, and died December 5, 1904.

The act of Congress approved March 3, 1905, (33 Stats., 1048), provides:

"That the Commission to the Five Civilized Tribes is authorized for sixty days after the date of the approval of this act to receive and consider applications for enrollment, of children, <u>born subsequent to May twenty-fifth, nineteen hundred and one, and prior to March fourth, nineteen hundred and five, and living on said latter date,</u> to citizens of the Creek tribe of Indians whose enrollment has been approved by the Secretary of the Interior prior to the approval of this act; and to enroll and make allotments to such children."

It is, therefore, ordered that the application for the enrollment of Alfred Sarty, deceased, as a citizen by blood of the Creek Nation is hereby dismissed.

                                          (Name Illegible) Commissioner.

Muskogee, Indian Territory.
JAN 4 1907

BIRTH AFFIDAVIT.

DEPARTMENT OF THE INTERIOR.
COMMISSION TO THE FIVE CIVILIZED TRIBES.

      IN RE APPLICATION FOR ENROLLMENT, as a citizen of the Creek Nation, of Mamie Sarty, born on the 2 day of July, 1902

Name of Father: Ned Sarty	a citizen of the	Creek	Nation.
Name of Mother: Eliza Sarty	a citizen of the	Creek	Nation.

                                    Postoffice   Coweta, I.T.

Applications for Enrollment of Creek Newborn
Act of 1905   Volume II

AFFIDAVIT OF ~~MOTHER~~. father

UNITED STATES OF AMERICA, Indian Territory, ⎫
    Western   DISTRICT. ⎭

    I, Ned Sarty, on oath state that I am 28 years of age and a citizen by blood, of the Creek Nation; that I am the lawful ~~wife~~ Husband of Eliza Sarty, who is a citizen, by blood of the Creek Nation; that a Female child was born to me on 2 day of July, 1902, that said child has been named Mamie Sarty, and is now living.

                                            Ned Sarty

Witnesses To Mark:
{

    Subscribed and sworn to before me this 10 day of March, 1905.

                                            Edw C Griesel
                                                Notary Public.

BIRTH AFFIDAVIT.

DEPARTMENT OF THE INTERIOR.
COMMISSION TO THE FIVE CIVILIZED TRIBES.

    IN RE APPLICATION FOR ENROLLMENT, as a citizen of the Creek Nation, of Mamie Sarty, born on the 2nd day of July, 1902

Name of Father: Ned Sarty   a citizen of the   Creek   Nation.
Name of Mother: Eliza Sarty, nee McCellop   a citizen of the Creek   Nation.

                          Postoffice   Coweta, I.T.

AFFIDAVIT OF MOTHER.

UNITED STATES OF AMERICA, Indian Territory, ⎫
    Western   DISTRICT. ⎭

    I, Eliza Sarty, on oath state that I am 24 years of age and a citizen by birth, of the Creek Nation; that I am the lawful wife of Ned Sarty, who is a citizen, by birth of the Creek Nation; that a female child was born to me on 2nd day of July, 1902, that said child has been named Mamie Sarty, and was living March 4, 1905.

                                            her
                                       Eliza x Sarty
Witnesses To Mark: mark
    { Joe *(Illegible)*
      B.F. Hughes

Applications for Enrollment of Creek Newborn
Act of 1905 Volume II

Subscribed and sworn to before me this 23rd day of May , 1905.

                            R.C. Allen
My Com. Ex. Mch. 15, 1908   Notary Public.

AFFIDAVIT OF ATTENDING PHYSICIAN OR MID-WIFE.

UNITED STATES OF AMERICA, Indian Territory, }
    Western   DISTRICT.

    I, Suzan Sarty , a mid-wife , on oath state that I attended on Mrs. Eliza Sarty , wife of Ned Sarty on the 2nd day of July , 1902 ; that there was born to her on said date a female child; that said child was living March 4, 1905, and is said to have been named Mamie Sarty .
                                                  her
                                         Suzan x Sarty
Witnesses To Mark: mark
{ Joe *(Illegible)*
{ B.F. Hughes

Subscribed and sworn to before me this 223rd day of May, 1905.

                            R.C. Allen
My Com. Ex. Mch. 15, 1908   Notary Public.

                                                        Cr NC-123
DEPARTMENT OF THE INTERIOR,
COMMISSIONER TO THE FIVE CIVILIZED TRIBES.

Muskogee, Indian Territory, July 19, 1905

    In the matter of the application for the enrollment of Gusta A. Hodge as a citizen by blood of the Creek Nation.

    Minnie L. Hodge, being duly sworn, testified as follows:

EXAMINATION BY THE COMMISSIONER:
Q What is your name? A Minnie L. Hodge.
Q What is your age? A 28.
Q What is your postoffice address? A Tulsa.
Q You are not a citizen of any tribe in Indian Territory? A No sir.
Q What is the name of this child you have here with you? A Gusta A. Hodge.
Q When was Gusta born? A The 21st day of August, 1902.
Q How old will she be the 21st of next month? A Theree[sic] years old.

Applications for Enrollment of Creek Newborn
Act of 1905 Volume II

Q How has it come that you made that affidavit here and stated that she was born the 12th of August, 1903? A I did not tell them; I told them the 21st of August, 1902—no, 1901. I made a mistake in one year.
Q And he made a mistake in the day? A Yes sir.
Q You signed it yourself, you know? A Yes sir.
Q You did not read it before you signed it? A When we went to sign the name, he liked to forgot me signing it.
Q Who was the midwife? A She was my mother.
Q Her name is--? A F—or Frances Wimberly.
Q The same mistake was made in her affidavit as it was in yours? A Yes sir.

John N Hodge, being duly sworn, testified as follows:

EXAMINATION BY THE COMMISSIONER:
Q What is your name? A John N. Hodge.
Q Are you a citizen of the Creek Nation? A Yes sir.
Q How old are you? A Thirty years old in June.
Q What is your father's name? A Alvin T. Hodge.
Q Mr. Hodge, you made affidavit before the Commission in which you state that this child was born in May, 1902; was that the correct month? A No sir; I said "about".
Q Since talking to your wife and thinking it over, you concluded it was born August 21, 1902? A Yes sir.
Q Is this your child? A Yes sir.

INDIAN TERRITORY, Western District.
I, J. Y. Miller, a stenographer to the Commissioner to the Five Civilized Tribes, hereby certify that the foregoing is a true and complete translation of my notes as same appear in my stenographic report of this case.

JY Miller

Sworn to and subscribed before me
this 19th day of July, 1905.   Edw C Griesel
Notary Public.

BIRTH AFFIDAVIT.
DEPARTMENT OF THE INTERIOR.
COMMISSION TO THE FIVE CIVILIZED TRIBES.

IN RE APPLICATION FOR ENROLLMENT, as a citizen of the CREEK Nation, of Gusta A. Hodge, born on or about the 25 day of May, 1902

Name of Father:	John N. Hodge	a citizen of the	Creek	Nation.
Name of Mother:	Minnie L. "	a citizen of the	U. S.	Nation.

Postoffice   Tulsa, I.T.

Applications for Enrollment of Creek Newborn
Act of 1905 Volume II

AFFIDAVIT OF ~~MOTHER~~.

UNITED STATES OF AMERICA, Indian Territory,
WESTERN DISTRICT.

I, John N. Hodge, on oath state that I am 29 years of age and a citizen by blood, of the Creek Nation; that I am the lawful ~~wife~~ hus of Minnie L. Hodge, who is a citizen, by ----- of the U.S. Nation; that a female child was born to me on or about 25 day of May, 1902, that said child has been named Gusta A. Hodge, and is now living.

John N. Hodge

Witnesses To Mark:

Subscribed and sworn to before me this 10 day of March, 1905.

Edw C Griesel
Notary Public.

DEPARTMENT OF THE INTERIOR,
COMMISSION TO THE FIVE CIVILIZED TRIBES.

IN RE Application for Enrollment, as a citizen of the Creek Nation, of Gusta A Hodge, born on the 21 day of Aug, 1902

Name of Father:	John N. Hodge	a citizen of the	Creek	Nation.
Name of Mother:	Minnie L. Hodge	a citizen of the	U. S.	Nation.

Postoffice   Tulsa, I.T.

AFFIDAVIT OF MOTHER.

UNITED STATES OF AMERICA, Indian Territory,
Western DISTRICT.

I, John N. Hodge, on oath state that I am 29 years of age and a citizen by blood, of the Creek Nation; that I am the lawful ~~wife~~ husband of Minnie L. Hodge, who is a citizen, by *(blank)* of the U.S. ~~Nation~~; that a female child was born to ~~me~~ her on or about 21 day of Aug, 1902, that said child has been named Gusta A. Hodge, and is now living.

John N. Hodge

Applications for Enrollment of Creek Newborn
Act of 1905 Volume II

Witnesses To Mark:
{

Subscribed and sworn to before me this 19 day of July, 1905.

                                   Henry G. Hains
                                   Notary Public.

BIRTH AFFIDAVIT.

DEPARTMENT OF THE INTERIOR.
COMMISSION TO THE FIVE CIVILIZED TRIBES.

IN RE APPLICATION FOR ENROLLMENT, as a citizen of the Creek Nation, of Gusta A. Hodge, born on the 12 day of August, 1903

Name of Father:	John N. Hodge	a citizen of the	Creek	Nation.
Name of Mother:	Minnie L. Hodge	a citizen of the	U. S.	Nation.

                     Postoffice   Tulsa, I.T.

AFFIDAVIT OF MOTHER.

UNITED STATES OF AMERICA, Indian Territory, }
       Western   DISTRICT.

I, Minnie L. Hodge, on oath state that I am 27 years of age and a citizen by Birth, of the U.S. Nation; that I am the lawful wife of Johnnie N. Hodge, who is a citizen, by Blood of the Creek Nation; that a Female child was born to me on 17" day of August, 1903, that said child has been named *(blank)*, and was living March 4, 1905.

                                 Minnie L. Hodge

Witnesses To Mark:
{

Subscribed and sworn to before me this 13" day of April, 1905.

     My Com Ex 7/3/1906   Robert E. Lynch
                                    Notary Public.

Applications for Enrollment of Creek Newborn
Act of 1905 Volume II

AFFIDAVIT OF ATTENDING PHYSICIAN OR MID-WIFE.

UNITED STATES OF AMERICA, Indian Territory,
Western DISTRICT.

I, Francis Wimberly , a Midwife , on oath state that I attended on Mrs. Minnie L Hodge , wife of John N. Hodge on the 17 day of August , 1903 ; that there was born to her on said date a Female child; that said child was living March 4, 1905, and is said to have been named Gusta A. Hodge

Frances Wimberly

Witnesses To Mark:

Subscribed and sworn to before me this 28 day of March, 1905.

My Com Ex 7/3/1906   Robert E. Lynch
                         Notary Public.

NC 123.

Muskogee, Indian Territory, July 1, 1905.

John N. Hodge,
  Tulsa, Indian Territory.

Dear Sir:

There are on file with the Commission affidavits executed by you, your wife, and Frances Wimberly, a midwife, in which the date of the birth of your minor child, Gusta A. Hodge, is given as August 12, 1903, and May 25, 1902.

For the purpose of correcting this discrepancy in the date of the birth of said child, you are advised that it will be necessary for you and the mother of said child to appear before the Commissioner to the Five Civilized Tribes at its office in Muskogee, Indian Territory, to be examined under oath.

Respectfully,

Commissioner.

NC 123.

Muskogee, Indian Territory, July 5, 1905.

John N. Hodge,
  Tulsa, Indian Territory.

Applications for Enrollment of Creek Newborn
Act of 1905 Volume II

Dear Sir:

There are on file with the Commission affidavits executed by you, your wife, and Frances Wimberly, a midwife, in which the date of the birth of your minor child, Gusta A. Hodge, is given as August 12, 1903, and May 25, 1902.

For the purpose of correcting this discrepancy in the date of the birth of said child, you are advised that it will be necessary for you and the mother of said child to appear before the Commissioner to the Five Civilized Tribes at its office in Muskogee, Indian Territory, to be examined under oath.

Respectfully,

Commissioner.

BIRTH AFFIDAVIT.

DEPARTMENT OF THE INTERIOR.
COMMISSION TO THE FIVE CIVILIZED TRIBES.

IN RE APPLICATION FOR ENROLLMENT, as a citizen of the CREEK Nation, of Moses Burnett, born on the 12 day of May, 1903

Name of Father: A. J. Burnett	a citizen of the U. S.	Nation.
Name of Mother: Mary Jane "	a citizen of the Creek	Nation.

Postoffice   Tulsa, I.T.

AFFIDAVIT OF ~~MOTHER~~. father

UNITED STATES OF AMERICA, Indian Territory,
WESTERN   DISTRICT.

I, A. J. Burnett, on oath state that I am 43 years of age and a citizen by -----, of the U. S. Nation; that I am the lawful ~~wife~~ hus of Mary Jane Burnett, who is a citizen, by blood of the Creek Nation; that a male child was born to me on 12 day of May, 1903, that said child has been named Moses Burnett, and is now living.

A.J. Burnett

Witnesses To Mark:
{

Subscribed and sworn to before me this 10" day of March, 1905.

Applications for Enrollment of Creek Newborn
Act of 1905   Volume II

Edw C Griesel
Notary Public.

BIRTH AFFIDAVIT.

DEPARTMENT OF THE INTERIOR.
COMMISSION TO THE FIVE CIVILIZED TRIBES.

    IN RE APPLICATION FOR ENROLLMENT, as a citizen of the Creek Nation, of Moses Burnett , born on the 12 day of May , 1903

Name of Father:	A. J. Burnett	a citizen of the U. S.	Nation.
Name of Mother:	Mary J Burnett	a citizen of the Creek	Nation.

                  Postoffice   Tulsa, Ind.Ter.

The enclosed affidavits are in lieu of an application filed for enrollment by A.J. Burnett 3/9/1905

AFFIDAVIT OF MOTHER.

UNITED STATES OF AMERICA, Indian Territory,
    Western   DISTRICT.

    I, Mary J. Burnett , on oath state that I am 21 years of age and a citizen by Blood , of the Creek   Nation; that I am the lawful wife of A. J. Burnett   , who is a citizen, by Birth of the U. S.   Nation; that a Male   child was born to me on 12" day of May , 1903, that said child has been named   Moses Burnett , and was living March 4, 1905.

Mary J. Burnett

Witnesses To Mark:

{

    Subscribed and sworn to before me this 18" day of March , 1905.

    Com Ex 7/3/1906   Robert E. Lynch
Notary Public.

AFFIDAVIT OF ATTENDING PHYSICIAN OR MID-WIFE.

UNITED STATES OF AMERICA, Indian Territory,
    Western   DISTRICT.

    I, Mary J Hodge   , a mid wife , on oath state that I attended on Mrs. Mary J. Burnett , wife of A. J. Burnett on the 12   day of May , 1903 ; that there was born to

Applications for Enrollment of Creek Newborn
Act of 1905 Volume II

her on said date a male child; that said child was living March 4, 1905, and is said to have been named Moses Burnett

Mary J. Hodge

Witnesses To Mark:
{

Subscribed and sworn to before me this 18 day of March, 1905.

Com Ex 7/3/1906

Robert E. Lynch
Notary Public.

REFER IN REPLY TO THE FOLLOWING:

N.C. 126

DEPARTMENT OF THE INTERIOR,
COMMISSIONER TO THE FIVE CIVILIZED TRIBES.

Muskogee, Indian Territory, November 18, 1905.

Annie Heneha,
    Coweta, Indian Territory.

Dear Madam:

There is herewith enclosed one copy of the order of the Commissioner to the Five Civilized Tribes, dated November 14, 1905, dismissing the application made by you for the enrollment of your minor child Katie Heneha, deceased, as a citizen by blood of the Creek Nation.

Respectfully,

Wm O. Beall

Acting Commissioner.

AG-126

N.C. 126   I.D.

DEPARTMENT OF THE INTERIOR,
COMMISSIONER TO THE FIVE CIVILIZED TRIBES.

In the matter of the application for the enrollment of Katie Heneha, deceased, as a citizen by blood of the Creek Nation.

ORDER

The record in this case shows that on March 10, 1905, Annie Heneha appeared

Applications for Enrollment of Creek Newborn
Act of 1905   Volume II

before the Commission to the Five Civilized Tribes and made application for the enrollment of her minor child, Katie Heneha, deceased, as a citizen by blood of the Creek Nation.

The evidence shows that said Katie Heneha, deceased, was born during the month of September, 1904, and that she died prior to March 4, 1905.

The act of Congress approved March 3, 1905, (33 Stats., 1048), provides:

"That the Commission to the Five Civilized Tribes is authorized for sixty days after the date of the approval of this act to receive and consider applications for enrollment, of children, born subsequent to May twenty-fifth, nineteen hundred and one, and prior to March fourth, nineteen hundred and five, and living on said latter date, to citizens of the Creek tribe of Indians whose enrollment has been approved by the Secretary of the Interior prior to the approval of this act; and to enroll and make allotments to such children."

It is, therefore, ordered that there is no authority of law for the enrollment of said Katie Heneha, deceased, as a citizen by blood of the Creek Nation, and that the application for her enrollment as such should be and the same is hereby dismissed.

Tams Bixby.
Commissioner.

Muskogee, Indian Territory.
NOV 14 1905

NC -
~~En~~. 127.

DEPARTMENT OF THE INTERIOR,
COMMISSION TO THE FIVE CIVILIZED TRIBES,
MUSKOGEE, I.T. MAY 20, 1905.

In the matter of the application for the enrollment of Leo J. Jobe, as a citizen of the Creek Nation.

Lewis N. B. Jobe, being duly sworn, testified as follows:

Examination by the Commission:
Q What is your name? A Lewis N.B. Jobe.
Q What is your age? A About 42.
Q What is your post office address? A Muskogee, Indian Territory.
Q You have a new born child, have you? A Yes sir.
Q Is that child's name Leo J. Jobe? A Yes sir.
Q Your wife made out an affidait[sic] relative to a child of hers and called it Leo J. Jobe, is that the same child? A Yes sir.

Applications for Enrollment of Creek Newborn
Act of 1905   Volume II

Lona Merrick, being duly sworn, states that the above and foregoing is a true and correct transcript of her stenographic notes as taken in said cause on said date.

Lona Merrick

Subscribed and sworn to before me this 22nd, day of May, 1905,

Edw C Griesel
Notary Public.

BIRTH AFFIDAVIT.

DEPARTMENT OF THE INTERIOR.
COMMISSION TO THE FIVE CIVILIZED TRIBES.

IN RE APPLICATION FOR ENROLLMENT, as a citizen of the Creek Nation, of John Leo Jobe, born on the 2nd day of April, 1902

Name of Father:	Lewis Jobe	a citizen of the Creek	Nation.
Name of Mother:	Mary E. Jobe	a citizen of the U.S.	Nation.

Postoffice   Muskogee, I.T.

Child Present Gr

AFFIDAVIT OF MOTHER.

UNITED STATES OF AMERICA, Indian Territory, ⎫
    Western   DISTRICT.   ⎭

I, Mary E. Jobe, on oath state that I am 36 years of age and a citizen by *(blank)*, of the U.S. Nation; that I am the lawful wife of Lewis Jobe, who is a citizen, by blood of the Creek Nation; that a male child was born to me on the 2nd day of April, 1902, that said child has been named John Leo Jobe, and was living March 4, 1905.

Mary E. Jobe

Witnesses To Mark:
{

Subscribed and sworn to before me 13 day of March, 1905.

Edw C Griesel
Notary Public.

Applications for Enrollment of Creek Newborn
Act of 1905 Volume II

AFFIDAVIT OF ATTENDING PHYSICIAN OR MID-WIFE.

UNITED STATES OF AMERICA, Indian Territory, }
Western DISTRICT.

I, James O. Callahan , a Physician , on oath state that I attended on Mrs. Mary E. Jobe , wife of Lewis Jobe on the 2nd day of April , 1902 ; that there was born to her on said date a male child; that said child was living March 4, 1905, and is said to have been named John Leo Jobe

J.O. Callahan

Witnesses To Mark:
{

Subscribed and sworn to before me this 13 day of March, 1905.

Edw C Griesel
Notary Public.

BIRTH AFFIDAVIT.

DEPARTMENT OF THE INTERIOR.
COMMISSION TO THE FIVE CIVILIZED TRIBES.

IN RE APPLICATION FOR ENROLLMENT, as a citizen of the CREEK Nation, of Leo J. Jobe, born on the 2 day of April , 1902

Name of Father:	Lewis N. B. Jobe	a citizen of the Creek	Nation.
Name of Mother:	Mollie G. "	a citizen of the U.S.	Nation.

Postoffice Muskogee

AFFIDAVIT OF ~~MOTHER~~. father

UNITED STATES OF AMERICA, Indian Territory, }
WESTERN DISTRICT.

I, Lewis N. B. Jobe , on oath state that I am 43 years of age and a citizen by blood , of the Creek Nation; that I am the lawful ~~wife~~ hus of Mollie G. Jobe , who is a citizen, by ----- of the U.S. Nation; that a male child was born to me on 2 day of April, 1902 , that said child has been named Leo J. Jobe , and is now living.

Lewis N. B. Jobe

Witnesses To Mark:
{

Applications for Enrollment of Creek Newborn
Act of 1905   Volume II

Subscribed and sworn to before me this 10 day of March, 1905.
Edw C Griesel
Notary Public.

NC 127.

Muskogee, Indian Territory, May 18, 1905.

Louis N.B. Jobe,
    Muskogee, Indian Territory.

Dear Sir:

    In the matter of the application for the enrollment of your minor child, Leo Jobe, as a citizen of the Creek Nation, you are advised that the Commission requires the affidavits of the mother and midwife or physician in attendance at the birth of said child.

    There is enclosed a blank form of birth affidavit, and in executing same care should be exercised to see that all blanks are properly filled, all names written in full and in the event that the persons signing the affidavits is unable to write, signatures by mark must be attested by two witnesses. Each affidavit must be executed before a Notary Public and the notarial seal and signature of the officer must be attached to each separate affidavit.

    Respectfully,

BC.   Chairman.

NC 127.

Muskogee, Indian Territory, May 19, 1905.

Louis N. B. Jobe,
    Muskogee, Indian Territory.

Dear Sir:

    In the matter of the application for the enrollment of Leo J. Jobe, as a citizen of the Creek Nation, you are advised that the Commission desires further evidence as to the birth of said child.

    You will be allowed thirty days from date within which to appear before the Commission at its office in Muskogee, Indian Territory, along with your wife, for the purpose of being examined under oath.

    Respectfully,

                                                      Chairman.

Applications for Enrollment of Creek Newborn
Act of 1905 Volume II

REFER IN REPLY TO THE FOLLOWING:
NC-128

DEPARTMENT OF THE INTERIOR,
COMMISSIONER TO THE FIVE CIVILIZED TRIBES.

Muskogee, Indian Territory, July 25, 1905.

Nancy Pigeon,
    Haskell, Indian Territory.

Dear Madam:

    It appears from the evidence on file, in the matter of the application for the enrollment of your minor child, you are advised that the Commission requires further evidence as to the birth of said child. of your daughter, that there is a discrepancy as to the name of said child. It appears from your affidavit executed before the Commission to the Five Civilized Tribes on March 9, 1905 that the name of said child is Elizabeth E. Davis while from your affidavit and the affidavit of Betty Bruner, midwife, which were filed with said Commission on April 12, 1905, it appears that the name of said child is Elizabeth Helen Davis.

    You are, therefore, requested to immediately inform this office as to the correct name of your said daughter returning your answer in the inclosed[sic] envelope.

                              Respectfully,

Env.

                              (Name Illegible) Commissioner

                    G.H. Chandler Mercantile Company
                          General Merchandise.

Hon. Tamas Bixby

                                                           Haskell, I.T. 7/28, 1905

    Chairman Dawes Com.
        Muskogee, I.T.

Sir:

    In reply to enclosed letter would beg to inform you that the error as to the childs[sic] name has been corrected once by answering a similar letter to yours of 25th inst. Once by phone and once by myself in person. On the last two occasions I was assured that the matter was satisfactorly[sic] explained and would be forwarded to Washington in that month (May) The correct name of the child is Elizabeth E. Davis. Please notify us at once if this is satisfactorly[sic] explained.

                                  (signed) Nancy Pigeon.

Applications for Enrollment of Creek Newborn
Act of 1905 Volume II

NC 128.

Muskogee, Indian Territory, May 18, 1905.

J. R. Davis,
Haskell, Indian Territory.

Dear Sir:

In the matter of the application for the enrollment of your minor child, Elizabeth E. Davis, as a citizen of the Creek Nation, you are advised that the Commission requires the affidavit of the midwife or physician in attendance at the birth of said child.

There is herewith enclosed a blank form of birth affidavit, and in executing same care should be exercised to see that all blanks are properly filled, all names written in full and in the event that the person signing the affidavit is unable to write, signature by mark must be attested by two witnesses. Each affidavit must be executed before a Notary Public and the notarial seal and signature of the officer must be attached to each separate affidavit.

Respectfully,

BC.	Chairman.

BIRTH AFFIDAVIT.

DEPARTMENT OF THE INTERIOR.
COMMISSION TO THE FIVE CIVILIZED TRIBES.

IN RE APPLICATION FOR ENROLLMENT, as a citizen of the CREEK Nation, of Elizabeth E. Davis, born on the 7 day of July, 1902

Name of Father: J. R. Davis	a citizen of the U.S. Nation.
Name of Mother: Nancy Pigeon	a citizen of the Creek Nation.

Postoffice   Haskell, I.T.

(Child present) HGH

AFFIDAVIT OF MOTHER.

UNITED STATES OF AMERICA, Indian Territory,
WESTERN DISTRICT.

I, Nancy Pigeon, on oath state that I am 30 years of age and a citizen by blood, of the Creek Nation; that I am the lawful wife of J. R. Davis, who is a citizen, by -----

Applications for Enrollment of Creek Newborn
Act of 1905   Volume II

of the   U. S. Nation; that a female   child was born to me on   7   day of July , 1902 , that said child has been named   Elizabeth E. Davis , and is now living.

Nancy Pigeon

Witnesses To Mark:

{

   Subscribed and sworn to before me this 9 day of March , 1905.

Edw C Griesel
Notary Public.

AFFIDAVIT OF ATTENDING PHYSICIAN OR MID-WIFE.

UNITED STATES OF AMERICA, Indian Territory, }   dead
    Western   DISTRICT.

   I,   , a   , on oath state that I attended on Mrs.   , wife of   on the   day of   , 190 ; that there was born to her on said date a male child; that said child is now living and is said to have been named

Witnesses To Mark:

{

   Subscribed and sworn to before me this 28 day of March, 1905.

Notary Public.

BIRTH AFFIDAVIT.

DEPARTMENT OF THE INTERIOR.
COMMISSION TO THE FIVE CIVILIZED TRIBES.

   IN RE APPLICATION FOR ENROLLMENT, as a citizen of the Creek Nation, of Elizabeth E. Davis , born on the 7th day of July , 1902

Name of Father: J. R. Davis   a citizen of the United States Nation.
Name of Mother: Nancy Pigeon   a citizen of the   Creek   Nation.

Postoffice   Haskell, I.T.

Applications for Enrollment of Creek Newborn
Act of 1905 Volume II

AFFIDAVIT OF MOTHER.

UNITED STATES OF AMERICA, Indian Territory,
Western DISTRICT.

    I, William T. Davis, on oath state that I am 52 years of age and a citizen ~~by~~ *(blank)*, of the United States ~~Nation~~; that I am the ~~lawful wife~~ step-father of Nancy Pigeon, who is a citizen, by blood of the Creek Nation; that a female child was born to ~~me~~ her on 7th day of July, 1902, that said child has been named Elizabeth E. Davis, and was living March 4, 1905. that said child's full name is Elizabeth Ellen Davis and that the affidavits heretofore filed with the Commission stating that the name of said child is Elizabeth Helen Davis are erroneous in regard to the name of said child.

                              William T. Davis

Witnesses To Mark:

    Subscribed and sworn to before me this 2" day of August, 1905.

                              Henry G. Hains
                              Notary Public.

BIRTH AFFIDAVIT.

DEPARTMENT OF THE INTERIOR.
COMMISSION TO THE FIVE CIVILIZED TRIBES.

    IN RE APPLICATION FOR ENROLLMENT, as a citizen of the Creek Nation, of Elizabeth Helen Davis, born on the 7th day of July, 1902
Name of Father: Russell Davis   a citizen of the   White   Nation.
Name of Mother: Nancy Pigeon   a citizen of the   Creek   Nation.

                      Postoffice   Haskell, I.T.

AFFIDAVIT OF MOTHER.

UNITED STATES OF AMERICA, Indian Territory,
Western DISTRICT.

    I, Nancy Pigeon, on oath state that I am 30 years of age and a citizen by Blood, of the Creek Nation; that I am the ~~lawful~~ common law wife of Russell Davis, who is ~~a citizen, by~~ white ----- of the ----- Nation; that a female child was born to me on 7th day of July, 1902, that said child has been named Elizabeth Helen Davis, and is now living.

                              Nancy Pigeon

Applications for Enrollment of Creek Newborn
Act of 1905   Volume II

Witnesses To Mark:
{

Subscribed and sworn to before me this 10th day of April , 1905.

Ralph Dresback
Notary Public.

AFFIDAVIT OF ATTENDING PHYSICIAN OR MID-WIFE.

UNITED STATES OF AMERICA, Indian Territory,
Western   DISTRICT.

I, Betty Bruner , a midwife , on oath state that I attended on Mrs. Nancy Pigeon , wife of Russell Davis on the 7th day of July , 1902 ; that there was born to her on said date a female child; that said child is now living and is said to have been named Elizabeth Helen Davis

her
Betty x Bruner
mark

Witnesses To Mark:
{ Isom Peters
{ E.B. Harris

Subscribed and sworn to before me this 10th day of April , 1905.

Ralph Dresback
Notary Public.

NC 129.

Muskogee, Indian Territory, May 18, 1905.

Thomas Morton,
  Bald Hill, Indian Territory.

Dear Sir:

In the matter of the application for the enrollment of your minor child, Roy Ray Morton, as a citizen of the Creek Nation, you are advised that the Commission requires the affidavits of the mother and midwife or physician in attendance at the birth of said children.

There are herewith enclosed two blank forms of birth affidavit, and in executing same care should be exercised to see that all blanks are properly filled, all names written in full and in the event that the persons signing the affidavits are unable to write,

Applications for Enrollment of Creek Newborn
Act of 1905   Volume II

signatures by mark must be attested by two witnesses. Each affidavit must be executed before a Notary Public and the notarial seal and signature of the officer must be attached to each separate affidavit.

Respectfully,

BC.   Chairman.

BIRTH AFFIDAVIT.

DEPARTMENT OF THE INTERIOR.
COMMISSION TO THE FIVE CIVILIZED TRIBES.

IN RE APPLICATION FOR ENROLLMENT, as a citizen of the Creek Nation, of Roy Ray Morton , born on the 31st day of May, 1902

Name of Father: Thomas Morton   a citizen of the   non citizen   Nation.
Name of Mother: Joanna Morton   a citizen of the   Creek   Nation.

Postoffice   Bald Hill, Indian Territory.

AFFIDAVIT OF MOTHER.

UNITED STATES OF AMERICA, Indian Territory, }
    Western   DISTRICT.

I, Joanna Morton, on oath state that I am 34 years of age and a citizen by birth , of the Creek   Nation; that I am the lawful wife of Thomas Morton , who is a citizen, by non citizen of the Creek   Nation; that a   male child was born to me on the 31st day of May , 1902 , that said child has been named Roy Ray Morton , and was living March 4, 1905.

Joanna Morton

Witnesses To Mark:
{

Subscribed and sworn to before me this 23rd day of May , 1905.

Mark L. Bozarth

My Com. Ex. Oct. 21st, 1906.   Notary Public.

Applications for Enrollment of Creek Newborn
Act of 1905 Volume II

AFFIDAVIT OF ATTENDING PHYSICIAN OR MID-WIFE.

UNITED STATES OF AMERICA, Indian Territory, }
    Western   DISTRICT.

    I, Aery Ann Berryhill , a mid-wife , on oath state that I attended on Mrs. Joanna Morton , wife of Thomas Morton on the 31st day of May , 1902 ; that there was born to her on said date a male child; that said child was living March 4, 1905, and is said to have been named Roy Ray Morton
                                          her
                                    Aery x Ann Berryhill
Witnesses To Mark: mark
  { John J. *(Illegible)*
    Mark L. Bozarth

    Subscribed and sworn to before me this 23rd day of May , 1905.

                              Mark L. Bozarth
My Com. Ex. Oct. 21st, 1906.   Notary Public.

BIRTH AFFIDAVIT.

DEPARTMENT OF THE INTERIOR.
COMMISSION TO THE FIVE CIVILIZED TRIBES.

    IN RE APPLICATION FOR ENROLLMENT, as a citizen of the Creek Nation, of Roy Ray Morton , born on the 31 day of May, 1902

Name of Father: Thomas Morton   a citizen of the U. S.   Nation.
Name of Mother: Joan   "   a citizen of the Creek   Nation.

                        Postoffice   Bald Hill, I.T.

(affiant presents certificate for land of Joanna & says she is too sick to come.) HGH
                      AFFIDAVIT OF ~~MOTHER~~. father

UNITED STATES OF AMERICA, Indian Territory, }
    WESTERN   DISTRICT.

    I, Thomas Morton , on oath state that I am 38 years of age and a citizen by ----- , of the U. S. Nation; that I am the lawful ~~wife~~ hus of Joan Morton , who is a citizen, by blood of the Creek Nation; that a male child was born to me on 31 day of May , 1902 , that said child has been named Roy Ray Morton , and is now living.
                                          His
                                  Thomas x Morton
Witnesses To Mark: mark
  { JY Miller
    EC Griesel

Applications for Enrollment of Creek Newborn
Act of 1905   Volume II

Subscribed and sworn to before me this 9 day of March, 1905.

                        Edw C Griesel
                        Notary Public.

BIRTH AFFIDAVIT.

DEPARTMENT OF THE INTERIOR.
COMMISSION TO THE FIVE CIVILIZED TRIBES.

IN RE APPLICATION FOR ENROLLMENT, as a citizen of the CREEK Nation, of Charley McNae, born on the 1 day of Aug, 1902

Name of Father:	Peter McNae	a citizen of the	Creek	Nation.
Name of Mother:	Lousanna "	a citizen of the	"	Nation.

                  Postoffice   Senora

AFFIDAVIT OF MOTHER.

UNITED STATES OF AMERICA, Indian Territory,
    WESTERN   DISTRICT.

I, Peter McNae, on oath state that I am 30 years of age and a citizen by blood, of the Creek Nation; that I am the lawful ~~wife~~ hus of Lousanna McNae, who is a citizen, by blood of the Creek Nation; that a male child was born to me on 1 day of Aug, 1902, that said child has been named Charley McNae, and was living March 4, 1905.

                        Peter McNae

Witnesses To Mark:
{

Subscribed and sworn to before me this 13 day of March, 1905.

                        Edw C Griesel
                        Notary Public.

BIRTH AFFIDAVIT.

DEPARTMENT OF THE INTERIOR.
COMMISSION TO THE FIVE CIVILIZED TRIBES.

IN RE APPLICATION FOR ENROLLMENT, as a citizen of the Creek Nation, of Charley McNae, born on the ----- day of Aug, 1902

Applications for Enrollment of Creek Newborn
Act of 1905 Volume II

Name of Father: Peter McNae   a citizen of the   Creek   Nation.
Name of Mother: Lozanna McNae   a citizen of the   Creek   Nation.

                       Postoffice   Henryetta, I.T.

AFFIDAVIT OF MOTHER.   (Child present)

UNITED STATES OF AMERICA, Indian Territory, }
     Western   DISTRICT.

     I, Lozanna McNae, on oath state that I am 30 years of age and a citizen by blood, of the Creek Nation; that I am the lawful wife of Peter McNae, who is a citizen, by blood of the Creek Nation; that a male child was born to me on ----- day of Aug, 1902, that said child has been named Charley McNae, and is now living.

                                            her
                              Lozanna x McNae
                                  mark

Witnesses To Mark:
{ EC Griesel
{ Jesse McDermott

     Subscribed and sworn to before me this 13" day of April, 1905.

                                J McDermott
                                    Notary Public.

AFFIDAVIT OF ATTENDING PHYSICIAN OR MID-WIFE.

UNITED STATES OF AMERICA, Indian Territory, }
     Western   DISTRICT.

     I, Polly Thomas, a midwife, on oath state that I attended on Mrs. Lozanna McNae, wife of Peter McNae on the ----- day of Aug, 1902; that there was born to her on said date a *(blank)* child; that said child is now living and is said to have been named Charley McNae

                                   her
                              Polly x Thomas
Witnesses To Mark: mark
{ EC Griesel
{ Jesse McDermott

     Subscribed and sworn to before me this 13 day of April, 1905.

                               J. McDermott
                                 Notary Public.

Applications for Enrollment of Creek Newborn
Act of 1905   Volume II

BIRTH AFFIDAVIT.

DEPARTMENT OF THE INTERIOR.
COMMISSION TO THE FIVE CIVILIZED TRIBES.

IN RE APPLICATION FOR ENROLLMENT, as a citizen of the CREEK Nation, of Marsey McNae, born on the 20 day of March, 1904

Name of Father: Peter McNae   a citizen of the   Creek   Nation.
Name of Mother: Lousanna   "   a citizen of the   "   Nation.

Postoffice   Senora

AFFIDAVIT OF MOTHER.

UNITED STATES OF AMERICA, Indian Territory,
WESTERN   DISTRICT.

I, Peter McNae, on oath state that I am 30 years of age and a citizen by blood, of the Creek Nation; that I am the lawful ~~wife~~ husb of Lousanna McNae, who is a citizen, by blood of the Creek Nation; that a male child was born to me on 20 day of March, 1904, that said child has been named Marsey McNae, and was living March 4, 1905.

Peter McNae

Witnesses To Mark:
{

Subscribed and sworn to before me this 13 day of March, 1905.

Edw C Griesel
Notary Public.

BIRTH AFFIDAVIT.

DEPARTMENT OF THE INTERIOR.
COMMISSION TO THE FIVE CIVILIZED TRIBES.

IN RE APPLICATION FOR ENROLLMENT, as a citizen of the Creek Nation, of Marcy McNae, born on the 20 day of Mar, 1904

Name of Father: Peter McNae   a citizen of the   Creek   Nation.
Name of Mother: Lozanna   "   a citizen of the   Creek   Nation.

Postoffice   Henryetta, I.T.

Applications for Enrollment of Creek Newborn
Act of 1905 Volume II

AFFIDAVIT OF MOTHER. (Child present)

UNITED STATES OF AMERICA, Indian Territory,
Western DISTRICT.

I, Lozanna McNae, on oath state that I am 30 years of age and a citizen by blood, of the Creek Nation; that I am the lawful wife of Peter McNae, who is a citizen, by blood of the Creek Nation; that a male child was born to me on 20" day of Mar, 1904, that said child has been named Marcy McNae, and is now living.

her
Lozanna x McNae
mark

Witnesses To Mark:
{ EC Griesel
  Jesse McDermott

Subscribed and sworn to before me this 13" day of Apr, 1905.

J McDermott
Notary Public.

AFFIDAVIT OF ATTENDING PHYSICIAN OR MID-WIFE.

UNITED STATES OF AMERICA, Indian Territory,
Western DISTRICT.

I, Polly Thomas, a midwife, on oath state that I attended on Mrs. Lozanna McNae, wife of Peter McNae on the 20 day of Mar, 1904; that there was born to her on said date a *(blank)* child; that said child is now living and is said to have been named Marcy McNae

her
Polly x Thomas
mark

Witnesses To Mark:
{ EC Griesel
  Jesse McDermott

Subscribed and sworn to before me this 13" day of Apr, 1905.

J. McDermott
Notary Public.

Applications for Enrollment of Creek Newborn
Act of 1905   Volume II

NC-131

Muskogee, Indian Territory, May 29, 1905.

W. L. Gilcrease,
   Mounds, Indian Territory.

Dear Sir:

In the matter of the application for the enrollment of your minor children, Elmer Lee and Mabel Gilcrease, as a citizen of the Creek Nation, there are on file with the Commission affidavits executed by M.D. Taylor, M. D. March 31, 1905 and stating that said children were born April 1, 1905. This is obviously an error.

For the purpose of correcting these affidavits, there are herewith enclosed two blank forms of birth affidavit. In executing same, care should be taken to see that all blanks are properly filled, all names spelled in full, and in the event that the person signing the affidavit is unable to write, signature by mark must be attested by two witnesses.

This matter should receive your prompt attention.

Respectfully,

Chairman.

BIRTH AFFIDAVIT.

DEPARTMENT OF THE INTERIOR.
COMMISSION TO THE FIVE CIVILIZED TRIBES.

IN RE APPLICATION FOR ENROLLMENT, as a citizen of the Creek Nation, of Bessie Gilcrease, born on the 2nd day of July, 1904

Name of Father: William L. Gilcrease   a non citizen of the Creek   Nation.
Name of Mother: Lizzie Gilcrease   a citizen of the   Creek   Nation.

Postoffice   Mounds, Indian Territory

Applications for Enrollment of Creek Newborn
Act of 1905 Volume II

AFFIDAVIT OF MOTHER.

UNITED STATES OF AMERICA, Indian Territory, }
Western DISTRICT.

I, Lizzie Gilcrease, on oath state that I am thirty one years of age and a citizen by blood, of the Creek Nation; that I am the lawful wife of William L. Gilcrease, who is a non citizen, by *(blank)* of the Creek Nation; that a female child was born to me on Second day of July, 1904, that said child has been named Bessie Gilcrease, and is now living.

Lizzie Gilcrease

Witnesses To Mark:
{

Subscribed and sworn to before me this 2Ist[sic] day of March, 1905.

D J Red
Notary Public.

AFFIDAVIT OF ATTENDING PHYSICIAN OR MID-WIFE.

UNITED STATES OF AMERICA, Indian Territory, }
Western DISTRICT.

I, J. W. Bronaugh, a Physician, on oath state that I attended on Mrs. Lizzie Gilcrease, wife of William L. Gilcrease on the second day of July, 1904[sic], 1*(blank)*; that there was born to her on said date a female child; that said child is now living and is said to have been named Bessie Gilcrease

J. W. Bronaugh, M.D.

Witnesses To Mark:
{

Subscribed and sworn to before me this 23rd day of March, 1905.

DJ Red
Notary Public.

(The above affidavit was copied again)

Applications for Enrollment of Creek Newborn
Act of 1905 Volume II

BIRTH AFFIDAVIT.

DEPARTMENT OF THE INTERIOR.
COMMISSION TO THE FIVE CIVILIZED TRIBES.

IN RE APPLICATION FOR ENROLLMENT, as a citizen of the CREEK Nation, of Bessie Gilcrease, born on the 2" day of July, 1904

Name of Father:	W.L. Gilcrease	a citizen of the	U.S.		Nation.
Name of Mother:	Lizzie "	a citizen of the		Creek	Nation.

Postoffice   Mounds, I.T.

AFFIDAVIT OF ~~MOTHER~~. father

UNITED STATES OF AMERICA, Indian Territory, ⎫
  WESTERN   DISTRICT. ⎭

I, W. L. Gilcrease, on oath state that I am 37 years of age and a citizen by ----- , of the U.S. Nation; that I am the lawful ~~wife~~ hus of Lizzie Gilcrease, who is a citizen, by blood of the Creek Nation; that a female child was born to me on 2" day of July, 1904, that said child has been named Bessie Gilcrease, and is now living.

                                        W.L. Gilcrease
Witnesses To Mark:
{

Subscribed and sworn to before me this 10" day of March, 1905.

                                        Edw C Griesel
                                          Notary Public.

BIRTH AFFIDAVIT.

DEPARTMENT OF THE INTERIOR.
COMMISSION TO THE FIVE CIVILIZED TRIBES.

IN RE APPLICATION FOR ENROLLMENT, as a citizen of the Creek Nation, of Mabel Gilcrease, born on the first day of April, 1903

Name of Father:	William L. Gilcrease	a non citizen of the	Creek	Nation.
Name of Mother:	Lizzie Gilcrease	a citizen of the	Creek	Nation.

Postoffice   *(blank)*

Applications for Enrollment of Creek Newborn
Act of 1905   Volume II

AFFIDAVIT OF MOTHER.

UNITED STATES OF AMERICA, Indian Territory,
Western District   DISTRICT.

I, Lizzie Gilcrease, on oath state that I am *(blank)* years of age and a citizen by blood , of the Creek Nation; that I am the lawful wife of William L. Gilcrease , who is a non citizen, by blood of the Creek Nation; that a female child was born to me on first day of April , 1903, that said child has been named Mabel Gilcrease , and was living March 4, 1905.

(No signature)

Witnesses To Mark:
{

Subscribed and sworn to before me this day of , 1905.

Notary Public.

AFFIDAVIT OF ATTENDING PHYSICIAN OR MID-WIFE.

UNITED STATES OF AMERICA, Indian Territory,
Western District   DISTRICT.

I, M. D. Taylor , a Physician , on oath state that I attended on Mrs. Lizzie Gilcrease , wife of William L. Gilcrease on the first day of April , 1903 ; that there was born to her on said date a female child; that said child was living March 4, 1905, and is said to have been named Mabel Gilcrease

M.D. Taylor, M.D.

Witnesses To Mark:
{

Subscribed and sworn to before me this 3rd day of June, 1905.

DJ Red

Notary Public.

BIRTH AFFIDAVIT.

DEPARTMENT OF THE INTERIOR.
COMMISSION TO THE FIVE CIVILIZED TRIBES.

IN RE APPLICATION FOR ENROLLMENT, as a citizen of the Creek Nation, of Mabel Gilcrease , born on the first day of April , 1903

Applications for Enrollment of Creek Newborn
Act of 1905   Volume II

Name of Father: William L. Gilcrease a non- a citizen of the   Creek   Nation.
Name of Mother: Lizzie Gilcrease   a citizen of the   Creek   Nation.

                            Postoffice   Mounds, Indian Territory

AFFIDAVIT OF MOTHER.

UNITED STATES OF AMERICA, Indian Territory,⎱
   Western   DISTRICT.⎰

    I, Lizzie Gilcrease, on oath state that I am thirty one years of age and a citizen by blood , of the Creek   Nation; that I am the lawful wife of William L. Gilcrease , who is a non- citizen, by *(blank)* of the Creek Nation; that a female   child was born to me on first   day of April , 1903 , that said child has been named Mabel Gilcrease , and is now living. This child as a twin.

                                    Lizzie Gilcrease

Witnesses To Mark:
⎰
⎱

    Subscribed and sworn to before me this 21st day of March , 1905.

                                  D J Red
                                        Notary Public.

AFFIDAVIT OF ATTENDING PHYSICIAN OR MID-WIFE.

UNITED STATES OF AMERICA, Indian Territory,⎱
   Western   DISTRICT.⎰

    I, M. D. Taylor , a Physician , on oath state that I attended on Mrs. Lizzie Gilcrease , wife of William L. Gilcrease on the first   day of April , 1905 ; that there was born to her on said date a female child; that said child is now living and is said to have been named Mabel Gilcrease

                                  M.D. Taylor, M.D.

Witnesses To Mark:
⎰
⎱

    Subscribed and sworn to before me this   21st day of March, 1905.

                                    DJ Red
                                        Notary Public.

Applications for Enrollment of Creek Newborn
Act of 1905 Volume II

BIRTH AFFIDAVIT.

DEPARTMENT OF THE INTERIOR.
COMMISSION TO THE FIVE CIVILIZED TRIBES.

IN RE APPLICATION FOR ENROLLMENT, as a citizen of the Creek Nation, of Elmer Lee Gilcrease, born on the first day of April, 1903

Name of Father: William L. Gilcrease   a non citizen of the Creek Nation.
Name of Mother: Lizzie Gilcrease   a citizen of the Creek Nation.

Postoffice Mounds, Ind. Ter.

AFFIDAVIT OF MOTHER.

UNITED STATES OF AMERICA, Indian Territory,
Western District   DISTRICT.

I, Lizzie Gilcrease, on oath state that I am *(blank)* years of age and a citizen by blood, of the Creek Nation; that I am the lawful wife of William L. Gilcrease, who is a non- citizen, by blood of the Creek Nation; that a male child was born to me on first day of April, 1903, that said child has been named Elmer Lee Gilcrease, and was living March 4, 1905.

(No signature)

Witnesses To Mark:
{

Subscribed and sworn to before me this day of , 190.

Notary Public.

AFFIDAVIT OF ATTENDING PHYSICIAN OR MID-WIFE.

UNITED STATES OF AMERICA, Indian Territory,
Western District   DISTRICT.

I, M. D. Taylor, a Physician, on oath state that I attended on Mrs. Lizzie Gilcrease, wife of William L. Gilcrease on the first day of April, 1903 ; that there was born to her on said date a male child; that said child was living March 4, 1905, and is said to have been named Elmer Lee Gilcrease

M.D. Taylor, M.D.

Witnesses To Mark:
{

Subscribed and sworn to before me this 3rd day of June, 1905.

Applications for Enrollment of Creek Newborn
Act of 1905 Volume II

DJ Red
Notary Public.

(The above affidavit copied again.)

BIRTH AFFIDAVIT.

DEPARTMENT OF THE INTERIOR.
COMMISSION TO THE FIVE CIVILIZED TRIBES.

IN RE APPLICATION FOR ENROLLMENT, as a citizen of the CREEK Nation, of Elmer Lee & Mabel Gilcrease, born on the 1 day of April, 1903

Name of Father:	W.L. Gilcrease	a citizen of the	U. S.	Nation.
Name of Mother:	Lizzie "	a citizen of the	Creek	Nation.

Postoffice   Mounds, I.T.

AFFIDAVIT OF ~~MOTHER~~. father

UNITED STATES OF AMERICA, Indian Territory, }
WESTERN   DISTRICT.

I, W. L. Gilcrease, on oath state that I am 37 years of age and a citizen by -----, of the U. S. Nation; that I am the lawful ~~wife~~ husb of Lizzie Gilcrease, who is a citizen, by blood of the Creek Nation; that a Boy & girl child wins was born to me on 1 day of April, 1903, that said children has been named Elmer Lee & Mabel Gilcrease, and ~~is~~ are now living.

W.L. Gilcrease

Witnesses To Mark:

Subscribed and sworn to before me this 10" day of March, 1905.

Edw C Griesel
Notary Public.

BIRTH AFFIDAVIT.

DEPARTMENT OF THE INTERIOR.
COMMISSION TO THE FIVE CIVILIZED TRIBES.

IN RE APPLICATION FOR ENROLLMENT, as a citizen of the Creek Nation, of Elmer Lee Gilcrease, born on the first day of April, 1903

Applications for Enrollment of Creek Newborn
Act of 1905   Volume II

Name of Father: William L. Gilcrease   a non-citizen of the   Creek   Nation.
Name of Mother: Lizzie Gilcrease   a citizen of the   Creek   Nation.

Postoffice   Mounds, Indian Territory

AFFIDAVIT OF MOTHER.

UNITED STATES OF AMERICA, Indian Territory, ⎫
   Western District   DISTRICT.   ⎭

I, Lizzie Gilcrease, on oath state that I am thirty one years of age and a citizen by blood , of the Creek Nation; that I am the lawful wife of William L. Gilcrease, who is a non- citizen, by *(blank)* of the Creek Nation; that a male child was born to me on first day of April , 1903 , that said child has been named Elmer Lee Gilcrease , and is now living. This child has a twin.

Lizzie Gilcrease

Witnesses To Mark:
{

Subscribed and sworn to before me this 2Ist[sic] day of March , 190.5

DJ Red
Notary Public.

AFFIDAVIT OF ATTENDING PHYSICIAN OR MID-WIFE.

UNITED STATES OF AMERICA, Indian Territory, ⎫
   Western   DISTRICT.   ⎭

I, M. D. Taylor , a Physician , on oath state that I attended on Mrs. Lizzie Gilcrease , wife of William L. Gilcrease on the first day of April , 1905[sic] ; that there was born to her on said date a male child; that said child is now living and is said to have been named Elmer Lee Gilcrease

M.D. Taylor, M.D.

Witnesses To Mark:
{

Subscribed and sworn to before me this 2Ist day of March, 1905.

DJ Red
Notary Public.

Applications for Enrollment of Creek Newborn
Act of 1905 Volume II

BIRTH AFFIDAVIT.

DEPARTMENT OF THE INTERIOR.
COMMISSION TO THE FIVE CIVILIZED TRIBES.

IN RE APPLICATION FOR ENROLLMENT, as a citizen of the CREEK Nation, of Lizzie Canard, born on the 13 day of April, 1903

Name of Father: Sam Canard   a citizen of the   Creek   Nation.
Name of Mother: Nancy   "   a citizen of the   Creek   Nation.

       Postoffice Wetumka[sic]

Child Present Gr

AFFIDAVIT OF MOTHER.

UNITED STATES OF AMERICA, Indian Territory,
 WESTERN DISTRICT.

  I, Nancy Canard, on oath state that I am about 29 years of age and a citizen by blood, of the Creek Nation; that I am the lawful wife of Sam Canard, who is a citizen, by blood of the Creek Nation; that a female child was born to me on 13 day of April, 1903, that said child has been named Lizzie Canard, and was living March 4, 1905.

            Her
         Nancy x Canard
Witnesses To Mark: mark
 { J McDermott
   EC Griesel

  Subscribed and sworn to before me this 13 day of March, 1905.

        Edw C Griesel
         Notary Public.

BIRTH AFFIDAVIT.

DEPARTMENT OF THE INTERIOR.
COMMISSION TO THE FIVE CIVILIZED TRIBES.

IN RE APPLICATION FOR ENROLLMENT, as a citizen of the Creek Nation, of Lizzie Canard, born on the 13 day of April, 1903

Name of Father: Sam Canard   a citizen of the   Creek   Nation.
Name of Mother: Nancy   "   a citizen of the   "   Nation.

       Postoffice Wetumka[sic]

Applications for Enrollment of Creek Newborn
Act of 1905 Volume II

AFFIDAVIT OF ~~MOTHER~~. father

UNITED STATES OF AMERICA, Indian Territory, }
Western DISTRICT.

I, Sam Canard, on oath state that I am 30 years of age and a citizen by blood, of the Creek Nation; that I am the lawful ~~wife~~ Husband of Sam[sic] Canard, who is a citizen, by blood of the Creek Nation; that a male child was born to me on 13 day of April, 1903, that said child has been named Lizzie Canard, and is now living.

His
Sam x Canard
mark

Witnesses To Mark:
{ J McDermott
{ EC Griesel

Subscribed and sworn to before me this 3 day of Mar, 1905.

Edw C Griesel
Notary Public.

BIRTH AFFIDAVIT.

DEPARTMENT OF THE INTERIOR.
COMMISSION TO THE FIVE CIVILIZED TRIBES.

IN RE APPLICATION FOR ENROLLMENT, as a citizen of the Creek Nation, of Lizzie Canard, born on the 12th[sic]day of April, 1903

Name of Father:	Sam Canard	a citizen of the	Creek	Nation.
Name of Mother:	Nancy Canard	a citizen of the	Creek	Nation.

Postoffice Wetumka IT

AFFIDAVIT OF MOTHER.

UNITED STATES OF AMERICA, Indian Territory, }
Western DISTRICT.

I, Nancy Canard, on oath state that I am about 24 years of age and a citizen by blood, of the Creek Nation; that I am the lawful wife of Sam Canard, who is a citizen, by blood of the Creek Nation; that a female child was born to me on 12th day of April, 1903, that said child has been named Lizzie Canard, and was living March 4, 1905.

Her
Nancy x Canard
mark

Applications for Enrollment of Creek Newborn
Act of 1905 Volume II

Witnesses To Mark:
{ Roby Canard
{ *(Illegible)* Canard

Subscribed and sworn to before me this 3rd day of June, 1905.

                               Jeff T. Canard
Com Ex Aug 2, 1906   Notary Public.

AFFIDAVIT OF ATTENDING PHYSICIAN OR MID-WIFE.

UNITED STATES OF AMERICA, Indian Territory,
    Western   DISTRICT.

    I, Rosanna Scott, a midwife, on oath state that I attended on Mrs. Nancy Canard, wife of Sam Canard on the 12th day of April, 1903; that there was born to her on said date a female child; that said child was living March 4, 1905, and is said to have been named   Lizzie Canard   her
                                            Rosanna x Scott
                                            mark

Witnesses To Mark:
{ Roby Canard
{ *(Illegible)* Canard

Subscribed and sworn to before me this 3rd day of June, 1905.

                               Jeff T. Canard
Com Ex Aug 2nd 1906   Notary Public.

COMMISSIONERS:
TAMS BIXBY,
THOMAS B. NEEDLES,
C.R. BRECKINBRIDGE.

DEPARTMENT OF THE INTERIOR,
COMMISSIONER TO THE FIVE CIVILIZED TRIBES.

REFER IN REPLY TO THE FOLLOWING:
HGH

NC 132.

WM. O. BEALL
Secretary

ADDRESS ONLY THE
COMMISSION TO THE FIVE CIVILIZED TRIBES.

                                    Muskogee, Indian Territory, May 18, 1905.

Sam Canard,
        Wetumka[sic], Indian Territory.

Dear Sir:

        In the matter of the application for the enrollment of your minor child, Lizzie Canard, as a citizen of the Creek Nation, you are advised that the Commission requires the affidavit of the midwife or physician in attendance at the birth of said child.

Applications for Enrollment of Creek Newborn
Act of 1905   Volume II

There is herewith enclosed a blank form of birth affidavit, and in executing same care should be exercised to see that all blanks are properly filled, all names written in full and in the event that the person signing the affidavit is unable to write, signature by mark must be attested by two witnesses. Each affidavit must be executed before a Notary Public and the notarial seal and signature of the officer must be attached to each separate affidavit.

Respectfully,

(Name Illegible)
BC.   Chairman.

NC-132

Muskogee, Indian Territory, June 7, 1905.

Nancy Canard,
    Wetumka[sic], Indian Territory.

Dear Madam:

There are on file with the Commission affidavits relative to the birth of your minor child, Lizzie Canard, in which the date of her birth is given as April 13 and April 12, 1903.

You are requested to advise the Commission as to the correct date of the birth of your said child.

Respectfully,

Commissioner in Charge.

BIRTH AFFIDAVIT.
DEPARTMENT OF THE INTERIOR.
COMMISSION TO THE FIVE CIVILIZED TRIBES.

IN RE APPLICATION FOR ENROLLMENT, as a citizen of the CREEK Nation, of Oliver Lee Withers, born on the 1 day of Oct , 1904

Name of Father:	Robert Withers	a citizen of the	U.S.	Nation.
Name of Mother:	Lydia "	a citizen of the	Creek	Nation.

Postoffice   Mounds, I.T.

251

Applications for Enrollment of Creek Newborn
Act of 1905   Volume II

AFFIDAVIT OF ~~MOTHER~~. father

UNITED STATES OF AMERICA, Indian Territory, }
  WESTERN   DISTRICT.

    I, Robert Withers, on oath state that I am 38 years of age and a citizen by ----- , of the U. S. Nation; that I am the lawful ~~wife~~ hus of Lydia Withers, who is a citizen, by blood of the Creek Nation; that a male child was born to me on 1 day of Oct, 1904, that said child has been named Oliver Lee Withers, and is now living.

                                                Robert Withers

Witnesses To Mark:
{

    Subscribed and sworn to before me this 10" day of March, 1905.

                                      Edw C Griesel
                                            Notary Public.

BIRTH AFFIDAVIT.

DEPARTMENT OF THE INTERIOR.
COMMISSION TO THE FIVE CIVILIZED TRIBES.

IN RE APPLICATION FOR ENROLLMENT, as a citizen of the Creek Nation, of Oliver Lee Withers, born on the first day of October, 1904

Name of Father: Robert O. Withers   a non- a citizen of the   Creek   Nation.
Name of Mother: Lydia Withers   a citizen of the   Creek   Nation.

                            Postoffice   Mounds, Indian Territory

---

AFFIDAVIT OF MOTHER.

UNITED STATES OF AMERICA, Indian Territory, }
  Western   DISTRICT.

    I, Lydia Withers, on oath state that I am twenty four years of age and a citizen by blood, of the Creek Nation; that I am the lawful wife of Robert O. Withers, who is a non- citizen, by *(blank)* of the Creek Nation; that a male child was born to me on first day of October, I904, 1*(blank)*, that said child has been named Oliver Lee Withers, and is now living.

                                             Lydia Withers

Witnesses To Mark:
{

    Subscribed and sworn to before me this 2Ist[sic] day of March, 1905.

Applications for Enrollment of Creek Newborn
Act of 1905 Volume II

DJ Red
Notary Public.

AFFIDAVIT OF ATTENDING PHYSICIAN OR MID-WIFE.

UNITED STATES OF AMERICA, Indian Territory,
　　Western　　　DISTRICT.

    I, J. W. Bronaugh , a Physician , on oath state that I attended on Mrs. Lydia Withers , wife of Robert O. Withers on the first day of October, I904 , 1*(blank)* ; that there was born to her on said date a male child; that said child is now living and is said to have been named Oliver Lee Withers

J.W. Bronaugh M.D.

Witnesses To Mark:

    Subscribed and sworn to before me this 23rd day of March, 1905.

DJ Red
Notary Public.

NC 134.

Muskogee, Indian Territory, May 18, 1905.

Frank Oliver,
    Coweta, Indian Territory.

Dear Sir:

    In the matter of the application for the enrollment of your minor child, Louis Oliver, as a citizen of the Creek Nation, you are advised that the Commission requires the affidavit of the midwife or physician in attendance at the birth of said child.

    There is herewith enclosed a blank form of birth affidavit, and in executing same care should be exercised to see that all blanks are properly filled, all names written in full and in the event that the person signing the affidavit is unable to write, signature by mark must be attested by two witnesses. Each affidavit must be executed before a Notary Public and the notarial seal and signature of the officer must be attached to each separate affidavit.

Respectfully,

BC.　　　　　　　　　　　　　　　　　　　　　　　　　　Chairman.

Applications for Enrollment of Creek Newborn
Act of 1905 Volume II

NC 134.

Muskogee, Indian Territory, May 29, 1905.

Frank Oliver,
    Coweta, Indian Territory.

Dear Sir:

    In the matter of the application for the enrollment of your minor child, Louis Oliver, as a citizen of the Creek Nation, you have been advised that the affidavit of the midwife or physician in attendance at the child's birth was required. If it is impossible to secure the affidavit of the midwife or physician, you are required to procure the affidavits of two disinterested witnesses as to the birth of said child disinterested witnesses relative to the birth of said child.

    There is herewith enclosed a blank form of birth affidavit to be executed by the midwife or physician (if procurable). In filling same out, care should be exercised to see that all blanks are properly filled, all names writton[sic] in full, and in the event that the person signing the affidavit is unable to write, signature by mark must be attested by two witnesses.

                      Respectfully,

                                Chairman.

BIRTH AFFIDAVIT.

DEPARTMENT OF THE INTERIOR.
COMMISSION TO THE FIVE CIVILIZED TRIBES.

      IN RE APPLICATION FOR ENROLLMENT, as a citizen of the Creek Nation, of Louis Oliver, born on the ----- day of April , 1904

Name of Father: Frank Oliver   a citizen of the   U.S.   Nation.
Name of Mother: Hatty Sarty Oliver   a citizen of the   Creek Nation.

                    Postoffice   Coweta

Child Present ECG

AFFIDAVIT OF MOTHER.

UNITED STATES OF AMERICA, Indian Territory, ⎱
    Western   DISTRICT.   ⎰

    I, Hatty Sarty Oliver , on oath state that I am 33 years of age and a citizen by blood, of the Creek Nation; that I am the lawful wife of Frank Oliver , who is a

Applications for Enrollment of Creek Newborn
Act of 1905   Volume II

citizen, by ----- of the U. S. Nation; that a male child was born to me on ----- day of April, 1904 , that said child has been named Louis Oliver , and is now living.

Hatty Sarty Oliver

Witnesses To Mark:
{

Subscribed and sworn to before me this 10 day of March , 1905.

Edw C Griesel
Notary Public.

BIRTH AFFIDAVIT.

DEPARTMENT OF THE INTERIOR.
COMMISSION TO THE FIVE CIVILIZED TRIBES.

IN RE APPLICATION FOR ENROLLMENT, as a citizen of the Creek Nation, of Louis Oliver, born on the 9 day of April , 1904

Name of Father: Frank Oliver   ~~a citizen of the   Nation~~.
Name of Mother: Hatty Oliver nee Sarty   a citizen of the   Creek   Nation.

Postoffice   Coweta I.T.

AFFIDAVIT OF MOTHER.

UNITED STATES OF AMERICA, Indian Territory, ⎤
    (blank)   DISTRICT.   ⎦

I, Hatty Oliver , on oath state that I am 33 years of age and a citizen by birth, of the Creek   Nation; that I am the lawful wife of Frank Oliver   , who is a citizen, by (blank) of the (blank) Nation; that a male child was born to me on 9 day of April, 1904 , that said child has been named Louis Oliver , and was living March 4, 1905.

Hatty Oliver

Witnesses To Mark:
{ Carl Lumpkin
{ P. B. McKellop

Subscribed and sworn to before me this 23 day of May , 1905.

My commission expires   R. W. Lumpkin
Jany 13th 1909   Notary Public.

255

Applications for Enrollment of Creek Newborn
Act of 1905 Volume II

BIRTH AFFIDAVIT.

DEPARTMENT OF THE INTERIOR.
COMMISSION TO THE FIVE CIVILIZED TRIBES.

IN RE APPLICATION FOR ENROLLMENT, as a citizen of the Creek Nation, of Louis Oliver, born on the 9th day of April, 1904

Name of Father: Frank Oliver   a non citizen of the *(blank)* Nation.
Name of Mother: Hatty Sarty Oliver   a citizen of the Creek Nation.

Postoffice Coweta I.T.

AFFIDAVIT OF MOTHER.

UNITED STATES OF AMERICA, Indian Territory,
    Western   DISTRICT.

     I, Hatty Sarty Oliver, on oath state that I am 33 years of age and a citizen by blood, of the Creek Nation; that I am the lawful wife of Frank Oliver, who is a non citizen, by *(blank)* of the *(blank)* Nation; that a male child was born to me on 9th day of April, 1904, that said child has been named Louis Oliver, and was living March 4, 1905.

                                                      Hatty Sarty Oliver

Witnesses To Mark:
    Joe Fennell
    Ellis Childers

     Subscribed and sworn to before me this *(blank)* day of June 14, 1905.

                                        RC Allen
My Com Ex. Mch. 15, 1908   Notary Public.

AFFIDAVIT OF ATTENDING PHYSICIAN OR MID-WIFE.

UNITED STATES OF AMERICA, Indian Territory,
    Western   DISTRICT.

                                         we know personally
     We ~~I~~, JM Braddock & Mollie Braddock, on oath state that ~~I attended on~~ Mrs. Hatty Oliver, wife of Frank Oliver on the 9th day of April, 1904; that there was born to her on or about said date a male child; that said child was living March 4, 1905, and is said to have been named Louis Oliver.

                                          John M. Braddock
                                          Mollie Braddock

Applications for Enrollment of Creek Newborn
Act of 1905   Volume II

Witnesses To Mark:
- Joe Fennell
- Ellis Childers

Subscribed and sworn to before me this 14th day of June, 1905.

                                 RC Allen

My Com Ex. Mch. 15, 1908   Notary Public.

                                      NC 135.

                  Muskogee, Indian Territory, May 18, 1905.

Jack Bell,
     Tulsa, Indian Territory.

Dear Sir:

    In the matter of the application for the enrollment of your minor child, Lelia May Bell, as a citizen of the Creek Nation, you are advised that the Commission requires the affidavit of the midwife or physician in attendance at the birth of said child.

    There is herewith enclosed a blank form of birth affidavit, and in executing same care should be exercised to see that all blanks are properly filled, all names written in full and in the event that the person signing the affidavit is unable to write, signature by mark must be attested by two witnesses. Each affidavit must be executed before a Notary Public and the notarial seal and signature of the officer must be attached to each separate affidavit.

                             Respectfully,

BC.   Chairman.

BIRTH AFFIDAVIT.

DEPARTMENT OF THE INTERIOR.
COMMISSION TO THE FIVE CIVILIZED TRIBES.

    IN RE APPLICATION FOR ENROLLMENT, as a citizen of the Creek Nation, of Lelia May Bell, born on the 10 day of April, 1904

Name of Father:	Jack Bell	a citizen of the	U.S.	Nation.
Name of Mother:	Clarissa Bell	a citizen of the	Creek	Nation.

                              Postoffice   Tulsa, Ind. Terr.

Applications for Enrollment of Creek Newborn
Act of 1905   Volume II

AFFIDAVIT OF MOTHER.

UNITED STATES OF AMERICA, Indian Territory,
   Western   DISTRICT.

I, Clarissa Bell , on oath state that I am 34 years of age and a citizen by Blood , of the Creek Nation; that I am the lawful wife of Jack Bell , who is a citizen, by U.S. of the by marriage of Creek Nation; that a Girl child was born to me on 10 day of April , 1904 , that said child has been named Lelia May Bell , and was living March 4, 1905.

                                Clarissa Bell
Witnesses To Mark:

Subscribed and sworn to before me this 23^d day of May , 1905.

                        (Name Illegible)
My Commission Expires Dec. 15, 1907   Notary Public.

AFFIDAVIT OF ATTENDING PHYSICIAN OR MID-WIFE.

UNITED STATES OF AMERICA, Indian Territory,
   Western   DISTRICT.

I, Mary J Hodge , a midwife , on oath state that I attended on Mrs. Clarissa Bell , wife of Jack Bell on the 10 day of April , 1904 ; that there was born to her on said date a Girl child; that said child was living March 4, 1905, and is said to have been named Lelia May Bell
                                    her
                            Mary J x Hodge
Witnesses To Mark: mark
   Lyda F Shipman
   Anna Van Pelt

Subscribed and sworn to before me this 23^d day of May, 1905.

                        (Name Illegible)
My Commission Expires Dec. 15, 1907   Notary Public.

Applications for Enrollment of Creek Newborn
Act of 1905   Volume II

BIRTH AFFIDAVIT.

DEPARTMENT OF THE INTERIOR.
COMMISSION TO THE FIVE CIVILIZED TRIBES.

IN RE APPLICATION FOR ENROLLMENT, as a citizen of the CREEK Nation, of Lelia May Bell, born on the 10 day of April, 1904

Name of Father:	Jack Bell	a citizen of the	U.S.	Nation.
Name of Mother:	Clarissa "	a citizen of the	Creek	Nation.

Postoffice   Tulsa

Child Present Gr

AFFIDAVIT OF MOTHER.

UNITED STATES OF AMERICA, Indian Territory, }
WESTERN   DISTRICT. }

I, Clarissa Bell, on oath state that I am 34 years of age and a citizen by blood, of the Creek Nation; that I am the lawful wife of Jack Bell, who is a citizen, by ----- of the U.S. Nation; that a female child was born to me on 10 day of April, 1904, that said child has been named Lelia May Bell, and is now living.

Clarissa Bell

Witnesses To Mark:
{

Subscribed and sworn to before me this 15 day of March, 1905.

Edw C Griesel
Notary Public.

BIRTH AFFIDAVIT.

DEPARTMENT OF THE INTERIOR.
COMMISSION TO THE FIVE CIVILIZED TRIBES.

IN RE APPLICATION FOR ENROLLMENT, as a citizen of the Creek Nation, of Lela May Bell, born on the 10 day of April, 1904

Name of Father:	Jack Bell	a citizen of the	U.S.	Nation.
Name of Mother:	Clarissa Bell	a citizen of the	Creek	Nation.

Postoffice   Tulsa, I.T.

Applications for Enrollment of Creek Newborn
Act of 1905   Volume II

AFFIDAVIT OF MOTHER.

UNITED STATES OF AMERICA, Indian Territory, }
Western   DISTRICT.

   I, Clarissa Bell , on oath state that I am 34 years of age and a citizen by blood, of the Creek Nation; that I am the lawful wife of Jack Bell , who is a citizen, by marriage of the Creek Nation; that a Girl child was born to me on 10th day of April, 1904 , that said child has been named Lela May Bell , and was living March 4, 1905.

Clarissa Bell

Witnesses To Mark:
{ *(Illegible)* T Hodge
{ Carl O. Magee

   Subscribed and sworn to before me this 16 day of March , 1905.

(Name Illegible)
My Commission Expires Dec. 15, 1907   Notary Public.

AFFIDAVIT OF ATTENDING PHYSICIAN OR MID-WIFE.

UNITED STATES OF AMERICA, Indian Territory, }
Western   DISTRICT.

   I, Mary J Hodge , a midwife , on oath state that I attended on Mrs. Clarissa Bell , wife of Jack Bell on the 10 day of April , 1904 ; that there was born to her on said date a Girl child; that said child was living March 4, 1905, and is said to have been named Lelia May Bell

Mary J Hodge

Witnesses To Mark:
{ Mary J Hodge
{ Carl O. Magee

   Subscribed and sworn to before me this 16 day of March, 1905.

(Name Illegible)
My Commission Expires Dec. 15, 1907   Notary Public.

Applications for Enrollment of Creek Newborn
Act of 1905 Volume II

NC 136.

Muskogee, Indian Territory, May 18, 1905.

Jonas Heneha,
    Coweta, Indian Territory.

Dear Sir:

    In the matter of the application for the enrollment of your minor child, John Heneha, as a citizen of the Creek Nation, you are advised that the Commission requires the affidavit of the midwife or physician in attendance at the birth of said child.

    There is herewith enclosed a blank form of birth affidavit, and in executing same care should be exercised to see that all blanks are properly filled, all names written in full and in the event that the person signing the affidavit is unable to write, signature by mark must be attested by two witnesses. Each affidavit must be executed before a Notary Public and the notarial seal and signature of the officer must be attached to each separate affidavit.

                                 Respectfully,

BC.   Chairman.

COMMISSIONERS:
TAMS BIXBY,
THOMAS B. NEEDLES,
C.R. BRECKINBRIDGE.

DEPARTMENT OF THE INTERIOR,
COMMISSIONER TO THE FIVE CIVILIZED TRIBES.

REFER IN REPLY TO THE FOLLOWING:

NC 136.

WM. O. BEALL
Secretary

ADDRESS ONLY THE
COMMISSION TO THE FIVE CIVILIZED TRIBES.

Muskogee, Indian Territory, May 31, 1905.

Annie Hinneha,
    Coweta, Indian Territory.

Dear Madam:

    There are on file with the Commission affidavits signed by you under the name of Annie Heneha and Annie Hinneha. You have been identified on the rolls as Annie Tiger, and your husband is identified as Jonas Hinneha.

    You are requested to sign the correct one of the two enclosed blank forms. When correctly signed and executed return same to the Commission in the enclosed envelope.

                                   Respectfully,
                                   Tams Bixby

LM 531.   Chairman.
BC.

Applications for Enrollment of Creek Newborn
Act of 1905   Volume II

NC 136.

Muskogee, Indian Territory, July 9, 1905.

Jonas Hinneha,
    Coweta, Indian Territory.

Dear Sir:

There are on file at this office affidavits signed by your wife under the name of Annie Heneha and Annie Hinneha.

She has been identified on the rolls as Annie Tiger, and you as Jonas Hinneha.

You are requested to have your wife sign the correct one of the two enclosed blank forms. When correctly signed and executed, return same to this office in the inclosed[sic] envelope.

                Respectfully,

LM-5-31   Commissioner.

BIRTH AFFIDAVIT.

DEPARTMENT OF THE INTERIOR.
COMMISSION TO THE FIVE CIVILIZED TRIBES.

IN RE APPLICATION FOR ENROLLMENT, as a citizen of the Creek Nation, of John Hinneha, born on the 28 day of August, 1904

Name of Father: Jonas Hinneha   a citizen of the   Creek   Nation.
Name of Mother: Annie Hinneha   a citizen of the   Creek   Nation.

                Postoffice   Okfuskee[sic], I.T.

AFFIDAVIT OF MOTHER.

UNITED STATES OF AMERICA, Indian Territory,
    Western   DISTRICT.

I, Annie Hinneha, on oath state that I am 29 years of age and a citizen by blood, of the Creek Nation; that I am the lawful wife of Jonas Hinneha, who is a citizen, by blood of the Creek Nation; that a male child was born to me on 28 day of August, 1904, that said child has been named John Hinneha, and was living March 4, 1905.

Applications for Enrollment of Creek Newborn
Act of 1905   Volume II

Annie Hinneha

Witnesses To Mark:
  { Carl Lumpkin
  { Roman Sarty

Subscribed and sworn to before me this 25 day of May, 1905.

RC Allen
My Com. Ex. Mch 15, 1908.   Notary Public.

AFFIDAVIT OF ATTENDING PHYSICIAN OR MID-WIFE.

UNITED STATES OF AMERICA, Indian Territory, }
  Western   DISTRICT.

I, Elsa Sarty, a mid-wife, on oath state that I attended on Mrs. Annie Hinneha, wife of Jonas Hinneha on the 28 day of August, 1904; that there was born to her on said date a male child; that said child was living March 4, 1905, and is said to have been named John Hinneha

                        her
                    Elsa x Sarty

Witnesses To Mark: mark
  { Carl Lumpkin
  { Roman Sarty

Subscribed and sworn to before me this 25 day of May, 1905.

RC Allen
My Com. Ex. Mch 15, 1908.   Notary Public.

BIRTH AFFIDAVIT.

DEPARTMENT OF THE INTERIOR.
COMMISSION TO THE FIVE CIVILIZED TRIBES.

IN RE APPLICATION FOR ENROLLMENT, as a citizen of the Creek Nation, of John Heneha, born on the ----- day of August, 1904

Name of Father:	Jonas Heneha	a citizen of the	Creek	Nation.
Name of Mother:	Annie Heneha	a citizen of the	Creek	Nation.

Postoffice   Coweta

Applications for Enrollment of Creek Newborn
Act of 1905 Volume II

Child is present

AFFIDAVIT OF MOTHER.

UNITED STATES OF AMERICA, Indian Territory,
Western DISTRICT.

    I, Annie Heneha, on oath state that I am 28 years of age and a citizen by blood, of the Creek Nation; that I am the lawful wife of Jonas Heneha, who is a citizen, by blood of the Creek Nation; that a male child was born to me on ----- day of August, 1904, that said child has been named John Heneha, and is now living.

                                            Annie Heneha

Witnesses To Mark:
{

    Subscribed and sworn to before me this 10 day of March, 1905.

                                          Edw C Griesel
                                              Notary Public.

BIRTH AFFIDAVIT.

DEPARTMENT OF THE INTERIOR.
COMMISSION TO THE FIVE CIVILIZED TRIBES.

    IN RE APPLICATION FOR ENROLLMENT, as a citizen of the Creek Nation, of Velma Dunzy, born on the 12 day of April, 1904

Name of Father: Jackson R. Dunzy   a citizen of the   Creek   Nation.
Name of Mother: Lucinda Dunzy   a citizen of the Creek   Nation.

                          Postoffice   Wetumka[sic]

AFFIDAVIT OF MOTHER.

UNITED STATES OF AMERICA, Indian Territory,
Western DISTRICT.

    I, Lucinda Dunzy, on oath state that I am 37 years of age and a citizen by blood, of the Creek Nation; that I am the lawful wife of Jackson R. Dunzy, who is a citizen, by blood of the Creek Nation; that a female child was born to me on 12th day of April, 1904, that said child has been named Velma Dunzy, and was living March 4, 1905, and is now living.

                                            Lucinda Dunzy

Applications for Enrollment of Creek Newborn
Act of 1905 Volume II

Witnesses To Mark:

{

Subscribed and sworn to before me this 22d day of May , 1905.

My Com Ex 7-1-1906   Jas A Long
                                                    Notary Public.

AFFIDAVIT OF ATTENDING PHYSICIAN OR MID-WIFE.

UNITED STATES OF AMERICA, Indian Territory, }
    Western   DISTRICT.

I, Jackson R. Dunzy , a *(blank)* , on oath state that I attended on Mrs. Lucinda Dunzy , wife of Jackson R. Dunzy on the 12 day of April , 1904 ; that there was born to her on said date a female child; that said child was living March 4, 1905, and ~~is said to have been~~ was named Velma Dunzy and is now living.

                                        Jackson R. Dunzy

Witnesses To Mark:

{

Subscribed and sworn to before me this 22d day of May, 1905.

My Com Ex 7-1-1906   Jas A Long
                                                    Notary Public.

BIRTH AFFIDAVIT.

DEPARTMENT OF THE INTERIOR.
COMMISSION TO THE FIVE CIVILIZED TRIBES.

IN RE APPLICATION FOR ENROLLMENT, as a citizen of the CREEK Nation, of Velma Dunzy, born on the 12 day of April , 1904

Name of Father:	Jackson R. Dunzy	a citizen of the	Creek	Nation.
Name of Mother:	Lucinda "	a citizen of the	Creek	Nation.

                              Postoffice   Wetumka[sic], I.T.

Applications for Enrollment of Creek Newborn
Act of 1905   Volume II

AFFIDAVIT OF ~~MOTHER~~. father

UNITED STATES OF AMERICA, Indian Territory, }
WESTERN DISTRICT. }

I, Jackson Dunzy, on oath state that I am 38 years of age and a citizen by blood, of the Creek Nation; that I am the lawful ~~wife~~ hus of Lucinda Dunzy, who is a citizen, by blood of the Creek Nation; that a female child was born to me on 12 day of April, 1904, that said child has been named Velma Dunzy, and is now living.

Jackson Dunzy

Witnesses To Mark:
{

Subscribed and sworn to before me this 10 day of March, 1905.

Edw C Griesel
Notary Public.

DEPARTMENT OF THE INTERIOR,
COMMISSION TO THE FIVE CIVILIZED TRIBES.
Hon. TAMS BIXBY, Commissioner.

....
In Re Enrollment :
  of Velma Dunzy, :
.................:

UNITED STATES OF AMERICA,   )
) SS.
WESTERN DISTRICT, INDIAN TERRITORY.)

John P. Bradbury being duly sworn says that he is an American citizen of the age of 47 years. and is the Post Master at the Town of Wetumka[sic], that he has known Jackson R. Dunzy and Lucinda Dunzy for the past four years and that on or about April 12, 1904, there was born to Jackson R. Dunzy and Lucinda Dunzy his wife a girl baby who was alive upon March 4th, 1905, and who is now alive and who is called Velma Dunzy, that affiant is in no manner interested in the matter of the enrollment of the said child upon the Rolls of the Creek Nation and only makes this affidavit in the interest of truth and justice.

John P. Bradbury

Subscribed and sworn to before me this 31, day of July, A. D. 1905.

My Com Ex   Jas A. Long
7-1-1906   Notary Public.

Applications for Enrollment of Creek Newborn
Act of 1905   Volume II

DEPARTMENT OF THE INTERIOR,
COMMISSION TO THE FIVE CIVILIZED TRIBES.
Hon. TAMS BIXBY, Commissioner.

....
   In Re Enrollment   :
           of   :
   Velma Dunzy,   :
..............................:

UNITED STATES OF AMERICA,   )
) SS.
WESTERN DISTRICT, INDIAN TERRITORY.)

     William H. Waggner[sic] being duly sworn says that he is an American citizen of the age of 44 years and that in the year 1904, he was living March 4, 1905 on with his family upon land belonging to one of the children of Jackson R. Dunzy and Lucinda Dunza[sic], his wife and that in the month of April, and about the month of April, of said year there was born to the said Jackson R. Dunzy and Lucinda Dunzy his wife, a girl baby which they named, VELMA DUNZY, and which baby was alive upon the Fourth day of March, A. D. 1905, and who is now alive.   That affiant has no interest in said matter of the enrollment of Velma Dunzy and makes this affidavit in the interest of truth and that justice may be done all parties.   That affiant does not now live on the lands of the said child of J. R. Dunzy.

                                          William H Waggener

Subscribed and sworn to before me this 5 day of Aug. A. D. 1905.

       My Com. Ex. 7-1-1906   Jas A. Long
                                      Notary Public.

                                                                       NC 137.

                              Muskogee, Indian Territory, May 18, 1905.

Jackson Dunzy,
     Wetumka[sic], Indian Territory.

Dear Sir:

     In the matter of the application for the enrollment of your minor child, Velma Dunzy, as a citizen of the Creek Nation, you are advised that the Commission requires the affidavit of the midwife or physician in attendance at the birth of said child.

     There is herewith enclosed a blank form of birth affidavit, and in executing same care should be exercised to see that all blanks are properly filled, all names written in full and in the event that the person signing the affidavit is unable to write, signature by mark

Applications for Enrollment of Creek Newborn
Act of 1905 Volume II

must be attested by two witnesses. Each affidavit must be executed before a Notary Public and the notarial seal and signature of the officer must be attached to each separate affidavit.

                        Respectfully,

BC.   Chairman.

NC-137.

                                  Muskogee, Indian Territory, July 25, 1905.

Jackson Dunzy,
    Wetumka[sic], Indian Territory.

Dear Sir:

      In the matter of the application for the enrollment of your daughter Velma Dunzy, born April 12, 1904, as a citizen by blood of the Creek Nation there are on file the affidavits of yourself and your wife Lucinda Dunzy as to the birth of said child, your affidavits appearing on the blank provided for the affidavit of the attending physician or midwife.

      You are advised if there was an attending physician or midwife at the birth of said Velma Dunzy it will be necessary for you to furnish this office with the affidavit of said physician or midwife; but if no physician or midwife attended at the birth of said child, it will be necessary for you to furnish the affidavits of two disinterested persons who know that said child was born to your said wife, giving the date of her birth and whether or not the said Velma Dunzy was living March 4, 1905 on March 4, 1905.

      This matter should have prompt attention.

                      Respectfully,

                                           Commissioner.

                                Muskogee, Indian Territory, August 12, 1905.

Jackson R. Dunzy,
    Wetumka[sic], Indian Territory.

Dear Sir:

      Receipt is acknowledge of your letter of August 5, 1905, enclosing affidavits relative to the birth of your minor child, Velma Dunzy.

Applications for Enrollment of Creek Newborn
Act of 1905 Volume II

Respectfully,

Acting Commissioner.

BIRTH AFFIDAVIT.

DEPARTMENT OF THE INTERIOR.
COMMISSION TO THE FIVE CIVILIZED TRIBES.

IN RE APPLICATION FOR ENROLLMENT, as a citizen of the CREEK Nation, of Liza Jane Dice , born on the 7 day of Feb , 1904

| Name of Father: | Jim Dice | a citizen of the | U S | Nation. |
| Name of Mother: | Dove " | a citizen of the | Creek | Nation. |

Postoffice   Weleetka I.T.

(child present) HGH

AFFIDAVIT OF MOTHER.

UNITED STATES OF AMERICA, Indian Territory,
WESTERN   DISTRICT.

I, Dove Dice , on oath state that I am 27 years of age and a citizen by blood , of the Creek Nation; that I am the lawful wife of Jim Dice , who is a citizen, by ----- of the U.S. Nation; that a female child was born to me on 7 day of Feb , 1904 , that said child has been named Liza Jane Dice , and is now living.

Her
Dove x Dice
mark

Witnesses To Mark:
- Zera Ellen Parrish
- EC Griesel

Subscribed and sworn to before me this 10 day of March , 1905.

Edw C Griesel
Notary Public.

BIRTH AFFIDAVIT.

DEPARTMENT OF THE INTERIOR.
COMMISSION TO THE FIVE CIVILIZED TRIBES.

IN RE APPLICATION FOR ENROLLMENT, as a citizen of the CREEK Nation, of Liza Jane Dice , born on the 7 day of Feb , 1904

| Name of Father: | Jim Dice | a citizen of the | U S | Nation. |
| Name of Mother: | Dove " | a citizen of the | Creek | Nation. |

Applications for Enrollment of Creek Newborn
Act of 1905 Volume II

Postoffice   Weleetka I.T.

Child Present ECG

AFFIDAVIT OF ~~MOTHER~~. father

UNITED STATES OF AMERICA, Indian Territory, }
WESTERN   DISTRICT.

I, Jim Dice , on oath state that I am 34 years of age and a citizen by ----- , of the U. S. Nation; that I am the lawful ~~wife~~ of Dove Dice , who is a citizen, by blood of the Creek Nation; that a female child was born to me on 7 day of Feb , 1904 , that said child has been named Liza Jane Dice , and is now living.

His
Jim x Dice
mark

Witnesses To Mark:
{ Zera Ellen Parrish
{ EC Griesel

Subscribed and sworn to before me this 10 day of March, 1905.

Edw C Griesel
Notary Public.

BIRTH AFFIDAVIT.

DEPARTMENT OF THE INTERIOR.
COMMISSION TO THE FIVE CIVILIZED TRIBES.

IN RE APPLICATION FOR ENROLLMENT, as a citizen of the Creek Nation, of Freddie James Dice, born on the 11 day of Aug, 1902

Name of Father:	James Dice	a citizen of the United States Nation.
Name of Mother:	Dove Dice	a citizen of the Creek Nation.

Postoffice   Weleetka Ind Ter

AFFIDAVIT OF MOTHER.

UNITED STATES OF AMERICA, Indian Territory, }
Western   DISTRICT.

I, Dove Dice, on oath state that I am 27 years of age and a citizen by birth , of the Creek Nation; that I am the lawful wife of James Dice , who is a citizen, by birth of the United States ~~Nation~~; that a male child was born to me on 11 day of August , 1903[sic] , that said child has been named Freddie James Dice , and was living March 4, 1905.

Applications for Enrollment of Creek Newborn
Act of 1905   Volume II

                                  Her
                              Dove x Dice
Witnesses To Mark: mark
{ R L Meaden
  N T Reynolds

Subscribed and sworn to before me this 24 day of May , 1905.

                              E E Lewis
                                      Notary Public.
My commission expires 5/20-1907

AFFIDAVIT OF ATTENDING PHYSICIAN OR MID-WIFE.

UNITED STATES OF AMERICA, Indian Territory,
    Western   **DISTRICT.**

    I, Kate Hutchinson, a midwife , on oath state that I attended on Mrs. Dove Dice , wife of James Dice on the 11 day of Aug , 1903[sic] ; that there was born to her on said date a male child; that said child was living March 4, 1905, and is said to have been named Freddie James Dice   her
                              Kate x Hutchinson
                                  mark
Witnesses To Mark:
{ R L Meaden
  N T Reynolds

Subscribed and sworn to before me this 24 day of May , 1905.

                              E E Lewis
                                      Notary Public.
My commission expires 5/20-1907

BIRTH AFFIDAVIT.
                        DEPARTMENT OF THE INTERIOR.
            COMMISSION TO THE FIVE CIVILIZED TRIBES.

    IN RE APPLICATION FOR ENROLLMENT, as a citizen of the CREEK Nation, of Freddy James Dice, born on the 11 day of Aug, 1902

| Name of Father: | Jim Dice | a citizen of the | U. S. | Nation. |
| Name of Mother: | Dove " | a citizen of the | Creek | Nation. |

                      Postoffice   Weleetka I.T.

Applications for Enrollment of Creek Newborn
Act of 1905 Volume II

(Child present)

AFFIDAVIT OF MOTHER.

UNITED STATES OF AMERICA, Indian Territory, }
WESTERN DISTRICT.

I, Dove Dice, on oath state that I am 27 years of age and a citizen by blood , of the Creek Nation; that I am the lawful wife of Jim Dice , who is a citizen, by ----- of the U. S. Nation; that a male child was born to me on 11 day of August , 1902 , that said child has been named Freddy James Dice , and is now living.

           Her
          Dove x Dice
Witnesses To Mark: mark
{ Zera Ellen Parrish
  EC Griesel

Subscribed and sworn to before me this 10 day of March , 1905.

         Edw C Griesel
           Notary Public.

BIRTH AFFIDAVIT.

DEPARTMENT OF THE INTERIOR.
COMMISSION TO THE FIVE CIVILIZED TRIBES.

IN RE APPLICATION FOR ENROLLMENT, as a citizen of the CREEK Nation, of Freddy James Dice , born on the 11 day of Aug , 1902

Name of Father: Jim Dice   a citizen of the U. S. Nation.
Name of Mother: Dove Dice a citizen of the Creek Nation.

        Postoffice Weleetka I.T.

Child Present ECG

AFFIDAVIT OF MOTHER. father

UNITED STATES OF AMERICA, Indian Territory, }
WESTERN DISTRICT.

I, Jim Dice , on oath state that I am 34 years of age and a citizen by ----- , of the U. S. Nation; that I am the lawful wife hus of Dove Dice , who is a citizen, by blood of the Creek Nation; that a boy child was born to me on 11 day of Aug , 1902 , that said child has been named Freddy James Dice , and is now living.

Applications for Enrollment of Creek Newborn
Act of 1905 Volume II

His mark
Jim x Dice

Witnesses To Mark:
- Zera Ellen Parrish
- EC Griesel

Subscribed and sworn to before me this 10 day of March, 1905.

Edw C Griesel
Notary Public.

BIRTH AFFIDAVIT.

DEPARTMENT OF THE INTERIOR.
COMMISSION TO THE FIVE CIVILIZED TRIBES.

IN RE APPLICATION FOR ENROLLMENT, as a citizen of the Creek Nation, of Freddie James Dice, born on the 11 day of Aug, 1902

Name of Father:	Jim Dice	a citizen of the United States ~~Nation~~.
Name of Mother:	Dove Dice	a citizen of the Creek Nation.

Postoffice   Weleetka Ind Ter

AFFIDAVIT OF MOTHER.

UNITED STATES OF AMERICA, Indian Territory,
Western Judicial   DISTRICT.

I, Dove Dice, on oath state that I am 27 years of age and a citizen by birth , of the Creek Nation; that I am the lawful wife of Jim Dice , who is a citizen, by birth of the America ~~Nation~~; that a Male child was born to me on 11th day of August ,1902 , that said child has been named Freddie James Dice , and was living March 4, 1905.

Her
Dove Dice x
mark

Witnesses To Mark:
- Nat Williams
- Chas Coachman

Subscribed and sworn to before me this 16th day of June , 1905.

My Commission Expires Aug 15th 1906   B.H. Mills
Notary Public.

Applications for Enrollment of Creek Newborn
Act of 1905 Volume II

AFFIDAVIT OF ATTENDING PHYSICIAN OR MID-WIFE.

UNITED STATES OF AMERICA, Indian Territory, }
  Western   DISTRICT.

I, Kate Hutchinson, a Mid Wife , on oath state that I attended on Mrs. Dove Dice , wife of Jim Dice on the 11th day of Aug ,1902 ; that there was born to her on said date a Male child; that said child was living March 4, 1905, and is said to have been named Freddie James Dice

her
Kate Hutchinson x
mark

Witnesses To Mark:
 { Nat Williams
   Chas Coachman

Subscribed and sworn to before me this 16th day of June , 1905.

My Commission Expires Aug 15th 1906   B.H. Mills
Notary Public.

NC 138.

Muskogee, Indian Territory, May 18, 1905.

Jim Dice,
  Weeletka[sic], Indian Territory.

Dear Sir:

In the matter of the application for the enrollment of your minor children, Freddy James and Liza Jane Dice, as citizens of the Creek Nation, you are advised that the Commission requires the affidavit of the midwife or physician in attendance at the birth of said children.

There are herewith enclosed two blank forms of birth affidavits, and in executing same care should be exercised to see that all blanks are properly filled, all names written in full and in the event that the persons signing the affidavits are unable to write, signatures by mark must be attested by two witnesses. Each affidavit must be executed before a Notary Public and the notarial seal and signature of the officer must be attached to each separate affidavit.

Respectfully,

BC.   Chairman.

Applications for Enrollment of Creek Newborn
Act of 1905 Volume II

NC-138

Muskogee, Indian Territory, May 29, 1905.

Jim Dice,
  Weleetka, Indian Territory.

Dear Sir:

In the matter of the application for the enrollment of your minor child, Freddie James Dice, as a citizen of the Creek Nation, there are on file with the Commission affidavits executed by yourself and Dove Dice, the mother of said child, and Kate Hutchinson, the midwife in attendance at its birth, in which the date of birth is given as August 11, 1902 and August 11, 1903.

For the purpose of correcting the date, there is herewith enclosed a blank form of birth affidavit, which should be executed by the mother of said child and the midwife in attendance at its birth, care being taken that the correct date is given, and to see that all blanks are properly filled, all names written in full, and in the event that either of the persons signing the affidavit is unable to write, signature by mark must be attested by two witnesses.

In the matter of the application for the enrollment of your minor child, Eliza Jane Dice, it is required that you furnish the affidavit of the midwife in attendance at the birth of said child. If that is impossible, you are requested to obtain the affidavits of two disinterested witnesses relative to the birth of said child.

Respectfully,

2 B A   Chairman.

N. C. 138   COPY

Wetumka[sic], Ind Ter 6th/16th 1905

Hon Tames Bixby,
  Muskogee, I.T.

Dear Sir: Enclosed you will find the Affidavit of Mother and Mid Wife of Freddie James Dice and as it is impossible to get the affidavit of the Mid Wife of Eliza Jane Dice the same will be forwarded later.

Yours Truly

her
Dove Dice X
mark

Witness
Nat Williams
Chas. Coachman

Applications for Enrollment of Creek Newborn
Act of 1905   Volume II

TERRITORY OF OKLAHOMA
ss
COUNTY OF PAYNE

    On this 13th day of March, 1905, personally appeared before the undersigned, a Notary Public in and for the aforesaid County and Territory, Mrs. A. J. Casada, who on her oath says that she is a midwife; that she was present at the birth of a child born to Mrs. O. C. Dale in the Creek Nation, Indian Territory, near Shafter, Oklahoma, on the 17th day of August, 1903, which child, a boy, the parents say they have named Charles Henry Dale.

her
Mrs. A. J. x Casada
mark

Subscribed and sworn to before me this 13th day of March, 1905.

Al Adams
Notary Public.

My Commission expires Jan. 6, 1907.

(Copy)

R 71
C.139.

H.S. GUTHRIDGE.

Fine dress Goods,		Staple and
Gents' Furnishings,		Fancy Groceries.
Hats, Caps, Boots,	dealer in	Queensware.
Shoes and Notions.		

GENERAL MERCHANDISE.

Yale, Oklahoma, May 31, 190__.

Gentlemen of the Daws[sic] Commission,

    Will just say in explanation of enclosed affidavit, that owing to an accident to her arm Mrs. Cassady could not sign her name to the other paper, but is able now to hold a pen, and in regard to the name of the child, the enrollment clerk did not ask for the full name, so my wife said Charley insteat[sic] of Charles Henry. Hope this will be satisfactory.

Yours Respt,

O.C.Dale

Yale

R.F.D. #2.

OK

Applications for Enrollment of Creek Newborn
Act of 1905 Volume II

COMMISSIONERS:
TAMS BIXBY,
THOMAS B. NEEDLES,
C.R. BRECKINRIDGE.

WM. O. BEALL
Secretary

**DEPARTMENT OF THE INTERIOR,
COMMISSIONER TO THE FIVE CIVILIZED TRIBES.**

REFER IN REPLY TO THE FOLLOWING:

NC-139

ADDRESS ONLY THE
COMMISSION TO THE FIVE CIVILIZED TRIBES.

Muskogee, Indian Territory, May 29, 1905.

Oliver Dale,
    Shafter, Indian Territory.

Dear Sir:

    The Commission is in receipt of the affidavit of Mrs. A. J. Casada, the midwife in attendance at the birth of your minor child, Charles Henry Dale. Said affidavit is signed by mark and the signatures of the two witnesses to said mark are omitted. In an affidavit filed with the Commission and executed by the mother of said child, its name is given as Charley Dale.

    You are advised that the Commission requires the affidavit of the midwife in the case. For this purpose, there is herewith enclosed a blank form of birth affidavit. In executing same, care should be taken to see that all blanks are properly filled, all names written in full, and in the event that the person signing the affidavit is unable to write, signature by mark must be attested by two witnesses.

    This matter should receive your prompt attention.

                               Respectfully,

                               Tams Bixby

1 B A   Chairman.

BIRTH AFFIDAVIT.

**DEPARTMENT OF THE INTERIOR.
COMMISSION TO THE FIVE CIVILIZED TRIBES.**

    IN RE APPLICATION FOR ENROLLMENT, as a citizen of the CREEK Nation, of Charley Dale, born on the 17 day of Aug., 1903

Name of Father:	Oliver Dale	a citizen of the	U.S.	Nation.
Name of Mother:	Izora "	a citizen of the	Creek	Nation.

Applications for Enrollment of Creek Newborn
Act of 1905   Volume II

Postoffice   Shafter, Okla.

(Child present)

AFFIDAVIT OF MOTHER.

UNITED STATES OF AMERICA, Indian Territory, }
WESTERN   DISTRICT.

I, Izora Dale , on oath state that I am 27 years of age and a citizen by blood , of the Creek Nation; that I am the lawful wife of Oliver Dale , who is a citizen, by ----- of the U. S. Nation; that a male child was born to me on 17 day of Aug , 1903 , that said child has been named Charley Dale , and is now living.

Izora Dale

Witnesses To Mark:
{

Subscribed and sworn to before me this 15 day of March , 1905.

Edw C Griesel
Notary Public.

BIRTH AFFIDAVIT.

DEPARTMENT OF THE INTERIOR.
COMMISSION TO THE FIVE CIVILIZED TRIBES.

IN RE APPLICATION FOR ENROLLMENT, as a citizen of the Creek Nation, of Charles Henry Dale , born on the 17th day of August , 1903

Name of Father:	O. C. Dale	a citizen of the United States Nation.
Name of Mother:	Izora E. Dale	a citizen of the Creek Nation.

Postoffice   Shafter, Okla. RFD #2

AFFIDAVIT OF MOTHER.

Oklahoma
UNITED STATES OF AMERICA, ~~Indian~~ Territory, }
Payne County   ~~DISTRICT.~~

I, Izora E Dale , on oath state that I am 27 years of age and a citizen by blood , of the Creek Nation; that I am the lawful wife of O. C. Dale , who is a citizen, by birth of the United States ~~Nation~~; that a male child was born to me on 17th day of August , 1903 , that said child has been named Charles Henry Dale , and was living March 4, 1905.

Izora E Dale

Applications for Enrollment of Creek Newborn
Act of 1905 Volume II

Witnesses To Mark:
{

    Subscribed and sworn to before me this 1st day of June, 1905.

                            Al Adams
                                    Notary Public.
              My Commission Expires Jan. 6, 1907

AFFIDAVIT OF ATTENDING PHYSICIAN OR MID-WIFE.
Oklahoma
UNITED STATES OF AMERICA, ~~Indian~~ Territory, }
    Payne County   ~~DISTRICT.~~ }

    I, Mrs. A. J. Casada, a midwife, on oath state that I attended on Mrs. Izora E Dale, wife of O. C. Dale on the 17th day of August, 1903; that there was born to her on said date a male child; that said child was living March 4, 1905, and is said to have been named Charles Henry Dale

                            Mrs. A. J. Casada

Witnesses To Mark:
{

    Subscribed and sworn to before me this 1st day of June, 1905.

                            Al Adams
                                  Notary Public.
              My Commission Expires Jan. 6, 1907

(The above affidavit was copied again)

    DEPARTMENT OF THE INTERIOR.

COMMISSION TO THE FIVE CIVILIZED TRIBES.

IN RE APPLICATION FOR ENROLLMENT, as a citizen of the Creek Nation, of Hettie Tiger, born on the 15th day of March 1904, comes Amos Tiger, aged 24 years, whose Post Office address is Okmulgee INd.[sic] Ter., and swears among other things, that he cnnot[sic] furnish the affidavit if Dr. J.F. Howard the attending physian[sic] at the birth of his child Hettie Tiger, for the reason that the said Dr. J.F. Howard is dead, and he requests that you accept the affidavit of Bertha Whitecotton the nurse in lieu thereof, this 14th day of July 1905.

                            Amos Tiger

Applications for Enrollment of Creek Newborn
Act of 1905 Volume II

Subscribed and sworn to before me this 14th day of July 1905, and I hereby certify that the said affiant Amos Tiger is a credable[sic] person and entitled to credit.

My commission expires July 8/06. B.H. Nicholas
Notary Public.

BIRTH AFFIDAVIT.

DEPARTMENT OF THE INTERIOR.
COMMISSION TO THE FIVE CIVILIZED TRIBES.

IN RE APPLICATION FOR ENROLLMENT, as a citizen of the CREEK Nation, of Hettie Tiger, born on the 15 day of March , 1904

Name of Father:	Amos Tiger	a citizen of the Creek	Nation.
Name of Mother:	Devotia "	a citizen of the U. S.	Nation.

Postoffice   Okmulgee

Child Present Gr

AFFIDAVIT OF MOTHER.

UNITED STATES OF AMERICA, Indian Territory,
WESTERN   DISTRICT.

I, Devotia Tiger , on oath state that I am 18 years of age and a citizen by ----- , of the U.S. Nation; that I am the lawful wife of Amos Tiger , who is a citizen, by blood of the Creek Nation; that a female child was born to me on 15 day of March , 1904 , that said child has been named Hettie Tiger , and was living March 4, 1905.

Devotia Tiger

Witnesses To Mark:

Subscribed and sworn to before me this 13 day of March , 1905.

Edw C Griesel
Notary Public.

father
AFFIDAVIT OF ~~ATTENDING PHYSICIAN OR MID-WIFE~~.

UNITED STATES OF AMERICA, Indian Territory,
Western   DISTRICT.

I, AmosTiger , a m , ~~on oath state that I~~ attended on Mrs.   , ~~wife~~ husband of Devotia Tiger   on the 15 day of March , 1904 ; that there was born to her on said date

Applications for Enrollment of Creek Newborn
Act of 1905 Volume II

a female child; that said child was living March 4, 1905, and is said to have been named Hettie Tiger

Amos Tiger

Witnesses To Mark:

{ Subscribed and sworn to before me this 13 day of March, 1905.

Edw C Griesel
Notary Public.

BIRTH AFFIDAVIT.

DEPARTMENT OF THE INTERIOR.
COMMISSION TO THE FIVE CIVILIZED TRIBES.

IN RE APPLICATION FOR ENROLLMENT, as a citizen of the Creek Nation, of Hettie Tiger, born on the 15th day of March, 1904

Name of Father: Amos Tiger   a citizen of the   Creek   Nation.
Name of Mother: Deovocha Tiger   a citizen of the   Creek   Nation.
by Marriage.

Postoffice   Okmulgee Ind. Ter.

AFFIDAVIT OF MOTHER.

UNITED STATES OF AMERICA, Indian Territory, }
   Western Judicial   DISTRICT.

I, Deovocha Tiger , on oath state that I am 18 years of age and a citizen by marriage , of the Creek Nation; that I am the lawful wife of Amos Tiger , who is a citizen, by birth of the Creek Nation; that a female child was born to me on 15th day of March , 1904 , that said child has been named Hettie Tiger , and was living March 4, 1905.

her
Deovocha x Tiger
mark

Witnesses To Mark:
{ H.C Beckman
  B.H. Nicholas

Subscribed and sworn to before me this 14th day of July , 1905.

My commission expires July 8/05.   B.H. Nicholas
Notary Public.

Applications for Enrollment of Creek Newborn
Act of 1905   Volume II

AFFIDAVIT OF ATTENDING PHYSICIAN OR MID-WIFE.

UNITED STATES OF AMERICA, Indian Territory,
Western Judicial   DISTRICT.

    I, Bertha Whitecotton , a nurse , on oath state that I attended on Mrs. Deovocha Tiger , wife of Amos Tiger on the 15th day of March , 1904 ; that there was born to her on said date a female child; that said child was living March 4, 1905, and is said to have been named Hettie Tiger

                                            Bertha Whitecotton

Witnesses To Mark:
    H.O. Beckman

    Subscribed and sworn to before me this 14th day of July , 1905.

My commission expires July 8/05.   B.H. Nicholas
                                                 Notary Public.

NC 140.

Muskogee, Indian Territory, May 18, 1905.

Amos Tiger,
    Okmulgee, Indian Territory.

Dear Sir:

    In the matter of the application for the enrollment of your minor child, Hettie Tiger, as a citizen of the Creek Nation, you are advised that the Commission requires the affidavit of the midwife or physician in attendance at the birth of said child.

    There is herewith enclosed a blank form of birth affidavit, and in executing same care should be exercised to see that all blanks are properly filled, all names written in full and in the event that the person signing the affidavit is unable to write, signature by mark must be attested by two witnesses. Each affidavit must be executed before a Notary Public and the notarial seal and signature of the officer must be attached to each separate affidavit.

                                            Respectfully,

BC.   Chairman.

Applications for Enrollment of Creek Newborn
Act of 1905   Volume II

Cr.NC-140

Muskogee, Indian Territory, July 19, 1905.

Devotia Tiger,
    Okmulgee, Indian Territory.

Dear Madam:

There are on file in this office affidavits relative to the birth of your minor child, Hettie Tiger, in which your name is given as Devotia and Deovocha Tiger.
You are requested to advise this office as to your correct name.

Respectfully,

Commissioner.

Cr.NC-140

Muskogee, Indian Territory, July 19, 1905.

Devotia Tiger,
    Okmulgee, Indian Territory.

Dear Madam:

There are on file in this office affidavits relative to the birth of your minor child, Hettie Tiger, in which your name is given as Devotia and Deovocha Tiger.

You are requested to advise this office as to your correct name.

Respectfully,

(Signed) Tasm[sic] Bixby

Commissioner.

Devocha Tiger, is my wife's name and she is the mother of Hettie Tiger.

Yours truly,

(Signed) Amos Tiger

Applications for Enrollment of Creek Newborn
Act of 1905   Volume II

DEPARTMENT OF THE INTERIOR,
COMMISSION TO THE.
NEAR SENORA, I.T. April 21, 1905.

In the matter of the application for the enrollment of certain new born children of "Snake" parents:

Louie Lowe, being duly sworn, testified as follows, through Official Interpreter, Alex Posey.

Examination by the Commission:
Q What is your name? A Louie Lowe.
Q What is your age? A 25.
Q What is your post office? A Henryetta.
Q Are you a citizen of the Creek Nation? A I am a member of the Okchiye Town and Fish Pond Town.

Statement: Lijah Toney, of Hickory Ground and Losanna Lowe, of Kialigee Town, have a child named Foley Toney, living, it is two years two months and twenty five days old. Their Post Office is Henryetta.

Peter Sloan a Seminole, and Lodie of Weogufky Town, have a child near three years old, and the youngest about a year old; the older named Lillie and the other's name is not know[sic], but it is a boy, both, are living. Their post office is Henryetta.

I think Cakocheo of Thlewarthle and Lucinda, of Eufaula, Indian Territory. Canadian, have a child that hasn't been filed for yet, it is about a year old, don't know it's[sic] name, it is a boy and living. Their Post Office is Senora, Indian Territory. but he nevers[sic] goes after his mail, it is usually returned.

Willie Harjo of Weogufty, and Sukie Harjo of Kisligee have one child, was born in either January or February of this year, and is now living. It's[sic] mother is dead, I don't know it's[sic] name but it is under the custody of Joe and Cinda Yahdihka, whose post office is Dustin.

Letka Chupco and Jenely, Leetka is of Fish Pond or Greenleaf and Janely of Kialigee Town; they have three children, one set of twins, both boys nearly three years old, and the youngest child is a girl born last October, the twins are named John and Johnson, and I don't know the name of the little girl; all three are living, post office, Senora, Indian Territory. I think you have now all the children in the neighborhood except those that will be born tonight;

(The above testimony was partly given by Lewis Harjo, of Senora, Indian Territory., about 35 years of age, who was duly sworn, through Official Interpreter).

Applications for Enrollment of Creek Newborn
Act of 1905 Volume II

Henry G. Hains, being duly sworn, on his oath, states that the above and foregoing is a true and correct transcript of his stenographic notes as taken in said cause on said date. Henry G. Hains

Subscribed and sworn to before me this 11th day of May, 1905.

Drennan C Skaggs
Notary Public.

C 1063

DEPARTMENT OF THE INTERIOR,
COMMISSION TO THE FIVE CIVILIZED TRIBES.
Senora, I. T, June 21, 1905.

In the matter of the application for the enrollment of Nettie Harjo as a citizen by blood of the Creek Nation.

LUCINDA TIGER, being duly sworn, testified as follows:

Through Alex Posey Official Interpreter:

BY COMMISSION:
Q What is your name? A Lucinda Tiger.
Q How old are you? A about thirty.
Q What is your post office address? A Henryetta.
Q Are you a citizen of the Creek Nation? A Yes, sir.
Q To what town do you belong? A Eufaula Canadian.
Q Do you know Willie and Sucky[sic] Harjo? A Yes, sir.
Q Have they a child for whom they have not made application? A Yes, sir.
Q What is the child's name? A Nettie. The child is living with me.
Q Is the mother of the child dead? A Yes, sir.
Q When did she die? A She died in February, this year.
Q Do you know when the child was born? A I do not know of my own personal knowledge when the child was born but the father tells me tha[sic] the child was born in July and will be two years old next July.
Q Is the child any relation of yours? A I am an aunt to the child.

The child is present and appear[sic] to be about two years old.

---ooo○○○ooo---

I, D. C. Skaggs, on oath state that the above and foregoing is a full and true transcript of my stenographic notes as taken in said cause on said date.

DC Skaggs

Subscribed and sworn to before me this ___ day of JUL 17 1905 1905.

Applications for Enrollment of Creek Newborn
Act of 1905 Volume II

Edw C Griesel
Notary Public.

BIRTH AFFIDAVIT.

DEPARTMENT OF THE INTERIOR.
COMMISSION TO THE FIVE CIVILIZED TRIBES.

IN RE APPLICATION FOR ENROLLMENT, as a citizen of the Creek Nation, of Nettie Harjo, born on the 20th day of July, 1903

Name of Father:	Willie Harjo	a citizen of the	Creek	Nation.
Name of Mother:	Sukey Harjo	a citizen of the	Creek	Nation.

Postoffice   Henryetta, Ind. Ter.

AFFIDAVIT OF MOTHER.

UNITED STATES OF AMERICA, Indian Territory,
Western Judicial   DISTRICT.

I, "Sukey Harjo is Deceased", on oath state that I am years of age and a citizen by , of the Creek Nation; that I am the lawful wife of , who is a citizen, by of the Creek Nation; that a child was born to me on day of , 190 , that said child has been named , and is now living.

Witnesses To Mark:
{

Subscribed and sworn to before me this day of , 1905.

Notary Public.

AFFIDAVIT OF ATTENDING PHYSICIAN OR MID-WIFE.

UNITED STATES OF AMERICA, Indian Territory,
Western Judicial   DISTRICT.

I, Nancy Scott, a woman , on oath state that I attended on Mrs. Sukey Harjo, wife of Willie Harjo on the 20th day of July , 1903 ; that there was born to her on said date a female child; that said child was living March 4, 1905, and is said to have been named Nettie Harjo   her
                                                            Nancy x Scott
                                                                  mark

Applications for Enrollment of Creek Newborn
Act of 1905   Volume II

Witnesses To Mark:
{ J H Osborne
{ J.E. Williams

Subscribed and sworn to before me this 20th day of May, 1905.

My Commission expires 22^d day of April 1907   William B. Morgan
                                                           Notary Public.

A.P McKellop came in with father and vouches for facts herein set forth.
BIRTH AFFIDAVIT.

DEPARTMENT OF THE INTERIOR.
COMMISSION TO THE FIVE CIVILIZED TRIBES.

IN RE APPLICATION FOR ENROLLMENT, as a citizen of the Creek Nation, of Nettie Harjo, born on the 20 day of July, 1903

Name of Father: Willie Harjo   a citizen of the   Creek   Nation.
Name of Mother: Sookey   "   a citizen of the   "   Nation.

                           Postoffice   Henrietta I.T.

AFFIDAVIT OF ~~MOTHER~~.

UNITED STATES OF AMERICA, Indian Territory, }
         Western   **DISTRICT.**

I, Willie Harjo, on oath state that I am 29 years of age and a citizen by blood, of the Creek Nation; that I am the lawful ~~wife~~ hus of Sookey Harjo, who ~~is~~ was a citizen, by blood of the Creek Nation; that a female child was born to me on 20 day of July, 1903, that said child has been named Nettie Harjo, and is now living.

                                                His
                                       Willie x Harjo
Witnesses To Mark: mark
{ A.P. McKellop
{ EC Griesel

Subscribed and sworn to before me this 10 day of March, 1905.

                                          Edw C Griesel
                                              Notary Public.

Applications for Enrollment of Creek Newborn
Act of 1905 Volume II

AFFIDAVIT OF ~~ATTENDING PHYSICIAN OR MID-WIFE~~. Acquaintance

UNITED STATES OF AMERICA, Indian Territory, }
Western DISTRICT.

I, A. P. McKellop , a citizen , on oath state that ~~I attended on Mrs.   , wife of~~ on the 20   day of July , 1903 ; ~~that~~ there was born to her on said date a female child; that said child is now living and is said to have been named Nettie Harjo and that wife and mid-wife are both dead.

A. P. McKellop

Witnesses To Mark:
{

Subscribed and sworn to before me this 10 day of March, 1905.

Edw C Griesel
Notary Public.

BIRTH AFFIDAVIT.

DEPARTMENT OF THE INTERIOR.
COMMISSION TO THE FIVE CIVILIZED TRIBES.

IN RE APPLICATION FOR ENROLLMENT, as a citizen of the Creek Nation, of Seta Harjo , born on the 17 day of Jan. , 1905

Name of Father: Willie Harjo   a citizen of the   Creek   Nation.
Name of Mother: Sookey   "   a citizen of the   "   Nation.

Postoffice   Henrietta

AFFIDAVIT OF ~~MOTHER~~.

UNITED STATES OF AMERICA, Indian Territory, }
Western DISTRICT.

I, Willie Harjo , on oath state that I am 29   years of age and a citizen by blood , of the Creek   Nation; that I am the lawful ~~wife~~ hus of Sookey Harjo , who is a citizen, by blood of the Creek   Nation; that a female   child was born to me on 17 day of Jan, 1905 , that said child has been named Seta Harjo   , and ~~is now living~~. and died 21st Feb. 1905

His
Willie x Harjo
mark

Witnesses To Mark:
{ A.P. McKellop
  EC Griesel

Applications for Enrollment of Creek Newborn
Act of 1905 Volume II

Subscribed and sworn to before me this 10 day of March, 1905.

                                                        Edw C Griesel
                                                        Notary Public.

NC 141.   JLD
DEPARTMENT OF THE INTERIOR,
COMMISSIONER TO THE FIVE CIVILIZED TRIBES.

In the matter of the application for the enrollment of Seta Harjo, deceased, as a citizen by blood of the Creek Nation.

STATEMENT AND ORDER.

The record in this case shows that on March 10, 1905, application was made, in affidavit form, for the enrollment of Seta Harjo, deceased, as a citizen by blood of the Creek Nation, under the provisions of the act of Congress approved March 3, 1905.

It appears that the affidavit filed in this matter that said Seta Harjo, deceased, was born January 17, 1905, and died February 21, 1905.

The act of Congress approved March 3, 1905, (33 Stats., 1048), provides:

"That the Commission to the Five Civilized Tribes is authorized for sixty days after the date of the approval of this act to receive and consider applications for enrollment, of children, <u>born subsequent to May twenty-fifth, nineteen hundred and one, and prior to March fourth, nineteen hundred and five, and living on said latter date,</u> to citizens of the Creek tribe of Indians whose enrollment has been approved by the Secretary of the Interior prior to the approval of this act; and to enroll and make allotments to such children."

It is, therefore, ordered that the application for the enrollment of said Seta Harjo, deceased, as a citizen by blood of the Creek Nation, be, and the same is, hereby dismissed.

                                        Tams Bixby Commissioner.

Muskogee, Indian Territory.
    JAN 4 – 1907

                                                                              NC 141.

                              Muskogee, Indian Territory, May 18, 1905.

Willie Harjo,

        Henryetta, Indian Territory.

Applications for Enrollment of Creek Newborn
Act of 1905 Volume II

Dear Sir:

In the matter of the application for the enrollment of your minor child, Nettie Harjo, as a citizen of the Creek Nation, you are advised that the Commission requires the affidavits of two disinterested witnesses as to the birth of said child disinterested witnesses as to the birth of said child.

There are herewith enclosed two blank forms of birth affidavit, and in executing same care should be exercised to see that all blanks are properly filled, all names written in full and in the event that the persons signing the affidavits are unable to write, signature by mark must be attested by two witnesses. Each affidavit must be executed before a Notary Public and the notarial seal and signature of the officer must be attached to each separate affidavit.

Respectfully,

BC.   Chairman.

NC 141.

Muskogee, Indian Territory, June 6, 1905.

Sookey Harjo,
    Henryetta, Indian Territory.

Dear Madam:

In the matter of the application for the enrollment of your minor child, Hettie[sic] Harjo, as a citizen of the Creek Nation, you are advised that the Commission requires the affidavit of a disinterested witness as to its birth.

There is herewith enclosed a blank form of birth affidavit, and in executing same care should be exercised to see that all blanks are properly filled, all names written in full and in the event that the person signing the affidavit is unable to write, signature by mark must be attested by two witnesses. Each affidavit must be executed before a Notary Public and the notarial seal and signature of the officer must be attached to each separate affidavit.

Respectfully,

1 BA   Commissioner in Charge

Applications for Enrollment of Creek Newborn
Act of 1905 Volume II

NC 142.

Muskogee, Indian Territory, May 18, 1905.

Sam Scott,
    Edna, Indian Territory.

Dear Sir:

    In the matter of the application for the enrollment of your minor children, Christianns[sic] and John Scott, as citizens of the Creek Nation, you are advised that the Commission requires the affidavit of the midwife or physician in attendance at the birth of said children.

    There is herewith enclosed a blank form of birth affidavit, and in executing same care should be exercised to see that all blanks are properly filled, all names written in full and in the event that the person signing the affidavit is unable to write, signature by mark must be attested by two witnesses. Each affidavit must be executed before a Notary Public and the notarial seal and signature of the officer must be attached to each separate affidavit.

                            Respectfully,

BC.   Chairman.

NC-142

Muskogee, Indian Territory, June 7, 1905.

Nancy Scott,
    Edna, Indian Territory.

Dear Madam:

    There are on file with the Commission affidavits in which the name of one of your new-born children is given as Christiana and Christie Annie.

    You are requested to advise the Commission as to the correct name of your said child.

                            Respectfully,

                                              Commissioner in Charge.

Applications for Enrollment of Creek Newborn
Act of 1905 Volume II

NC 142

COPY

Edna I. T. 6-12-05

Commission to the Five Civilized Tribes,
    Muskogee, I.T.

    Gentlemen:

    You are requested me to gave correct name of my child her name is Chrristie Annie Scott.

        Yours Resptfy.

        Nancy Scott

        Edna I. T.

BIRTH AFFIDAVIT.

DEPARTMENT OF THE INTERIOR.
COMMISSION TO THE FIVE CIVILIZED TRIBES.

    IN RE APPLICATION FOR ENROLLMENT, as a citizen of the Creek Nation, of Christie Annie Scott, born on the 25 day of Dec., 1903

Name of Father:	Sam Scott	a citizen of the Creek	Nation.
Name of Mother:	Nancy Scott	a citizen of the Creek	Nation.

        Postoffice   Edna, I.T.

Child present

AFFIDAVIT OF MOTHER.

UNITED STATES OF AMERICA, Indian Territory,
    Western   **DISTRICT.**

    I, Nancy Scott, on oath state that I am 30 years of age and a citizen by Blood, of the Creek Nation; that I am the lawful wife of Sam Scott, who is a citizen, by Blood of the Creek Nation; that a female child was born to me on 25 day of Dec., 1903, that said child has been named Christie Annie Scott, and is now living.

                her
            Nancy x Scott
Witnesses To Mark: mark
    { Sam'l Bright
      James K. Kepley

Applications for Enrollment of Creek Newborn
Act of 1905 Volume II

Subscribed and sworn to before me this 2nd day of June , 1905.

My Com. Ex. July 14 – 1906.

(Illegible) Barker
Notary Public.

AFFIDAVIT OF ATTENDING PHYSICIAN OR MID-WIFE.

UNITED STATES OF AMERICA, Indian Territory, ⎱
    Western   DISTRICT. ⎰

I, Lucy Scott , a midwife , on oath state that I attended on Mrs. Nancy Scott , wife of Sam Scott on the 25 day of Dec. , 1903 ; that there was born to her on said date a female child; that said child is now living and is said to have been named Christie Annie Scott

her
Lucy x Scott
mark

Witnesses To Mark:
  { Sam'l Bright
    James K Kepley

Subscribed and sworn to before me this 2nd day of June, 1905.

My Com. Ex. July 14 – 1906.

(Illegible) Barker
Notary Public.

BIRTH AFFIDAVIT.

DEPARTMENT OF THE INTERIOR.
COMMISSION TO THE FIVE CIVILIZED TRIBES.

IN RE APPLICATION FOR ENROLLMENT, as a citizen of the CREEK Nation, of Christiana Scott, born on the 25 day of Dec. , 1903

| Name of Father: | Sam Scott | a citizen of the | Creek | Nation. |
| Name of Mother: | Nancy " | a citizen of the | " | Nation. |

Postoffice   Edna, I.T.

Father and 1 child present

AFFIDAVIT OF MOTHER.

UNITED STATES OF AMERICA, Indian Territory, ⎱
    WESTERN   DISTRICT. ⎰

I, Nancy Scott , on oath state that I am 41 years of age and a citizen by blood , of the Creek Nation; that I am the lawful wife of Sam Scott , who is a citizen, by

Applications for Enrollment of Creek Newborn
Act of 1905 Volume II

blood of the Creek Nation; that a female child was born to me on 25 day of Dec., 1903, that said child has been named Christiana Scott, and is now living.

                                            her
                                    Nancy x Scott

Witnesses To Mark: mark
  { J McDermott
    EC Griesel

Subscribed and sworn to before me this 15 day of March, 1905.

                                        Edw C Griesel
                                        Notary Public.

BIRTH AFFIDAVIT.

DEPARTMENT OF THE INTERIOR.
COMMISSION TO THE FIVE CIVILIZED TRIBES.

IN RE APPLICATION FOR ENROLLMENT, as a citizen of the CREEK Nation, of John Scott, born on the 25 day of March, 1902.

Name of Father:	Sam Scott	a citizen of the	Creek	Nation.
Name of Mother:	Nancy "	a citizen of the	"	Nation.

                            Postoffice   Edna, I.T.

Father and (child present)

AFFIDAVIT OF MOTHER.

UNITED STATES OF AMERICA, Indian Territory, }
    WESTERN   DISTRICT.   }

I, Nancy Scott, on oath state that I am 41 years of age and a citizen by blood, of the Creek Nation; that I am the lawful wife of Sam Scott, who is a citizen, by blood of the Creek Nation; that a male child was born to me on 25 day of March, 1902, that said child has been named John Scott, and is now living.

                                          Her
                                  Nancy x Scott

Witnesses To Mark: mark
  { J McDermott
    E.C. Griesel

Subscribed and sworn to before me this 15 day of March, 1905.

                                        Edw C Griesel
                                        Notary Public.

Applications for Enrollment of Creek Newborn
Act of 1905   Volume II

BIRTH AFFIDAVIT.

DEPARTMENT OF THE INTERIOR.
COMMISSION TO THE FIVE CIVILIZED TRIBES.

IN RE APPLICATION FOR ENROLLMENT, as a citizen of the Creek Nation, of John Scott, born on the 25 day of March, 1902

Name of Father:	Sam Scott	a citizen of the	Creek	Nation.
Name of Mother:	Nancy Scott	a citizen of the	Creek	Nation.

Postoffice   Edna, I.T.

Child present

AFFIDAVIT OF MOTHER.

UNITED STATES OF AMERICA, Indian Territory,
Western   DISTRICT.

I, Nancy Scott, on oath state that I am 30 years of age and a citizen by Blood, of the Creek Nation; that I am the lawful wife of Sam Scott, who is a citizen, by Blood of the Creek Nation; that a male child was born to me on 25 day of March, 1902, that said child has been named John Scott, and was living March 4, 1905.

                                            her
                                     Nancy x Scott
Witnesses To Mark: mark
{ Sam'l Bright
  James K. Kepley

Subscribed and sworn to before me this 2nd day of June, 1905.

                                      (Illegible) Barker
My Com. Ex. July 14 – 1906.   Notary Public.

AFFIDAVIT OF ATTENDING PHYSICIAN OR MID-WIFE.

UNITED STATES OF AMERICA, Indian Territory,
Western   DISTRICT.

I, Jeannette Foster, a midwife, on oath state that I attended on Mrs. Nancy Scott, wife of Sam Scott on the 25 day of March, 1902; that there was born to her on said date a male child; that said child was living March 4, 1905, and is said to have been named John Scott

                                            her
                                     Jeannette x Foster
Witnesses To Mark: mark
{ Sam'l Bright
  James K Kepley

Applications for Enrollment of Creek Newborn
Act of 1905   Volume II

Subscribed and sworn to before me this 2nd day of June, 1905.

My Com. Ex. July 14 – 1906.

(Illegible) Barker
Notary Public.

BIRTH AFFIDAVIT.

DEPARTMENT OF THE INTERIOR.
COMMISSION TO THE FIVE CIVILIZED TRIBES.

IN RE APPLICATION FOR ENROLLMENT, as a citizen of the CREEK Nation, of Betty McHenry , born on the 24 day of Oct. , 1904

Name of Father:	Louis McHenry	a citizen of the	Creek	Nation.
Name of Mother:	Silla "	a citizen of the	"	Nation.

Postoffice   Weer

AFFIDAVIT OF ~~MOTHER~~. father

UNITED STATES OF AMERICA, Indian Territory,
WESTERN   DISTRICT.

I, Louis McHenry , on oath state that I am 39 years of age and a citizen by blood, of the Creek Nation; that I am the lawful ~~wife~~ hus of Silla McHenry , who is a citizen, by blood of the Creek Nation; that a female child was born to me on 24 day of Oct. , 1904 , that said child has been named Betty McHenry , and is now living.

Lewis McHenry

Witnesses To Mark:

Subscribed and sworn to before me this 15 day of March, 1905.

Edw C Griesel
Notary Public.

Applications for Enrollment of Creek Newborn
Act of 1905 Volume II

BIRTH AFFIDAVIT.

DEPARTMENT OF THE INTERIOR.
COMMISSION TO THE FIVE CIVILIZED TRIBES.

IN RE APPLICATION FOR ENROLLMENT, as a citizen of the Creek Nation, of Bettie McHenry, born on the 24th day of Oct., 1904

Name of Father:	Louis McHenry	a citizen of the	Creek	Nation.
Name of Mother:	Silla McHenry	a citizen of the	Creek	Nation.

Postoffice Weer, I.T.

AFFIDAVIT OF MOTHER.

UNITED STATES OF AMERICA, Indian Territory,
Western DISTRICT.

I, Silla McHenry, on oath state that I am 36 years of age and a citizen by birth, of the Creek Nation; that I am the lawful wife of Louis McHenry, who is a citizen, by birth of the Creek Nation; that a female child was born to me on 24th day of Oct., 1904, that said child has been named Bettie McHenry, and is now living.

         her
        Silla x McHenry
Witnesses To Mark: mark
 { J. B. Downs
   Joe Fennell

Subscribed and sworn to before me this 4th day of April, 1905.

        R C Allen
          Notary Public.
My Com. Ex. Mch. 15, 1908.

AFFIDAVIT OF ATTENDING PHYSICIAN OR MID-WIFE.

UNITED STATES OF AMERICA, Indian Territory,
Western DISTRICT.

I, B.F. Ball, a Physician, on oath state that I attended on Mrs. Silla McHenry, wife of Louis McHenry on the 24th day of October, 1904; that there was born to her on said date a female child; that said child is now living and is said to have been named Bettie McHenry

        B.F. Ball

Applications for Enrollment of Creek Newborn
Act of 1905 Volume II

Witnesses To Mark:

{

Subscribed and sworn to before me this 5th day of April, 1905.

(Illegible) Day
Notary Public.

My Commission Expires March 10, 1907

BIRTH AFFIDAVIT.

DEPARTMENT OF THE INTERIOR.
COMMISSION TO THE FIVE CIVILIZED TRIBES.

IN RE APPLICATION FOR ENROLLMENT, as a citizen of the Creek Nation, of Abbie McHenry, born on the 11 day of November, 1902

Name of Father:	Louis McHenry	a citizen of the	Creek	Nation.
Name of Mother:	Silla McHenry	a citizen of the	Creek	Nation.

Postoffice   Weer, I.T.

AFFIDAVIT OF MOTHER.

UNITED STATES OF AMERICA, Indian Territory, }
Western   DISTRICT.

I, Silla McHenry, on oath state that I am 36 years of age and a citizen by birth, of the Creek Nation; that I am the lawful wife of Louis McHenry, who is a citizen, by birth of the Creek Nation; that a female child was born to me on 11th day of November, 1902, that said child has been named Abbie McHenry, and is now living.

                                                  her
                                       Silla x McHenry

Witnesses To Mark: mark
{ J. B. Downs
  Joe Fennell

Subscribed and sworn to before me this 4th day of April, 1905.

                                          R C Allen
                                          Notary Public.

My Com. Ex. Mch. 15, 1908.

Applications for Enrollment of Creek Newborn
Act of 1905   Volume II

AFFIDAVIT OF ATTENDING PHYSICIAN OR MID-WIFE.

UNITED STATES OF AMERICA, Indian Territory, ⎫
    Western   DISTRICT.   ⎬

    I, Bettie Sarty, a midwife, on oath state that I attended on Mrs. Silla McHenry, wife of Louis McHenry on the 11th day of November, 1902; that there was born to her on said date a female child; that said child is now living and is said to have been named Abbie McHenry

                                              Bettie Sarty

Witnesses To Mark:

{ Subscribed and sworn to before me this 4th day of April, 1905.

                                    RC Allen
                                                Notary Public.

My Com Ex Mch 15, 1908

BIRTH AFFIDAVIT.

DEPARTMENT OF THE INTERIOR.
COMMISSION TO THE FIVE CIVILIZED TRIBES.

    IN RE APPLICATION FOR ENROLLMENT, as a citizen of the CREEK Nation, of Abbie McHenry, born on the 11 day of Nov., 1902

Name of Father:	Louis McHenry	a citizen of the	Creek	Nation.
Name of Mother:	Silla "	a citizen of the	"	Nation.

                            Postoffice   Weer

AFFIDAVIT OF MOTHER.

UNITED STATES OF AMERICA, Indian Territory, ⎫
    WESTERN   DISTRICT.⎬

    I, Louis McHenry, on oath state that I am 39 years of age and a citizen by blood, of the Creek Nation; that I am the lawful ~~wife~~ husb of Silla McHenry, who is a citizen, by blood of the Creek Nation; that a female child was born to me on 11 day of Nov., 1902, that said child has been named Abbie McHenry, and is now living.

                                        Luois[sic] McHenry

Witnesses To Mark:
{

Applications for Enrollment of Creek Newborn
Act of 1905 Volume II

Subscribed and sworn to before me this 15 day of March, 1905.

                                      Edw C Griesel
                                      Notary Public.

United States of America }
Indian Territory } ss
Western District }

    Eliza McMillan, being first duly sworn on her oath deposes and says: My name is Eliza McMillan, I am 44 years old, I reside 2 miles West of Checotah, IT. I am by profession a mid-wife. I was present in my capacity as mid-wife at the birth of Vivian McIntosh, the youngest child of Thomas F. McIntosh and Kate McIntosh, his wife, I have known the parents of this child for over three years, the child, a girl, was born on the 6th day of September 1904, and is now living with its parents at their home 4 1/2 miles North East of Checotah, Creek Nation, Indian Territory, both of its parents are citizens by blood of the Creek Nation.

                                      her
                              Eliza x McMillan
Witnesses to mark: mark
   (Name Illegible)
   (Name Illegible)

Subscribed and sworn to before me this 13th day of March A.D. 1905.

                                    Charles Buford
My Commission expires July 3rd 1906.   Notary Public.

United States of America }
Indian Territory } ss
Western District }

    W. A. Reid, being first duly sworn, on his oath deposes and says: My name is W.A. Reid, I am 35 years old, my residence is Checotah, I.T. I am a practicing physician and surgeon. I have known Thomas F. McIntosh and Kate McIntosh, his wife, for the last 12 years, they live on their farm about 4 1/2 miles North East of Checotah, I.T. I attended Mrs. Kate McIntosh at the birth of her next to the youngest child, a daughter, this child was born on the 12th day of March AD 1902 at the home of its parents and was given the name of Edith Edna McIntosh, I was present at the birth of this child in my professional capacity. This child is living at home with its parents at the present time. Both parents are citizens by blood of the Creek Nation.

                                      W A Reid

Applications for Enrollment of Creek Newborn
Act of 1905   Volume II

Subscribed and sworn to before me this 13th day of March AD 1905.

                                        Charles Buford

My Commission expires July 3rd 1906.   Notary Public.

BIRTH AFFIDAVIT.

DEPARTMENT OF THE INTERIOR.
COMMISSION TO THE FIVE CIVILIZED TRIBES.

IN RE APPLICATION FOR ENROLLMENT, as a citizen of the Creek Nation, of Edith Edna McIntosh, born on the 12th day of March, 1902

| Name of Father: | Thomas F. McIntosh | a citizen of the | Creek | Nation. |
| Name of Mother: | Kate McIntosh | a citizen of the | Creek | Nation. |

                          Postoffice   Checotah, Ind. Ter.

AFFIDAVIT OF MOTHER.

UNITED STATES OF AMERICA, Indian Territory,
    Western   **DISTRICT.**

    I, Kate McIntosh, on oath state that I am 29 years of age and a citizen by blood, of the Creek or Muskogee Nation; that I am the lawful wife of Thomas F. McIntosh, who is a citizen, by blood of the Creek or Muskogee Nation; that a female child was born to me on twelfth (12th) day of March, 1902, that said child has been named Edith Edna McIntosh, and was living March 4, 1905.

                                        Kate McIntosh

Witnesses To Mark:

    Subscribed and sworn to before me this 13th day of March AD 1905.

                                      Charles Buford

My Commission expires July 3rd 1906.   Notary Public.

Applications for Enrollment of Creek Newborn
Act of 1905 Volume II

BIRTH AFFIDAVIT.

DEPARTMENT OF THE INTERIOR.
COMMISSION TO THE FIVE CIVILIZED TRIBES.

IN RE APPLICATION FOR ENROLLMENT, as a citizen of the Creek Nation, of Vivian McIntosh, born on the 6th day of September, 1904

Name of Father:	Thomas F. McIntosh	a citizen of the	Creek	Nation.
Name of Mother:	Kate McIntosh	a citizen of the	Creek	Nation.

Postoffice   Checotah, Ind. Ter.

AFFIDAVIT OF MOTHER.

UNITED STATES OF AMERICA, Indian Territory, }
    Western   DISTRICT.   }

I, Kate McIntosh , on oath state that I am 29 years of age and a citizen by blood , of the Creek or Muskogee Nation; that I am the lawful wife of Thomas F. McIntosh , who is a citizen, by blood of the Creek or Muskogee Nation; that a female child was born to me on sixth (6th) day of September, 1904, that said child has been named Vivian McIntosh , and was living March 4, 1905.

                              Kate McIntosh

Witnesses To Mark:
{

Subscribed and sworn to before me this 13th day of March AD 1905.

                              Charles Buford
My Commission expires July 3rd 1906.   Notary Public.

NC 143.

Muskogee, Indian Territory, May 18, 1905.

Cornelius Boudinot,
    Coweta, Indian Territory.

Dear Sir:

    In the matter of the application for the enrollment of your minor child, Mitchell Boudinot, as a citizen of the Creek Nation, you are advised that the commission requires

Applications for Enrollment of Creek Newborn
Act of 1905 Volume II

the affidavits of the mother and midwife or physician in attendance at the birth of said child.

There is herewith enclosed a blank form of birth affidavit, and in executing same care should be exercised to see that all blanks are properly filled, all names written in full and in the event that the person signing the affidavit is unable to write, signature by mark must be attested by two witnesses. Each affidavit must be executed before a Notary Public and the notarial seal and signature of the officer must be attached to each separate affidavit.

Respectfully,

BC. Chairman.

BIRTH AFFIDAVIT.

DEPARTMENT OF THE INTERIOR.
COMMISSION TO THE FIVE CIVILIZED TRIBES.

IN RE APPLICATION FOR ENROLLMENT, as a citizen of the CREEK Nation, of Mitchel Boudinot, born on the 18th day of February, 1903

Name of Father: Cornelius Boudinot   a citizen of the   Creek   Nation.
Name of Mother: Susanna Boudinot   a citizen of the   Creek   Nation.

Postoffice   Coweta Indian Territory

AFFIDAVIT OF MOTHER.

UNITED STATES OF AMERICA, Indian Territory, ⎱
    WESTERN   DISTRICT. ⎰

I, Susanna Boudinot, on oath state that I am twenty seven years of age and a citizen by blood, of the Creek Nation; that I am the lawful wife of Cornelius Boudinot, who is a citizen, by Blood of the Creek Nation; that a male child was born to me on 18th day of February, 1903, that said child has been named Mitchel Boudinot, and is now living.

Susanna Boudinot

Witnesses To Mark:
   ⎰ Ellis Childers
   ⎱ J.F. Johnson

Subscribed and sworn to before me this 20th day of February, 1905.

B.J. Beavers
Notary Public.

My commission expires 12/19/1908

Applications for Enrollment of Creek Newborn
Act of 1905 Volume II

AFFIDAVIT OF ATTENDING PHYSICIAN OR MID-WIFE.

UNITED STATES OF AMERICA, Indian Territory, ⎫
    Western   DISTRICT. ⎬

I, Jenny Berryhill , a midwife , on oath state that I attended on Mrs. ~~Cornelius~~ Susanna Boudinot , wife of Cornelius Boudinot on the 18th day of February , 1903 ; that there was born to her on said date a male child; that said child is now living and is said to have been named Mitchel Boudinot

                                  her
                       Jenny x Berryhill

Witnesses To Mark: mark
  ⎰ Ellis Childers
  ⎱ J.F. Johnson

Subscribed and sworn to before me this 20th day of February , 1905.

                          B.J. Beavers
                            Notary Public.
My commission expires Dec. 19-1908

BIRTH AFFIDAVIT.

DEPARTMENT OF THE INTERIOR.
COMMISSION TO THE FIVE CIVILIZED TRIBES.

IN RE APPLICATION FOR ENROLLMENT, as a citizen of the CREEK Nation, of Mitchell Boudinot , born on the 18 day of Feb. , 1903

Name of Father: Cornelius Boudinot   a citizen of the Creek   Nation.
Name of Mother: Susana   "   a citizen of the "   Nation.

                Postoffice   Coweta

AFFIDAVIT OF ~~MOTHER.~~ father

UNITED STATES OF AMERICA, Indian Territory, ⎫
    WESTERN   DISTRICT. ⎬

I, ~~Mitchell~~ Cornelius Boudinot , on oath state that I am 33 years of age and a citizen by blood , of the Creek Nation; that I am the lawful ~~wife~~ husb of Susana Boudinot , who is a citizen, by blood of the Creek Nation; that a male child was born to me on 18 day of Feb. , 1903 , that said child has been named Mitchell Boudinot , and is now living.

Applications for Enrollment of Creek Newborn
Act of 1905 Volume II

Cornelius Boudinot

Witnesses To Mark:
{

Subscribed and sworn to before me this 15 day of March, 1905.

Edw C Griesel
Notary Public.

BIRTH AFFIDAVIT.

DEPARTMENT OF THE INTERIOR.
COMMISSION TO THE FIVE CIVILIZED TRIBES.

IN RE APPLICATION FOR ENROLLMENT, as a citizen of the Creek Nation, of Mitchel Boudinot, born on the 28 day of February, 1903

Name of Father: Cornelius Boudinot   a citizen of the Creek Nation.
Name of Mother: Susana Boudinot a citizen of the Creek Nation.

Postoffice   *(blank)*

AFFIDAVIT OF MOTHER.

UNITED STATES OF AMERICA, Indian Territory, }
  Western Judicial   DISTRICT. }

I, Susana Boudinot, on oath state that I am 25 years of age and a citizen by blood, of the Creek Nation; that I am the lawful wife of Cornelius Boudinot, who is a citizen, by Blood of the Creek Nation; that a male child was born to me on 28 day of February, 1903, that said child has been named Mitchel Boudinot, and was living March 4, 1905.

Susanna Boudinot

Witnesses To Mark:
{

Subscribed and sworn to before me this 18th day of August, 1905.

My term Expires   W.A. Brigham
Oct. 28" 1906   Notary Public.

Applications for Enrollment of Creek Newborn
Act of 1905 Volume II

AFFIDAVIT OF ATTENDING PHYSICIAN OR MID-WIFE.

UNITED STATES OF AMERICA, Indian Territory, }
Western Judicial DISTRICT.

I, Jenny Berryhill , a midwife , on oath state that I attended on Mrs. Susanna Boudinot , wife of Cornelius Boudinot on the 28" day of February , 1903 ; that there was born to her on said date a male child; that said child was living March 4, 1905, and is said to have been named Mitchel Boudinot

                                  her
                                Jenny x Berryhill

Witnesses To Mark: mark
  { G.W. Farris
    Louella Brigham

Subscribed and sworn to before me this 17" day of August , 1905.

My term Expires   W.A. Brigham
  Oct. 28" 1906   Notary Public.

BIRTH AFFIDAVIT.

DEPARTMENT OF THE INTERIOR.
COMMISSION TO THE FIVE CIVILIZED TRIBES.

IN RE APPLICATION FOR ENROLLMENT, as a citizen of the CREEK Nation, of Joseph Asbury, born on the 11 day of Jan. , 1902

Name of Father:	Thomas Asbury (dead)	a citizen of the	Creek	Nation.
Name of Mother:	Elliza "	a citizen of the	"	Nation.

                              Postoffice   Beggs

(Child present)

AFFIDAVIT OF MOTHER.

UNITED STATES OF AMERICA, Indian Territory, }
    WESTERN   DISTRICT.

I, Eliza Asbury, on oath state that I am 31 years of age and a citizen by blood , of the Creek Nation; that I am the lawful wife of Thomas Asbury (dead) , who is a citizen, by blood of the Creek Nation; that a male child was born to me on 11 day of Jan. , 1902 , that said child has been named Joseph Asbury , and is now living.

                                        Her
                                Eliza x Asbury
                                    mark

Applications for Enrollment of Creek Newborn
Act of 1905   Volume II

Witnesses To Mark:
- J. McDermott
- EC Griesel

Subscribed and sworn to before me this 15 day of March , 1905.

Edw C Griesel
Notary Public.

BIRTH AFFIDAVIT.

DEPARTMENT OF THE INTERIOR.
COMMISSION TO THE FIVE CIVILIZED TRIBES.

IN RE APPLICATION FOR ENROLLMENT, as a citizen of the Creek Nation, of Joseph Asbury, born on the 11 day of Jan. , 1902

Name of Father:	Thomas Asbury (dead)	a citizen of the	Creek	Nation.
Name of Mother:	Elliza "	a citizen of the	"	Nation.

Postoffice   Beggs

AFFIDAVIT OF MOTHER.

UNITED STATES OF AMERICA, Indian Territory,
    DISTRICT.

I, ..., on oath state that I am ...... years of age and a citizen by ...., of the .... Nation; that I am the lawful wife of ...., who is a citizen, by .... of the .... Nation; that a .... child was born to me on ...... day of ...., 1......, that said child has been named ...., and was living March 4, 1905.

Witnesses To Mark:

Subscribed and sworn to before me this ...... day of ...., 1905.

Notary Public.

Applications for Enrollment of Creek Newborn
Act of 1905   Volume II

AFFIDAVIT OF ATTENDING PHYSICIAN OR MID-WIFE.

UNITED STATES OF AMERICA, Indian Territory, }
Western DISTRICT.

I, Sallie Asbury, a midwife, on oath state that I attended on Mrs. Eliza Asbury, wife of Thomas Asbury on the 14" day of January, 1902 ; that there was born to her on said date a male child; that said child was living March 4, 1905, and is said to have been named Joseph Asbury

Her
Sallie x Asbury
mark

Witnesses To Mark:
{ Walter W Morton
 H.W. Reid

Subscribed and sworn to before me this 4 day of October, 1905.

Wm P Morton
Notary Public.

My Com. Expires *(Illegible)*

BIRTH AFFIDAVIT.

DEPARTMENT OF THE INTERIOR.
COMMISSION TO THE FIVE CIVILIZED TRIBES.

IN RE APPLICATION FOR ENROLLMENT, as a citizen of the Creek Nation, of Joseph Asbury, born on the *(blank)* day of January, 1902

Name of Father: Thomas Asbury   a citizen of the   Creek Nation.
Name of Mother: Elliza Asbury   a citizen of the   Creek Nation.

Postoffice   Beggs, I.T.

AFFIDAVIT OF MOTHER.

UNITED STATES OF AMERICA, Indian Territory, }
Western DISTRICT.

I, Eliza Asbury, on oath state that I am 31 years of age and a citizen by blood, of the Creek Nation; that I am the lawful wife of Thomas Asbury (dead), who is a citizen, by blood of the Creek Nation; that a male child was born to me on 14 day of January, 1902, that said child has been named Joseph Asbury, and was living March 4, 1905.

Eliza x Asbury

Applications for Enrollment of Creek Newborn
Act of 1905   Volume II

Witnesses To Mark:
{ H.W. Reid
{ Chas Roach

Subscribed and sworn to before me this 28 day of October , 1905.

Wm P Morton
Notary Public.

My Com. Expires July 23-06

AFFIDAVIT OF ATTENDING PHYSICIAN OR MID-WIFE.

UNITED STATES OF AMERICA, Indian Territory,
     Western   DISTRICT.

I, Sallie Asbury , a midwife , on oath state that I attended on Mrs. Eliza Asbury, wife of Thomas Asbury on the 14" day of January , 1902 ; that there was born to her on said date a male child; that said child was living March 4, 1905, and is said to have been named Joseph Asbury

her
Sallie x Asbury
mark

Witnesses To Mark:
{ H.W. Reid
{ Chas Roach

Subscribed and sworn to before me this 28" day of October, 1905.

Wm P Morton
Notary Public.

My Com. Expires July 23-06

NC-146.

Muskogee, Indian Territory, September 11, 1905.

Eliza Asbury,
     Beggs, Indian Territory

Dear Madam:

In the matter of the application for the enrollment of your minor child, Joseph Asbury, as a citizen of the Creek Nation, you are advised that it will be necessary for you to file with this office, the affidavit of the midwife in attendance at the birth of said child.

Applications for Enrollment of Creek Newborn
Act of 1905 Volume II

There is herewith enclosed a blank for proof of birth partially filled out. In having same executed care should be taken that affiant signs her name as given in the body of the affidavit and that the notary public signs and affixes his official seal to same.

This matter should receive your prompt attention.

                Respectfully,

AG-7-11-44   Acting Commissioner.

NC-146.

                Muskogee, Indian Territory, October 16, 1905.

Eliza Asbury,
    Beggs, Indian Territory.

Dear Madam:

In the matter of the application for the enrollment of your minor child, Joseph Asbury, as a citizen by blood of the Creek Nation it appears from your affidavit that said Joseph Asbury was born January 11, 1902, and from the affidavit of the midwife, in attendance at his birth, that said child was born January 14, 1902.

There is herewith inclosed[sic] a form of birth affidavit, partially filled out, which you are requested to have executed giving the correct date of the birth of said child. In having same executed care should be taken that affiants sign their names as given in the body of the affidavits and that the notary public signs and affixes his official seal to same.

This matter should receive your prompt attention.

                Respectfully,

                                    Commissioner.

OTD-1
Env.

NC-146.

                Muskogee, Indian Territory, October 19, 1905.

Eliza Asbury,
    Beggs, Indian Territory.

Dear Madam:

Applications for Enrollment of Creek Newborn
Act of 1905   Volume II

In the matter of the application for the enrollment of your minor child, Joseph Asbury, as a citizen by blood of the Creek Nation, it appears from your affidavit that said Joseph Asbury was born January 11, 1902. From the affidavit of Sallie Asbury, the midwife in attendance at his birth, it appears that said child was born January 14, 1902.

In order that this discrepancy may be corrected there is herewith inclosed[sic] from[sic] of birth affidavit which has been partially filled out. You are requested to have same executed before a notary public and when so executed return it to this office in the inclosed[sic] envelope. Be careful to see that the notary public attaches his name and seal to each affidavit. In case any signature is by mark the same must be attested by two disinterested witnesses.

Respectfully,

Commissioner.

OTD-8
Env.

NC 147.

Muskogee, Indian Territory, May 18, 1905.

Jefferson Webster,
    Okmulgee, Indian Territory.

Dear Sir:

In the matter of the application for the enrollment of your minor child, Seeley Webster, as a citizen of the Creek Nation, you are advised that the Commission requires the affidavits of the mother and two disinterested witnesses as to the birth of said child.

There are herewith enclosed three blank forms of birth affidavit, and in executing same care should be exercised to see that all blanks are properly filled, all names written in full and in the event that the persons signing the affidavits are unable to write, signatures by mark must be attested by two witnesses. Each affidavit must be executed before a Notary Public and the notarial seal and signature of the officer must be attached to each separate affidavit.

Respectfully,

BC.   Chairman.

Applications for Enrollment of Creek Newborn
Act of 1905   Volume II

United States of America, Indian Territory,
Western Judicial District.

On this day personally appeared before me, the undersigned Notary Public, duly commissioned and acting as such, Thomas Kannard and Taylor Hardrige, who being by me first duly sworn on their oaths deposed and say, that they are acquainted with Jeff Webster and Mattie Webster, his wife, that there was born to Mattie Webster on the 1st day of October, 1902, a female child and that said child was named Seeley Webster, and was living March 4, 1905 on the 4th day of March, 1905, and is still living. Taylor Hardridge for himself states that at the time of the birth of said child he was living March 4, 1905 at the home of Jeff Webster and remebers[sic] the birth of said child and that he has this day seen said child and knows it to be the identical child born on the 1st day of October, and that it is the child of Mattie Webster, wife of said Jeff Webster.

Thomas Kannard states that he had known said child since ts birth and has this day also seen said child and that it is living.

Thomas Kannard
his
Taylor x Hardridge
mark

Sworn and subscribed to before me this 17th day of June, 1905.
My Commission Expires April 27th, 1908.

George C Bridleman
Notary Public.

Witness to Taylor Hardridge mark:
George C Bridleman
J.H. Winston

BIRTH AFFIDAVIT.

DEPARTMENT OF THE INTERIOR.
COMMISSION TO THE FIVE CIVILIZED TRIBES.

IN RE APPLICATION FOR ENROLLMENT, as a citizen of the Creek Nation, of Seeley Webster, born on the 1st day of October, 1902

Name of Father: Jeff Webster   a citizen of the   Creek   Nation.
Name of Mother: Mattie Webster   a citizen of the   Creek   Nation.

Postoffice   Sharp, Indian Territory

Applications for Enrollment of Creek Newborn
Act of 1905   Volume II

AFFIDAVIT OF MOTHER.

UNITED STATES OF AMERICA, Indian Territory, }
    Western   DISTRICT.

    I, Mattie Webster , on oath state that I am 26 years of age and a citizen by Blood, of the Creek Nation; that I am the lawful wife of Jeff Webster , who is a citizen, by Blood of the Creek Nation; that a Female child was born to me on 1st day of October , 1902 , that said child has been named Seeley Webster , and was living March 4, 1905.

                                       Mattie Webster

Witnesses To Mark:
{

    Subscribed and sworn to before me this day of , 1905.

                                       George C Bridleman
                                             Notary Public.

My Com Exp. April 27" 1908.

BIRTH AFFIDAVIT.

DEPARTMENT OF THE INTERIOR.
COMMISSION TO THE FIVE CIVILIZED TRIBES.

    IN RE APPLICATION FOR ENROLLMENT, as a citizen of the CREEK Nation, of Seeley Webster, born on the 1 day of Oct , 1902

Name of Father: Jefferson Webster   a citizen of the   Creek   Nation.
Name of Mother: Mattie   "   a citizen of the   "   Nation.

                             Postoffice   Okmulgee

AFFIDAVIT OF ~~MOTHER~~. father

UNITED STATES OF AMERICA, Indian Territory, }
    WESTERN   DISTRICT.

    I, Jefferson Webster , on oath state that I am 30 years of age and a citizen by blood , of the Creek Nation; that I am the lawful ~~wife~~ husb of Mattie Webster , who is a citizen, by blood of the Creek Nation; that a female child was born to me on 1 day of Oct. , 1902 , that said child has been named Seeley Webster , and is now living.

                                       Jeff Webster

Witnesses To Mark:
{

Applications for Enrollment of Creek Newborn
Act of 1905 Volume II

Subscribed and sworn to before me this 11 day of March, 1905.

>Edw C Griesel
>Notary Public.

AFFIDAVIT OF ATTENDING PHYSICIAN OR MID-WIFE.

UNITED STATES OF AMERICA, Indian Territory,
.... **DISTRICT.**

No Midwife or Doctor present

I, ..., a ...., on oath state that I attended on Mrs. ...., wife of .... on the .... day of ...., 1.......; that there was born to her on said date a .... child; that said child is now living and is said to have been named ....

Witnesses To Mark:
{ ....
....

Subscribed and sworn to before me this .... day of ...., 1........

>................................
>Notary Public.

BIRTH AFFIDAVIT.

DEPARTMENT OF THE INTERIOR.
COMMISSION TO THE FIVE CIVILIZED TRIBES.

IN RE APPLICATION FOR ENROLLMENT, as a citizen of the Creek Nation, of Jimmie Yaholar, born on the 10 day of July, 1904

Name of Father:	Josey Yaholar	a citizen of the	Creek Nation.
Name of Mother:	Petsey Yaholar	a citizen of the	Creek Nation.

Postoffice   Weleetka

AFFIDAVIT OF MOTHER.

UNITED STATES OF AMERICA, Indian Territory,
Western   **DISTRICT.**

I, Petsey Yaholar, on oath state that I am 40 years of age and a citizen by blood, of the Creek Nation; that I am the lawful wife of Josey Yaholar, who is a

Applications for Enrollment of Creek Newborn
Act of 1905   Volume II

citizen, by blood of the Creek Nation; that a Male child was born to me on 10 day of July , 1904 , that said child has been named Jimmie Yaholar , and was living March 4, 1905.

                                                her
                                       Petsey x Yaholar

Witnesses To Mark: mark
         his
{ Tothir x Harjo
        mark
  William Alligator

Subscribed and sworn to before me this 20 day of Sept , 1905.

                                        Amos R Robison
                                           Notary Public.
                                      My com Expires Feb 11/1909

AFFIDAVIT OF ATTENDING PHYSICIAN OR MID-WIFE.

UNITED STATES OF AMERICA, Indian Territory, ⎫
      Western   DISTRICT.   ⎭

I, Yobarhahey , a Female , on oath state that I attended on Mrs. Petsey Yaholar, wife of Josey Yaholar on the 20 day of July , 1904 ; that there was born to her on said date a male child; that said child was living March 4, 1905, and is said to have been named Jimmie Yaholar

                                           her
                                      x Yobarhahey

Witnesses To Mark: mark
       his
{ Tothir x Harjo
      mark
  William Alligator

Subscribed and sworn to before me this 20 day of Sept, 1905.

                                        Amos R Robison
                                           Notary Public.
                                      My com Expires Feb 11/1909

BIRTH AFFIDAVIT.
                                  DEPARTMENT OF THE INTERIOR.
                      COMMISSION TO THE FIVE CIVILIZED TRIBES.

IN RE APPLICATION FOR ENROLLMENT, as a citizen of the CREEK Nation, of Jimmie Yaholar , born on the 10 day of July , 1904

Applications for Enrollment of Creek Newborn
Act of 1905 Volume II

Name of Father: Josey Yaholar   a citizen of the   Creek   Nation.
Name of Mother: ~~Patty~~ Betsy "   a citizen of the   "   Nation.

Postoffice   Weleetka,

AFFIDAVIT OF MOTHER.

UNITED STATES OF AMERICA, Indian Territory,
WESTERN DISTRICT.

    I, Josey Yaholar, on oath state that I am 51 years of age and a citizen by blood, of the Creek Nation; that I am the lawful ~~wife~~ husband of Betsey Yaholar, who is a citizen, by blood of the Creek Nation; that a male child was born to me on 10 day of July, 1904, that said child has been named Jimmie, and was living March 4, 1905.

                            His
                      Josey x Yaholar
Witnesses To Mark: mark
  { Austin Chissoe
    EC Griesel

    Subscribed and sworn to before me this 13 day of March, 1905.

                      Edw C Griesel
                        Notary Public.

NC-148.

                Muskogee, Indian Territory, July 26, 1905.

Josey Yaholar,
    Weleetka, Indian Territory.

Dear Sir:

    On March 13, 1905 you appeared before the Commission to the Five Civilized Tribes and made application for the enrollment of your son Jimmie Yaholar, born July 10, 1904, as a citizen by blood of the Creek Nation and at that time submitted your affidavit only as to the birth of said child.
    You are advised that before the rights of said child as a citizen by blood of the Creek Nation can be finally determined it will be necessary for you to file with this office the affidavit of the mother of said child and the attending midwife at his birth.

    For that purpose a blank for proof of birth is inclosed[sic] herewith. In having the same executed be careful to see that all blanks are properly filled, all names written in full and that the notary public before whom the affidavits are acknowledged attaches his

Applications for Enrollment of Creek Newborn
Act of 1905   Volume II

seal and name to such affidavit, in case any signature is by mark it must be attested by two disinterested witnesses.

Respectfully,

B C   Commissioner.
Env.

NC. 149.

DEPARTMENT OF THE INTERIOR,
COMMISSION TO THE FIVE CIVILIZED TRIBES.
MUSKOGEE, I.T., June 5, 1905.

In the matter of the application for the enrollment of Susan Damet as a citizen by blood of the Creek Nation.

John P. Damet, being duly sworn, testified as follows:

Examination by the Commission:
Q What is your name? A John P. Damet.
Q What is your age: A 32.
Q What is your post office address? A Wagoner.
Q Have you a child –a new born child by the name of Susan Damet? A Yes sir.
Q When was that child born? A 27th of February, 1905.
Q Now how do you know it was on the 27th of February, did you write it down in a book or make a record of any kind at all? A Yes sir.
Q What day of the week was it born? A Monday morning, late Sunday night or early Monday morning.
Q Do you know how many days there are in February? A Either 28 or 29.
Q Are you sure t was born in February? A Yes sir.
Q How old was it? A Something about a week old.
Q Are you sure it wasn't born in March, that it was born in February? A Yes sir.
Q Is the child living? A Yes sir.
Q It is living today? A Yes sir.

-------oOo-------

Annie Baker, being duly sworn, testified as follows:
Q Are you any kin to John Baker? A No sir.
Q Do you know his child Susan? A Yes sir.
Q How old are you? A 19
Q What is your post office? A Wagoner.
Q When was it born? A 27th of February, Monday morning.
Q You were there, were you? A No sir, but I saw the child soon after it was born.
Q When did you see the child the last time? A This morning.

Applications for Enrollment of Creek Newborn
Act of 1905 Volume II

Q You know she was born on the 27th of February? A Yes sir.
Q About how old is that child now? A Not quite four months old.
Q It will be four months old the 27th of this monrth[sic]? Is that what you say? A Yes sir.

    Lida Fisher, being duly sworn, testified as follows:

Q What is your name? A Lida Fisher.
Q You live at Wagoner? A Yes sir.
Q Do you know John P. Damet? A Yes sir.
Q Do you know his child Susan? A Yes sir.
Q Do you know when Susan was born? A Born February 27, 1905.
Q Are you sure of that? A Yes sir.
Q You are no kin to him are you? A No sir.
Q Not interested in this case in anyway? A No sir.

  Lona Merrick, being duly sworn, states that the above and foregoing is a true and correct transcript of her stenographic notes as taken in said cause on said date.

          Lona Merrick

Subscribed and sworn to before me this 6th day of June, 1905.

          Edw C Griesel
            Notary Public.

BIRTH AFFIDAVIT.

DEPARTMENT OF THE INTERIOR.
COMMISSION TO THE FIVE CIVILIZED TRIBES.

  IN RE APPLICATION FOR ENROLLMENT, as a citizen of the Creek Nation, of Susan Damet, born on the 27 day of Feb, 1905

Name of Father:	John P Damet	a citizen of the	U.S.	Nation.
Name of Mother:	Eliza Damet	a citizen of the	Creek	Nation.

        Postoffice Wagoner

Child Present Gr

AFFIDAVIT OF MOTHER.

UNITED STATES OF AMERICA, Indian Territory, ⎫
 Western   DISTRICT.   ⎭

  I, Eliza Damet , on oath state that I am 21 years of age and a citizen by blood , of the Creek Nation; that I am the lawful wife of John P. Damet , who is a citizen, by -----

Applications for Enrollment of Creek Newborn
Act of 1905   Volume II

of the U.S. Nation; that a Female child was born to me on 27 day of Feb , 1905 , that said child has been named Susan Damet , and is now living.

Eliza Damet

Witnesses To Mark:
{

Subscribed and sworn to before me this 20 day of March , 1905.

Edw C Griesel
Notary Public.

AFFIDAVIT OF ATTENDING PHYSICIAN OR MID-WIFE.

UNITED STATES OF AMERICA, Indian Territory,
    Western   DISTRICT.

I, Lizzie Baker , a midwife , on oath state that I attended on Mrs. Eliza Damet , wife of John P Damet on the 27 day of Feb , 1905 ; that there was born to her on said date a Female child; that said child is now living and is said to have been named Susan Damet

Lizzie Baker

Witnesses To Mark:
{

Subscribed and sworn to before me this 20 day of Mar, 1905.

Edw C Griesel
Notary Public.

BIRTH AFFIDAVIT.

DEPARTMENT OF THE INTERIOR.
COMMISSION TO THE FIVE CIVILIZED TRIBES.

IN RE APPLICATION FOR ENROLLMENT, as a citizen of the CREEK Nation, of Susan Damet, born on the 27 day of Feb , 1905

Name of Father:	John P Damet	a citizen of the U.S.	Nation.
Name of Mother:	Eliza "	a citizen of the Creek	Nation.

Postoffice   Wagoner, IT

Applications for Enrollment of Creek Newborn
Act of 1905 Volume II

AFFIDAVIT OF ~~MOTHER~~. father

UNITED STATES OF AMERICA, Indian Territory, }
WESTERN DISTRICT.

I, John P Damet , on oath state that I am 30 years of age and a citizen by ----- , of the U.S. Nation; that I am the lawful ~~wife~~ husband of Eliza Damet , who is a citizen, by blood of the Creek Nation; that a female child was born to me on 27" day of Feb , 1905 , that said child has been named Susan Damet , and is now living.

                                                John P Damet

Witnesses To Mark:
{

Subscribed and sworn to before me this 11 day of March, 1905.

                                                Edw C Griesel
                                                    Notary Public.

BIRTH AFFIDAVIT.

DEPARTMENT OF THE INTERIOR.
COMMISSION TO THE FIVE CIVILIZED TRIBES.

IN RE APPLICATION FOR ENROLLMENT, as a citizen of the Creek Nation, of William F Damet, born on the 30 day of Apr, 1903

Name of Father:	John P Damet	a citizen of the	U.S.	Nation.
Name of Mother:	Eliza "	a citizen of the	Creek	Nation.

                                      Postoffice   Wagoner

Child Present Gr

AFFIDAVIT OF MOTHER.

UNITED STATES OF AMERICA, Indian Territory, }
Western DISTRICT.

I, Eliza Damet , on oath state that I am 21 years of age and a citizen by blood , of the Creek Nation; that I am the lawful wife of John P. Damet , who is a citizen, by ----- of the U.S. Nation; that a Male child was born to me on 30 day of Apr , 1903 , that said child has been named William F. Damet , and is now living.

                                                Eliza Damet

Witnesses To Mark:
{

Applications for Enrollment of Creek Newborn
Act of 1905   Volume II

Subscribed and sworn to before me this 20 day of March, 1905.

            Edw C Griesel
            Notary Public.

AFFIDAVIT OF ATTENDING PHYSICIAN OR MID-WIFE.

UNITED STATES OF AMERICA, Indian Territory, ⎫
 Western   DISTRICT.   ⎬
           ⎭

  I, Elmira Burress, a Mid Wife, on oath state that I attended on Mrs. Eliza Damet, wife of John P Damet on the 30 day of Apr, 1903; that there was born to her on said date a Male child; that said child is now living and is said to have been named William F. Damet

            Elmira Burress

Witnesses To Mark:
{

Subscribed and sworn to before me this 20 day of Mar, 1905.

            Edw C Griesel
            Notary Public.

BIRTH AFFIDAVIT.

DEPARTMENT OF THE INTERIOR.
COMMISSION TO THE FIVE CIVILIZED TRIBES.

  IN RE APPLICATION FOR ENROLLMENT, as a citizen of the CREEK Nation, of William F. Damet, born on the 30 day of Apr, 1903

| Name of Father: | John P Damet | a citizen of the | *(Illegible)* | Nation. |
| Name of Mother: | Eliza " | a citizen of the | Creek | Nation. |

       Postoffice Wagoner

AFFIDAVIT OF ~~MOTHER~~. father

UNITED STATES OF AMERICA, Indian Territory, ⎫
 WESTERN   DISTRICT. ⎬

  I, John P Damet, on oath state that I am 30 years of age and a citizen by -----, of the U.S. Nation; that I am the lawful ~~wife~~ husband of Eliza Damet, who is a citizen, by blood of the Creek Nation; that a male child was born to me on 30" day of Apr, 1903, that said child has been named William F. Damet, and is now living.

Applications for Enrollment of Creek Newborn
Act of 1905 Volume II

John P Damet

Witnesses To Mark:
{

Subscribed and sworn to before me this 11 day of March, 1905.

Edw C Griesel
Notary Public.

NC 149.

Muskogee, Indian Territory, May 18, 1905.

John D. Damet,
Wagoner, Indian Territory.

Dear Sir:

In the matter of the application for the enrollment of your minor child, Susan Damet, as a citizen of the Creek Nation, you are advised that the Commission desires the testimony of yourself and of two disinterested witnesses as to the date of the birth of said child.

You will be allowed thirty days from date within which to appear before the Commission at its office in Muskogee, Indian Territory, with said witnesses for the purpose of being examined under oath.

Respectfully,

Chairman.

BIRTH AFFIDAVIT.

DEPARTMENT OF THE INTERIOR.
COMMISSION TO THE FIVE CIVILIZED TRIBES.

IN RE APPLICATION FOR ENROLLMENT, as a citizen of the Creek Nation, of Thelma Agnes Minter , born on the 2 day of Jany , 1904

Name of Father:	Mark Minter	a citizen of the Creek	Nation.
Name of Mother:	Birdie "	a citizen of the U.S.	Nation.

Postoffice   Muskogee

Applications for Enrollment of Creek Newborn
Act of 1905   Volume II

(Child present)

AFFIDAVIT OF MOTHER.

UNITED STATES OF AMERICA, Indian Territory, }
Western   DISTRICT.

I, Birdie Minter , on oath state that I am 22 years of age and a citizen by ----- , of the U.S. Nation; that I am the lawful wife of Mark Minter , who is a citizen, by blood of the Creek Nation; that a female child was born to me on 2 day of Jany , 1904 , that said child has been named Thelma Agnes Minter , and was living March 4, 1905.

             Birdie Minter

Witnesses To Mark:
{

Subscribed and sworn to before me this 8" day of June , 1905.

             Henry G. Hains
              Notary Public.

BIRTH AFFIDAVIT.

DEPARTMENT OF THE INTERIOR.
COMMISSION TO THE FIVE CIVILIZED TRIBES.

IN RE APPLICATION FOR ENROLLMENT, as a citizen of the Creek Nation, of Thelma Agnes Minter , born on the 2 day of Jany , 1904

Name of Father: Mark Minter   a citizen of the   Creek   Nation.
Name of Mother: Birdie   "   a citizen of the   U.S.   Nation.

      Postoffice   Muskogee

AFFIDAVIT OF ~~MOTHER~~. father

UNITED STATES OF AMERICA, Indian Territory, }
Western   DISTRICT.

I, Mark Minter, on oath state that I am 25 years of age and a citizen by blood , of the Creek Nation; that I am the lawful ~~wife~~ husband of Birdie Minter , who is a citizen, by ----- of the U.S. Nation; that a female child was born to me on 2" day of January, 1904 , that said child has been named Thelma Agnes Minter , and was living March 4, 1905.

             Mark Minter

Witnesses To Mark:
{

Applications for Enrollment of Creek Newborn
Act of 1905 Volume II

Subscribed and sworn to before me this 3rd day of June, 1905.

         Henry G. Hains.
         Notary Public.

BIRTH AFFIDAVIT.

DEPARTMENT OF THE INTERIOR.
COMMISSION TO THE FIVE CIVILIZED TRIBES.

IN RE APPLICATION FOR ENROLLMENT, as a citizen of the CREEK Nation, of Thelma Agnes Minter, born on the 2 day of Jan., 1904

Name of Father:	Mark Minter	a citizen of the	Creek	Nation.
Name of Mother:	Birdie "	a citizen of the	U.S.	Nation.

      Postoffice Muskogee

(Child present) HGH

AFFIDAVIT OF MOTHER.

UNITED STATES OF AMERICA, Indian Territory, }
  WESTERN   DISTRICT.

  I, Birdie Minter, on oath state that I am 22 years of age and a citizen by -----, of the U.S. Nation; that I am the lawful wife of Mark Minter, who is a citizen, by blood of the Creek Nation; that a female child was born to me on 2 day of Jan., 1904, that said child has been named Thelma Agnes Minter, and is now living.

         Mark Minter

Witnesses To Mark:
{

  Subscribed and sworn to before me this 11 day of March, 1905.

         Edw C Griesel
         Notary Public.

        Father
AFFIDAVIT OF ~~ATTENDING PHYSICIAN OR MID-WIFE~~.

UNITED STATES OF AMERICA, Indian Territory, }
  Western   DISTRICT.

         married to
  I, Mark Minter, am 25, ~~on oath state that I attended on Mrs~~. Bertie Minter, ~~wife of~~ & on the 2 day of Jan., 1904; that there was born to her on said date a female child; that said child is now living and is said to have been named Thelma Agnes Minter.

Applications for Enrollment of Creek Newborn
Act of 1905 Volume II

Birdie Minter

Witnesses To Mark:

{

Subscribed and sworn to before me this 11 day of March, 1905.

Edw C Griesel
Notary Public.

BIRTH AFFIDAVIT.

DEPARTMENT OF THE INTERIOR.
COMMISSION TO THE FIVE CIVILIZED TRIBES.

IN RE APPLICATION FOR ENROLLMENT, as a citizen of the Creek Nation, of Thelma Agnes Minter, born on the 2 day of Jan, 1904

Name of Father:	Mark Minter	a citizen of the	Creek	Nation.
Name of Mother:	Bertie "	a citizen of the	U.S.	Nation.

Postoffice Muskogee

AFFIDAVIT OF MOTHER.

UNITED STATES OF AMERICA, Indian Territory,
DISTRICT.

I, ..., on oath state that I am ..... years of age and a citizen by ...., of the .... Nation; that I am the lawful wife of ...., who is a citizen, by .... of the .... Nation; that a .... child was born to me on ..... day of ...., 1......., that said child has been named ...., and was living March 4, 1905.

Witnesses To Mark:

{

Subscribed and sworn to before me this ..... day of ...., 1905.

Notary Public.

Applications for Enrollment of Creek Newborn
Act of 1905   Volume II

AFFIDAVIT OF ATTENDING PHYSICIAN ~~OR MID-WIFE~~.

UNITED STATES OF AMERICA, Indian Territory,　⎫
　　Western　　　DISTRICT.　　　　　　　　⎬
　　　　　　　　　　　　　　　　　　　　　⎭

　　　I, M. F. Williams , a Physician , on oath state that I attended on Mrs. Bertie Minter , wife of Mark Minter on the 2 day of Jan , 1904 ; that there was born to her on said date a female child; that said child is now living and is said to have been named Thelma Agnes Minter.

　　　　　　　　　　　　　　　　　M. F. Williams, M.D.

Witnesses To Mark:
⎰
⎱

　　　Subscribed and sworn to before me this 23 day of March, 1905.

　　　　　　　　　　　　　　Edw C Griesel
　　　　　　　　　　　　　　　　　Notary Public.

　　　　　　　　　　　————————

　　　　　　　　　　　　　　　　　　NC. 150

　　　　　　Muskogee, Indian Territory, May 27, 1905.

Mark Minter,
　　Muskogee, Indian Territory.

Dear Sir:

　　　In the matter of the application for the enrollment of your minor child, Thelma Agnes Minter, as a citizen of the Creek Nation, you are required to appear before the Commission, at its office, in Muskogee, Indian Territory, together with your wife, Birdie Minter, for the purpose of furnishing proper proof relative to the birth of said child.

　　　　　　　　　　　Respectfully,

　　　　　　　　　　　　　　　　　Chairman.

Index

[ILLEGIBLE]
   Arthur L 5
   Dug 28
   Jas A 151
   Job 145
   Joe 216
   John 62
   John J 234
   Mitchell 189
   O S 33,35
   A R 59
   W A, MD 6
   W M 142
   Wm 53,55,56,57,58,59,60,61
ADAMS, Al 275,278
ADCOCK, J H 138
ALLEN
   Cora L 2,6
   Cora Lou 1,3,4,5,6
   Cora Lue 1,4,5
   Eliza H 2,11
   John W 1,2,3,4,5,6,7,8
   Millard E 1,2,3,7
   R C 216,217,255,256,262, 296,297,298
   Vetrus 3,4,6,7,8
   Violet 5,6,7,8
ALLIGATOR, William 313
ANDERSON
   Emma 175,176,177,178,179
   Lydia 175,178,179
   Lydia C 175,176,177
   Malinda 126,127
   Solomon 175,176,177,178
ASBURY
   Eliza 305,306,307,308,309
   Elliza 305,307
   Joseph 304,305,306,307,308,309
   Sallie 306,307,309
   Thomas 305,306,307
ASHLEY
   Amanda S 196
   Hettie E 138
BAGLY, Louis 158
BAILEY, Ella 163
BAKER
   Annie 316

   Henry 207,208
   John 316
   Lizzie 317
   Millie 208
   Wm 209
BALL, B F 296
BARKER, [Illegible] 291,292,294
BARNETT
   Jansie 144,145
   Jennie 147
   Jensey 143,145,147,148,149
   Jincy 143,144
   Joe 143,144,145,147,148,149
   Joseph 146
   Wanney 143,144,145,146,148
   Wannie 145,147,149
BARNEY, Bessie 116
BARTON, R S 126,127
BAUGH
   John 71
   Rachel 73
   Willie E 71
BEALL, Wm O 224
BEAVER
   Eliza Techarna 146
   Jackson 145
BEAVERS, B J 69,70,302
BECKMAN
   H C 280
   H O 281
BEER, W M 84
BELL
   Alice 111
   Clarissa 257,258,259
   Jack 111,256,257,258,259
   Lela May 258
   Lelia May 256,257,258
BERRYHILL
   Aery Ann 234
   Jennie 189
   Jenny 302,304
BHIRHOLAS 44,45,47
BIGHEAD
   Lizzie 100,101,102,103
   Millie 101,102,103
   Standwaitie 101,102
   Stanwaitie 103

Index

Stanwaitte 100
BIGPOND
   Daniel 101
   Nancy 102
BIRD, Mary 68,71
BIXBY
   Hon Tames 274
   Hon Tams 229
   Mr Tams 26
   Tams 42,48,147,148,224,260, 266,276,288
   Tasm 282
BLAKEMORE, W F 39
BOUDINOT
   Cornelius 301,302,303,304
   Mitchel 302,303,304
   Mitchell 301,303
   Susana 303,304
   Susanna 302,304
BOUGH
   John 71,72,73
   Rache 73
   Rachel 72,73
   Rachel Childers 71,72
   Willie E 72
   Willie Edward 71,72,73
BOWERS
   A E 138
   Fred... 103,104,105,106,108,109,112
   Ida 104,106,108,109,110
   Lewis 106
   Paul 103,104,105,106,107,108, 109,110,111,112
   Paul W 108,110
   Rebecca 106
BOZARTH, Mark L 234
BRADBURY, John P 265
BRADDOCK
   J M 256
   John M 256
   Mollie 256
BRENNAN, Francis R 145
BREWER, Theo F 192
BRIAN
   Charley M 138
   Charlie 137,139
   Hettie E 137,138,139,140

   John William 137,139
   Mary Ellen 137,139,140
BRIDLEMAN, George C 310,311
BRIGHAM
   Louella 304
   W A 304
BRIGHT, Sam'l 291,292,294
BRONAUGH
   J W 240,252
   J W, MD 240,252
BRUNER
   Adaline 126,127,128
   Betty 232
   Billie 125,126
   Billy 127,128
   Ella 171,173,174,175
   Joseph 49,50
   Lucy 171,172,173,174
   Miller 170,171,172,173,174
   Mineffie 170,171,172,173
   Richard Douglas 125,126,127,128
BRYAN
   Charlie 140
   Hettie E 140
   S A 12
   S A, MD 12
BUFORD, Charles 299,300,301
BUKEY, Fred 132,134,135
BURL, Mary 111
BURNETT
   A J 221,222,223
   Mary J 223
   Mary Jane 221,222
   Moses 221,222,223
BURRESS, Elmira 319
BURTON
   Ethel V 152
   Ethel Victoria 153
   Lydia Belle 158
   Mollie E 152,153,154,155
   R O 152,153,154,155
   Robert O 151,152,154
   Robert Owen 153,155
   Wynema O 154
   Wynema Owen 155
BUTTES, Robt L 85,86
BYRD, Mary 66,71

Index

BYRT, Mary.................................66,67
CABLE
   Adam M.................................200,201
   Mary I....................................200,201
   Virgie Plimmer.....................200,201
CAGLE, Thomas J.........................151
CAIN, W A............20,21,22,28,29,141
CAKOCHEO..................................283
CALLAHAN
   Bentn...192
   Benton.................................193,194
   Cecilia..................................193,194
   Etta Sibyl.............................169,170
   J O...................38,169,170,193,226
   J O, MD.................................38,193
   James O...............167,168,169,226
   Mary E........................168,169,170
   Mary Elizabeth.....................168,169
   Mary R...169
   S B, Jr..192
   Sam...............................192,193,194
CALLEN, R......................................68,69
CAMPBELL
   Dan...111
   A E..141
CANARD
   [Illegible]....................................249
   Jeff T..249
   Lizzie....................247,248,249,250
   Nancy...................247,248,249,250
   Roby..249
   Sam.......................247,248,249,250
CARLILE, Joicie...............................115
CARR, Eli..13
CARTER
   Annie.....................31,32,33,34,35
   Henry........................29,30,31,32,34
   Henry C..............................32,33,35
   Jennie.........................29,31,32,33
   Susie......................29,30,34,35,36
CARWILE, Johny............................111
CASADA, Mrs A J............275,276,278
CASMEAN, E D......................33,35,36
CASSADY, Mrs.............................275
CASTELL, W R................................101
CASTELLO......................................131
   Geo C.................................132,133

George C............................129,136
Mabel.............129,130,132,133,136
Nettie..............129,130,132,133,136
CASTILLO......................................130
   G C.................131,132,134,135,136
   Mabel.....................................131,135
   Mabelle.......................................128
   Mable.............131,132,134,135,136
   Nettie.......128,131,132,134,135,136
   Walter..128
CHAMBLIS, J J...............................138
CHAMBLISS, J J, MD....................138
CHAPPEL, Walter W.....................162
CHAPPELL, Walter W...................163
CHEEK
   L 161
   M J...161
CHENUBBE, Sawdubby..........19,20,21
CHENUBBEE
   Martha..23
   Susie...23
CHENUBBIA, Susie..........................17
CHENUBIA, Susie............................22
CHENUBIE
   Martha......................................24,25
   Susie...24,25
CHILDERS, Ellis..............255,256,302
CHISSOE..66
   Austin..314
CHUNBIA, Ollie................................21
CHUPCO
   Janely..283
   Jenely..283
   John..283
   Johnson.......................................283
   Leetka...283
   Letka...283
CLARK
   [Illegible]......................................90
   Charles..111
   Jessie................................53,60,61
CLINTON
   Fred S......................................94,95
   Fred S, MD..............................94,95
COACHMAN, Chas...........272,273,274
COLBERT, Joe.................................173
COLLINS, Chas H............................159

Index

CONGER, J D 85,86
COOLEDGE, E F 207,208
COOPER
   Effie...................................77,78,79
   Eliza..77,79
   Grant................................77,78,79,80
   Liza.................................78,79,80
   Rosana...90
   W C 130
   W G 128,131,132,134,135,136
   Wheeler 77,79,80
CORNELIUS
   Julia..111
   Winey...................................164,165
   Winney..162
COUNTERMAN
   R M...................................153,155
   R M, MD 154,155
COVEY, Mary J 186,187
COWE
   Effa.....................................202,203
   Melinda......................................202
   Mrs Sarty 203
   Sarty 201,202,203
COX, Mitchell..............................111
DALE
   Charles Henry........275,276,277,278
   Charley 276,277
   Izora...................................276,277
   Izora E 277,278
   Mrs O C 275
   O C 275,277,278
   Oliver.................................276,277
DAMET
   Eliza..............316,317,318,319,320
   John P 315,316,317,318,319,320
   Susan 315,316,317,318,320
   William F.....................318,319,320
DANN, Mary..................................178
DARLING, A M......................33,35,36
DAVIS
   Elizabeth E 228,229,230,231
   Elizabeth Ellen...........................231
   Elizabeth Helen 228,231,232
   J R.................................229,230,231
   Russell 232
   William T 231

DAY
   [Illegible]...................................296
   James S......................................189
DENNEY, Lizzie............................181
DICE
   Dove 268,269,270,271,273,274
   Eliza Jane....................................274
   Freddie James.269,270,272,273,274
   Freddy James.................270,271,273
   James....................................269,270
   Jim 268,269,271,273,274
   Jime 270
   Liza Jane......................268,269,273
DONONVAN, Irwin 76
DONOVAN, Irwin 52,75,79,80
DOWNS, J B 296,297
DRESBACK, Ralph 173,232
DREW
   Alice 53,54,56,58,59,60
   Alice T......................55,56,57,59
   Amos 74,75
   Clarence................................74,75
   Earl B...53
   Earl E............................58,59,60,61
   Earnest..52
   Ernest.........53,54,55,56,57,58,59,60
   Nettie 74,75
   Ray W..53
   Roy W 53,54,55,56,57
   Sallie................................54,56,57
DUNFORD, Phil D 203
DUNN, Tripper..............................161
DUNZA, Lucinda..........................266
DUNZY
   J R...266
   Jackson 265,266,267
   Jackson R........263,264,265,266,267
   Lucinda..........263,264,265,266,267
   Velma 263,264,265,266,267
EARLEY, Lizzie 116
ELLIS, Nellie 211
ERLY, Lizzie..................................116
ESCO, Sarah M 141
ESCOE
   Sarah M 141,142
   Walter J 140,141,142
   William Albert..............140,141,142

Index

ESKRIDGE, C C 194
EVANS, Charley 20
EWERS, Albert 115,118,119
FARR
    Carrel 47
    Mollie 47
FARRIS, G W 304
FENNELL, Joe 68,255,256,296,297
FISHER, Lida 316
FIXICO
    Icey 61,62
    Pefeney 62
    Pefeny 61,62
FLETCHER, Caroline 65
FOSTER, Jeannette 294
FOWLER
    J A 85,86
    J A, MD 86
FOX, Willie 146
FRIDAY
    Berry 96,97,99,100
    Clarence 96,97,98,99,100
    Susan 99
FRYDAY
    Berry 95,96
    Clarence 95,96
    Susan 95,96
GILCREASE
    Bessie 240,241
    Elmer Lee 239,244,245,246,247
    Lizzie 240,241,242,243,244, 245,246
    Mabel 239,242,243,245
    W L 239,241,245
    William L 240,242,243,244,245,246
GOODEN
    Charley 89,90,91
    Charlie 88
    Jacob 88,89,90,91
    Louisa 89,90,91
    Susan 95,96,97,98,99,100
GRAY, Daniel 111
GRAYSON
    Ethel 111
    Isaac 111
    James L 122,123,124
    Matilda 123

    Matilfs 124
    Pearl 122,123,124
GRIESEL
    E C .... 19,27,32,34,73,76,87,88, 144,172,214,236,237,238,239,247,248 ,268,269,271,272,286,287,292,293, 305,314
    Edw C .... 1,3,4,5,6,10,13,14,16,17, 19,20,24,27,28,32,34,41,43,45,46,51, 52,55,57,60,64,67,73,91,92,97,103, 104,113,127,128,133,139,140,142,144 ,148,149,153,154,157,160,172,174, 176,177,180,183,184,185,188,190,193 ,194,195,197,198,200,201,205,207, 214,215,218,222,225,226,227,230,235 ,236,238,241,246,247,248,251,254, 258,263,265,268,269,271,272,277,279 ,280,284,286,287,292,293,295,298, 303,305,312,314,316,317,318,319,320 ,323,324
GRIFFIN, Bonnie 111
GROOM, L D 118,119
GUTHRIDGE, H S 275
HAERRIS, E B 232
HAIKEY
    Jessie 75,76
    John 75,76
    Susannah 76
    Sussannah 75,76
HAINS
    H G 25,27,121
    Henry 40
    Henry G 18,38,39,219,231, 283,321,322
HALL
    David 23,25
    A H 141
    Marley 25,26,27
    Martha 26,27,28
    Mollie 26,28,29
    Sandy 25,26,27,28
HAMILTON, Robt W 178
HARDIN, Bettie 167
HARDRIDGE, Taylor 310
HARDRIGE, Taylor 310
HARJO
    Hettie 289

Index

Lewis 283
Nettie 284,285,286,287,288
Sartarpe 25
Seta 287,288
Sookey 286,287,289
Sucky 284
Sukey 285
Sukie 283
Tothir 313
Willie 283,284,285,286,287,288
HARLAN, John 167
HARRED, Mary L 43,45
HARRIS, V B 84,85,86
HARRISON, R P 166,167
HASKELL, Revel, Jr 154,156
HAYNES
   Suke 79
   Sukey 75,76,80
HENDERSON, Mary 116
HENDRICKSON
   Elija 116
   Elijah 113,114,115,116,121,122
   Joe 121
   Joseph 113,114,115,116,117,118,
   119,120,121,122
   Mary 112,114,115,116,117,118,
   119,120,121,122
   Peter.. 112,113,117,118,119,120,121
   Peter Jackson 113
HENEHA
   Annie 223,224,260,261,262,263
   John 260,262,263
   Jonas 260,262,263
   Katie 223,224
HENRY
   Allen 181
   Charles 275
   Charley 275
HERROD, Mary L 43,45
HILL, Richard D 96
HINNEHA
   Annie 260,261,262
   John 261,262
   Jonas 260,261,262
HODGE
   [Illegible] T 259
   Alvin T 217

Gusta A 217,218,219,220,221
John N 217,218,219,220,221
Johnnie N 220
Mary J 223,257,259
Minnie L 217,218,219,220
HOLT, Z I J 66,72
HOWARD, Dr J F 278
HUGHES, B F 216
HUTCHINSON, Kate 270,273,274
ISAC, Amie 96
ISHMAEL
   Eva J 182,184,185
   James L 182,183,186,187
   James M ... 182,183,184,185,186,187
   Maude 182,183,184,185,186,187
JACOBS
   Elsey B 211,212
   Elsie B 210,211
   John A 210,211,212
   Mary 210,211
JAMES, Mose 111
JETTON, Robt 20,21,22,28
JOBE
   John Leo 225,226
   Leo 227
   Leo J 225,226,227,228
   Lewis 225,226
   Lewis N B 227,228
   Mary E 225,226
   Mollie G 227
JOHNSON
   H F 115,116,117,118,119
   Homer L 116
   I F 189
   J F 302
   P H 115,116
JOHNSTON, H G 207,208
JONES
   Malinda 82
   S F 82
KANNARD, Thomas 310
KELLY, Annie 128
KEPLEY, James K 291,292,294
LAGOW, Nannie 118
LAND
   Helen 47,48,49,50,51,52
   Joseph H 47,48,49,50,51,52

Index

Joseph Henry 49
Salina 48,49,50,51,52
Salina G 51
LANGLEY, J R 50
LARRABEE, C F 110
LAWLEY, Fanny 84
LEATH
   Ida Jane 84,85,86
   James Henry 84,85
   Jessie May 85,86
   Thomas Jefferson 84,85,86
LEE
   Dr John 201
   John 201
LEWIS, E E 270
LIGHTLE, Joseph M 40
LLOYD, L F 84,86
LONG, Jas A 264,265,266
LOONEY
   Fannie 81,82,83,84
   Josiah 80,82,83
   Sullivan 80,81,82,83
LOWE
   Losanna 283
   Louie 282
LUCINDA 283
LUMPKIN
   Carl 255,262
   R W 255
LYFORD
   H O 49,51
   H O, MD 49
LYNCH, Robert E 93,94,95,220,223
MAGEE
   Carl C 60,61
   Carl O 259
MAHALEY 66
MANN, Lola 162
MANTOOTH, S A 208,210
MARTIN
   John 189,190
   Johnson 187,188,189,190,191
   Loney 187,188,189,191
   Lonie 188
   Lovey 191
   Susana 188,189
   Susanna 187,188,189,190

A Z 62,63
MASON, W Y 50
MCCASLIN, Canzada 27
MCCELLOP, Eliza 216
MCCLELLAND, Annie 111
MCCORMICK, Mary 44
MCCOY, Henry 145,146
MCDERMOTT
   J 19,25,67,75,76,78,79,80,
   83,87,88,134,144,172,236,237,238,
   239,247,248,292,293,305
   Jesse 23,66,103,148,149,236,
   237,238,239
MCHENRY
   Abbie 297,298
   Bettie 295,296
   Betty 295
   Lewis 295
   Louis 295,296,297,298
   Silla 295,296,297,298
MCINTOSH
   Edith Edna 299,300
   Kate 299,300,301
   Thomas F 299,300
   Vivian 299,300,301
MCKELLOP
   A P 286,287
   P B 255
MCKINNN, Amanda S 196
MCKINNON
   Amanda S 195,197
   Archibald 195,196
   Lila Bell 196
   Lila Belle 197
   R W 195,197
MCMILLAN, Eliza 298,299
MCNAE
   Charley 235,236,237
   Lousana 235
   Lousanna 237
   Lozanna 236,237,238,239
   Marcy 238,239
   Marsey 237
   Peter 235,236,237,238,239
MEADEN, R L 270
MERRICK
   Edward 39,121,122,123,124

Index

Lona 16,225,316
MILLER
   George 96
   J T 218
   J Y 24,32,34,67,105,176
   L M 211,212
   Sam H 212
MILLS, B H 272,273
MINTER
   Bertie 323,324
   Birdie 321,322,323
   Mark 321,322,323,324
   Thelma Agnes 321,322,323,324
MITCHELL, W C 160,161
MITCHENER
   W C 196
   W C, MD 196
MOORE
   Augusta R 199
   J W 62
MORGAN
   Annie 111
   William B 286
MORTON
   Joan 234,235
   Joanna 233,234
   Jonn 235
   Roy Ray 233,234,235
   Thomas 233,234,235
   Walter W 306
   Wm P 306,307
MOTT, M L 107
MURPHY
   Eva Dorcas 37,41
   Eva Doris 36,37,39,40
   Eva Dorris 38
   Nettie 37,38,39,40
   William S 36,37,38,40
   Wm S 38,39,40,41
NERO, L E 65
NICHOLAS
   B 42
   B H 278,280,281
NOBLE
   Ben 68
   Minnie 66,69,70
OGLESBY

   Harry 120
   W J 120,121
   Will 120
OLIVER
   Frank 252,253,254,255,256
   Hatty 254,255,256
   Hatty Sarty 254,255
   Louis 253,254,255,256
OSBORNE, J H 285
PALMER
   Daniel 41,42,45,46
   Daniel B 42,46,47
   Eliza 42,44,46,47
   James W 42,44
   Jim 41,42,43
   John 41,42,43,45,46
   John W 44,46,47
   Liza 41,42,43,45,46
   Sarah 47
PARNASKEY, Taylor 88
PARRISH
   Zera E 105
   Zera Ellen 104,113,268,269,271,272
PATTERSON, John B 82,83
PEARCE, Sarah E 59,60,61
PEMBERTON, [Illegible] 82
PERRYMAN, James 69,70
PETERS
   Isom 173,232
   Louisa 173
PIERCE, Sarah E 59
PIGEON, Nancy .. 228,229,230,231,232
PLUMLEE
   R S 135,136
   R S, MD 135,136
POLLARD
   A J 72,73
   A J, MD 72,73
PORTER
   Edith 205
   Edith P 203,204,205,206,208,209
   L Ray 203,206,207,208,209,210
   L Roy 204
   Sam ... 203,204,205,206,207,208,209
   Sam N 208,209,210
   Susan 204,205,206,207,208,209
   Susan N 208,210

Index

Susie 205
POSEY, Alex 282,284
PROCTOR, Toney E 178
RED, D J 240,241,243,244,245, 246,247,252
REID
   H W 306,307
   W A 299
RENFRO
   Alef Adalaid 11,13,14
   Alef Adelaide 15
   Bettie 12,13,14,15
   Elza Tillman 12,13
   Will 13,14
   William D 11,12,14,15
REYNOLDS, N T 270
RILEY, E E 209,210
ROACH, Chas 307
ROBERTSON, R A 207
ROBISON
   Amos 313
   Amos R 84
ROGERS, N C 169,170
ROOK, Wm P 186,187
ROSS, Joshua 12
RUBLE, George W 15
RYAN
   Eliza 42
   Liza 42
SARTY
   Alfred 213,214,215
   Bettie 297
   Eliza 213,214,215,216
   Elsa 262
   Hatty 254
   Mamie 213,215,216
   Ned 69,70,213,214,215,216
   Roman 262
   Suzan 216
SCHAD, J L 208,210
SCOTT
   Bosie 205
   Christiana 290,292
   Christianns 289
   Christie Annie 290,291
   John 289,293,294
   Lucy 291

Nancy 285,290,291,292,293,294
Rosanna 249
Sam 289,291,292,293,294
Winey 203
SELF, William B 111
SHELBY
   David 148,149
   Davis 103
SHERRILL
   Chas M 2,6,10,11
   Gracie 8,9,10,11
   Mattie M 9,10,11
   William 8,9,10,11
SHIPMAN, Luda F 257
SILER, T M 206
SIMMONS, Peggy 62
SIMON
   Caesar 66,67,69,70
   George 66,67,68,69,70,71
   Mary 67,69,70,71
   Mary Byrd 69,71
   Mary Byrt 66
SIMPSON, Eskelle 15
SKAGGS
   D C 284
   Drennan C 153,155,158,283
SLOAN
   Lillie 283
   Lodie 283
   Peter 283
SMALLEY
   [Illegible] 135
   L E 132
SMART, Walter 84,86
SMITH
   Alvin 111
   Daniel B 197,198,199
   Emma 159,160
   Enoch 179,180
   Enoch O 180,181
   Enox 181
   Janie 179,180,181
   Mary I 198,199
   Oliver R 179,180,181
   Oliver Russell 180,181
   Ruth 197,198,199
   Stephen 159,160

Index

Steven 159,160
Terry Stephen 161
Terry Steven 159,160
SNELSON
   Dr A J 28,141
   A J 33,35,36
   A J, MD 29,141
   O J 26
STEPHENS
   Green 16,17,18,20,21,22
   Johnnie 15,16,17,21,22,23
   Millie 15,16,17,18,20,21,22,23
   Rachel 16
   Willie 15,16,18,20,21,22,23
STEVEN
   Green 16
   Johnnie 16
   Millie 16
STEVENS
   Green 19
   Mary 113
   Millie 19
   Willie 19
STROUVELLE
   Alice Kendall 92,93,94
   C E 92,93,94,95
   Charles Edward 95
   Charles Edward, Jr. 92
   Charley Edward 94
   Mrs C E (Barnett) 94
   Susanne Barett 94
   Susanne Barnett 92,93
   Susanne Barnette 95
SUDDUTH, William 68
SWEENEY, Miss Secelia 192
TAYLOR
   M D 243,245,246
   M D, MD 4,239,242,244,245,247
TERRYMAN, John W 53
THOMAS, Polly 237,239
THOMPSON, Sam G 167
TIGER
   Amos 278,279,280,281,282
   Annie 260,261
   Deovocha 280,282
   Devocha 282
   Devotia 279,281,282

Ethan Allen H 149,150,151
Ethan Allen Hitchcock 151
Hettie 278,279,280,281,282
John E 150,151
Johnson E 149,150,151
Lena E 150,151
Lucinda 284
Veovocha 281
TONEY
   Lijah 283
   Roley 283
TURNBOW, Aaron 209
TURNER
   G S 121
   G S, MD 119,121
   George S 119
   Thomas F 205
   Thos F 206
VAN PELT, Anna 59,257
VAUGHAN, Moses 111
WAGGENER, William H 266
WAGGNER, William H 266
WALKER, Wester 111
WASHINGTON, Winey 87
WATERFORD
   Dr R H 123
   R H, MD 124
WEBSTER
   Jeff 310,311,312
   Jefferson 309,311
   Mattie 310,311
   Seeley 309,310,311
WHITECOTTO, Bertha 281
WHITECOTTON, Bertha 278,280
WHITFIELD, Millie 15
WILLIAMS
   Charley 63,64,65
   J E 285
   John B 138
   M F 323
   M F, M 324
   Mary 64,65
   Mary M 63,64,65
   Mat 65
   Matt 63,64,65
   Nat 63,64,151,272,273,274
WILSON

```
        C H .............................. 156,157,158
        James ............................................ 112
        Lydia ...................................... 156,157
        Lydia Belle ................................. 158
        Oleta .......................... 156,157,158
WIMBERLY
        Frances ................................ 217,221
        Francis ......................................... 220
WINSTON
        J H ................................................ 310
        Jas A ..................................... 167,168
WISDOM, W T ................. 168,169,170
WITHERS
        Lydia ..................................... 251,252
        Oliver Lee ............................ 251,252
        Robert .......................................... 251
        Robert O .............................. 251,252
WOFFORD, Josie ............................ 111
WOLF
        Jim ............ 161,162,163,164,165,166
        John ................ 161,162,163,164,165
        John H ......................................... 166
        Minnie .......................... 162,164,165
        Winey ................................... 163,165
        Winnie ................................. 161,162
YAHDIHKA
        Cinda ............................................ 283
        Joe ................................................ 283
YAHOLA
        Haffy ................................... 86,87,88
        Jennetta ............................. 86,87,88
        Winey ................................. 86,87,88
YAHOLAR
        Betsey ........................................... 314
        Betsy ............................................ 314
        Jimmie .......................... 312,313,314
        Josey .............................. 312,313,314
        Petsey .................................. 312,313
YAR-MAH-LEE ............................. 111
YOBARHAHEY ............................. 313
```